The End of
WELFARE

M000207330

The End of
WELFARE

Fighting Poverty in the Civil Society

Michael Tanner

CATO
INSTITUTE
Washington, D.C.

Copyright © 1996 by the Cato Institute.
All rights reserved.

Library of Congress Cataloging-in-Publication Data

Tanner, Michael, 1956–
   The end of welfare : fighting poverty in the civil society /
Michael Tanner.
     p.   cm.
   Includes bibliographical references and index.
   ISBN 1-882577-37-X. — ISBN 1-882577-38-8
   1. Public welfare—United States.   2. Welfare recipients—
Employment—United States.   3. Welfare state.   I. Title.
HV95.T36   1996
362.5'8'0973—dc20   96-36010
                                                             CIP

Cover Design by Mark Fondersmith.

Printed in the United States of America.

CATO INSTITUTE
1000 Massachusetts Ave., N.W.
Washington, D.C. 20001

Contents

Acknowledgments

This book would not have been possible without the assistance of many people. In particular, I want to thank my research assistant, Naomi Lopez, whose work appears on almost every page. I also want to thank all those who read the mauscript and offered invaluable suggestions, particularly Tom G. Palmer, director of special projects at the Cato Institute. Others deserving thanks include Nancy Lord and Cato's president Edward H. Crane and executive vice president David Boaz as well as my copyeditor, Elizabeth W. Kaplan, who did her best to straighten out my mangled syntax. Finally, I must thank Ellen, who not only added greatly to the book but has taught me so much about caring, compassion, and love.

Introduction

Just a few minutes' drive from the White House and Capitol Hill, where welfare policies are made, lie the slums of Washington, D.C., where those policies are carried out. The policies launched by successive presidents and Congresses have had the best of intentions. Yet in the streets of Anacostia, the failure of the welfare state is starkly visible.

That failure can be seen in the faces of unemployed youths selling drugs in the shadows of boarded-up storefronts. It can be seen in teenage mothers dropping out of school and raising children who will end up in poverty themselves. It can be seen in the children—abused, neglected, hungry.

Since the start of the War on Poverty in 1965, the federal and state governments have spent more than $5.4 trillion trying to ease the plight of the poor. What we have received for that massive investment is, primarily, more poverty.

Our welfare system is unfair to everyone: to taxpayers, who must pick up the bill for failed programs; to society, whose mediating institutions of community, church, and family are increasingly pushed aside; and most of all to the poor, who are trapped in a system that destroys opportunity for themselves and hope for their children.

Welfare began with the best of intentions. But as the saying goes, the road to hell is paved with good intentions. Noble goals and good intentions are not enough. Welfare programs must be judged on their results—results that have been a dismal, tragic failure.

That failure is now acknowledged virtually across the political and ideological spectrum. Yet, as the debate over the 1996 welfare reform bill showed, both liberals and conservatives remain locked into the paradigms of the past. Both liberals and conservatives continue to believe that government can solve the problem of poverty in America. To be sure, they would use government in different ways, but both ultimately believe in the primacy of a political solution to poverty.

1

Liberals continue to see government as an engine for redistributing wealth. By and large they would continue to pour money into existing or new programs. If they believe programs need to be reformed, they think restructuring is all that is needed. The failures of the past, they believe, were the result of poor management, not poor ideas.

Conservatives take two approaches to welfare reform. One group—the green-eyeshade conservatives—seeks to make welfare programs less costly and more efficient. They target "fraud, waste, and abuse" and call for reducing welfare benefits and transferring programs to state control.

The second group of conservatives seeks to use welfare as a tool of social engineering to fight "behavioral poverty." Incongruously, they believe that a government that has a hard time delivering the mail can develop a set of incentives and disincentives that will change the behavior of the poor, forcing them to adopt conservative social norms.

The history of government welfare should tell us that both conservatives and liberals are wrong. The answer to poverty does not lie with government. If we are serious about fighting poverty and creating opportunity for all Americans, we must think outside the box of traditional government programs. We must develop a new paradigm based, not on government and political society, but on civil society.

Unlike government, or political society, which is ultimately based on force or coercion, civil society is based on voluntary cooperation and persuasion. It provides the widest possible latitude for individuals to live their lives without interference so long as they do not violate the rights of others. Civil society would not use government either to redistribute wealth or to shape the poor's behavior.

That does not mean that civil society would be indifferent to the plight of the poor. Rather, civil society recognizes that the belief in government's ability to engineer society is, in the words of Nobel prize–winning economist F. A. Hayek, a "fatal conceit." Government is incapable of successfully fighting poverty.

In contrast, civil society would emphasize the creation of wealth and prosperity. It would increase the opportunity for all Americans to achieve their portion of the American dream. While stressing self-reliance and individual initiative, it would also provide a vigorous network of private, localized, nonbureaucratic charities that are far more capable than is government of helping those people who need temporary assistance.

Americans are already the most generous people on earth, contributing more than $120 billion per year to organized private charity. History and the American character suggest that the people would more than rise to the occasion and meet the needs of the poor. At the same time, the removal of the destructive incentives of the current welfare system would mean that fewer people would need help. Fewer children would be born to single mothers unready and unable to support them. More poor people would find the road out of poverty through work and education.

While eliminating welfare, civil society would also eliminate barriers to economic growth and job creation. That means reducing regulations and cutting taxes to spur economic growth. Civil society would be less concerned with making poverty comfortable than with making prosperity available.

We should not pretend that necessary changes to our social welfare system will come easily or painlessly. But come they must. We cannot afford to continue subsidizing a culture of long-term dependence. We must avoid bringing more people into a cycle of welfare, illegitimacy, fatherlessness, crime, more illegitimacy, and more welfare. A compassionate society can find other ways to deal with the problem of people who need temporary assistance to get through hard times. As is the case with other social pathologies, such as child abuse or alcoholism, we must break the cycle or watch the problem spread through succeeding generations. Above all, we must remember that it is the children growing up in welfare-ravaged neighborhoods who are the true victims of our social welfare policies.

As this book goes to press, Congress has passed, and President Clinton has indicated that he will sign, welfare reform legislation (the Personal Responsibility and Work Opportunity Reconciliation Act of 1996). Unfortunately, that legislation falls far short of what is needed to truly break the cycle of poverty in America. It is time to recognize that welfare cannot be reformed. It should be ended. Some say that would be too cruel, that it's punishing the victim. But what could be crueler than sacrificing another generation to our current social welfare muddle?

1. Poverty in America

According to the Bureau of the Census, 39 million Americans, or approximately 15.1 percent of the U.S. population, currently live in poverty. However, that figure may tell us far less than it seems to.

The first question, of course, is what do we mean by poverty? Adam Smith defined it as the "want of necessities," defining necessities as "not only the commodities which are indispensably necessary for the support of life, but whatever the custom of the country renders it indecent for creditable people, even of the lowest order, to be without."[1] The National Research Council, in attempting to develop a new national poverty standard, recently updated that definition slightly, calling poverty a lack of "family resources necessary to obtain a minimally adequate standard of living, defined appropriately for the United States today."[2]

In both cases poverty is defined in the context of a nation's wealth, customs, and general standard of living. Poverty, after all, is relative. The equivalent of Calcutta's slums or Somalia's starving children does not exist in the United States.

Some welfare critics, such as Robert Rector of the Heritage Foundation, make much of that fact, pointing out that the poor in the United States are generally far from destitute. For example, poor Americans have more housing space and are less likely to be overcrowded than is the average citizen of Western Europe. In fact, nearly 40 percent of poor Americans own their own homes. Nearly 64 percent of poor families own a car, 56 percent own a microwave oven, and 25 percent have automatic dishwashers. Fully 91 percent of poor U.S. families

---

[1]Adam Smith, *An Inquiry into the Nature and Causes of the Wealth of Nations* (1776; New York: Random House, Modern Library, 1993), p. 47.

[2]Constance F. Citro and Robert T. Michael, *Measuring Poverty: A New Approach* (Washington: National Academy Press, 1995), p. 19.

have a color television, and 29 percent own two or more.[3] Hardly Somalia.

But we cannot take satisfaction from comparisons with India or Somalia. In a country as rich as ours, the mere fact that people are not starving is not enough. Indeed, in many ways the juxtaposition of poverty and wealth in this country makes things worse. The starving child in Somalia may not be aware of all that he is missing, but the poor child in America is.

One cannot deny the very real consequences of being poor in America. For example, poor children suffer from health problems and have slower cognitive development than do nonpoor children.[4] Child abuse, crime, and a host of social ills can be linked to poverty.[5]

Even though any definition of poverty is going to be arbitrary and fail to tell the full story, some statistical measure of poverty remains necessary. The current official government definition of poverty is an income less than three times as large as the amount needed to purchase a low-cost package of food.[6] That definition was developed by the Social Security Administration in 1965 on the basis of a 1955 study that indicated that the average American family spent approximately one-third of its income on food.[7] According to that standard, the 1994 poverty standard for a family of four was

---

[3]Robert Rector, "How the Poor Really Live: Lessons for Welfare Reform," Heritage Foundation Backgrounder no. 875, January 31, 1992; and Robert Rector, "Facts about America's Poor," Heritage Foundation FYI no. 6, December 23, 1993.

[4]See, for example, C. Deutsch, "Social Class and Child Development," in *Review of Child Development Research*, ed. B. M. Caldwell and M. Rischetti (Chicago: University of Chicago Press, 1973); F. Riessman, *The Culturally Deprived Child* (New York: Harper & Row, 1962); G. Lesser et al., *Mental Abilities of Children from Different Social Classes and Ethnic Groups*, Society for Research in Child Development Monograph 30 (Chicago: University of Chicago Press, 1965), pp. 1–115; Elsie Moore, "The Child of Poverty," in *Child Poverty and Public Policy*, ed. Judith A. Chafel (Washington: Urban Institute, 1993), pp. 167–201.

[5]See, for example, Joan Vondra, "Childhood Poverty and Child Maltreatment," in ibid., pp. 127–66;

[6]Using the U.S. Department of Agriculture's "Economy Food Plan." See U.S. House of Representatives, Committee on Ways and Means, *1994 Green Book: Background Material and Data on Programs within the Jurisdiction of the Committee on Ways and Means* (Washington: Government Printing Office, 1994), pp. 1152–53.

[7]Molly Orshansky, "Counting the Poor: Another Look at the Poverty Profile," *Social Security Bulletin* 28 (1965): 3–29.

Table 1.1
POVERTY STANDARDS, 1994

Family Size	Poverty Standard ($)
1	7,547
2	9,661
3	11,821
4	15,141
5	17,900
6	20,235
7	22,923
8	25,427
9+	30,300

SOURCE: Bureau of the Census, *Income, Poverty, and Valuation of Noncash Benefits: 1994,* Current Population Reports, Series P60-189 (Washington: Government Printing Office, 1996), Table A-2, p. A-4.

NOTE: Weighted averages include poverty thresholds for single and married heads of household. For example, four individuals could be a single parent and three children or married parents and two children.

$15,141.[8] Larger and smaller families, of course, have different poverty standards. Table 1.1 provides a breakout of poverty standards by family size as of 1994.

That method of determining poverty has come under a great deal of criticism from both liberals and conservatives. Conservatives point out that the definition of income does not include noncash government benefits such as food stamps, public housing, and Medicaid. (It does include cash benefits such as Aid to Families with Dependent Children.) Failure to include those benefits severely understates the amount of income that the poor actually have available. For example, Bruce Bartlett of the National Center for Policy Analysis points out that the poor actually spend $1.70 for every $1.00 the Census Bureau says they have.[9] If all noncash government benefits were included in a person's income, the percentage of

[8]Bureau of the Census, *Income, Poverty, and Valuation of Noncash Benefits: 1994,* Current Population Reports, Series P60-189 (Washington: Government Printing Office, 1996), Table A-2, p. A-4.

[9]Bruce Bartlett, "How Poor Are the Poor?" *American Enterprise,* January–February 1996, p. 58, citing data from the U.S. Department of Labor.

Americans living in poverty would decrease from 14.5 percent to 11.5 percent, a difference of nearly 8 million people.[10]

In addition, the poverty level fails to measure various kinds of income that the poor receive from informal sources, including a thriving underground economy. There is substantial evidence that many poor people have unreported income. For example, a study of welfare recipients in Chicago; Charleston, South Carolina; and Cambridge, Massachusetts, found that welfare actually accounted for only 57 percent of their income. The remainder came from gifts from friends, relatives, and absent fathers (21 percent), unreported work (10 percent), Supplemental Security Income and foster care (6 percent), illegal activities including prostitution and drug sales (3 percent), and other (3 percent).[11] That income does not show up in reports to the Bureau of the Census.

At the same time, some people on the left note that the proportion of family expenditures for food has declined since the 1950s; food now takes only one-sixth of the average household budget.[12] Many household goods that are common today were rare or nonexistent in 1955. Moreover, expenses for such things as child care, health care, and transportation are not adequately represented. Those costs are made particularly significant by the increased entry of women into the workforce.[13] In addition, because the value of the food package remains relatively stable, generally rising only with inflation, it fails to measure "relative poverty," the growing gap between the poor and those above them on the economic ladder. Thus poverty may appear relatively stable, even as the poor fall further and further behind the average family.[14]

Observers on both sides point out that the formula does not consider taxes, which decrease disposable income and leave families

[10]Bureau of the Census, *Income, Poverty, and Noncash Benefits: 1994*, Table L, p. xxiv.

[11]Christopher Jencks and Kathryn Edin, "The Real Welfare Problem," *American Prospect* 1, no. 1 (Spring 1990): 31–50.

[12]Frances Fox Piven and Richard Cloward, *Regulating the Poor: The Functions of Public Welfare* (New York: Vintage, 1993), p. 363.

[13]Patricia Ruggles, "Measuring Poverty," *Focus* 14 (January 1992): 1–9.

[14]Sheldon Danziger, "Fighting Poverty and Reducing Welfare Dependency: A Challenge for the 1990's," Paper presented at the Rockefeller Foundation Conference on Welfare Reform, New York, February 16–18, 1988.

poorer.[15] The impact of taxes on the income of poor people is considerable. The Bureau of the Census has estimated that, in 1994, for example, deducting taxes from income would have increased the percentage of Americans in poverty from 15.1 percent to 23.2 percent.[16]

The official poverty standard does not adequately reflect regional variations in the cost of living. After all, it costs considerably more to live in California or New York than it does in Alabama or Mississippi. Some cities such as New York City and Washington, D.C., are even more costly. Thus a family may be able to live above poverty in one area of the country, while a family with an identical income may be poor in another area.[17]

Despite the criticism, there is no consensus on a better method of defining poverty. The Bureau of the Census alone has proposed no fewer than 30 alternative definitions, which would put the percentage of Americans living in poverty as low as 8.5 percent and as high as 21.1 percent.[18]

Many liberals have suggested a "relative" measure of poverty, such as the number of people who earn less than half the median wage.[19] Such a measure would have the advantage of recognizing that poverty in America is not simply a lack of food, clothing, shelter, and similar necessities. But relative measurements, which reveal more about inequality than about actual poverty, present their own set of problems. Relative measures take no account of the poor's actual condition. For example, if the income of every American were to double, the poor would be substantially better off than they are

---

[15]Citro and Michael.

[16]Bureau of the Census, *Measuring the Effect of Benefits and Taxes on Income and Poverty*, Current Population Reports, Series P60-182 (Washington: Government Printing Office, 1992), p. 6.

[17]H. H. Nelson, "An Interstate Cost of Living Index," *Educational Evaluation and Policy Analysis* 13 (January 1991): 103–11.

[18]Bureau of the Census, *Measuring the Effect of Benefits and Taxes on Income and Poverty: 1990*, Current Population Reports, Series P160-167-RD (Washington: Government Printing Office, 1991), pp. 40–41, 182–83.

[19]See, for example, Sheldon Danziger and Peter Gottschalk, *America Unequal* (Cambridge, Mass.: Harvard University Press, 1995); David Ellwood, *Poor Support: Poverty in the American Family* (New York: Basic Books, 1988); and Valerie Polakow, *Lives on the Edge: Single Mothers and Their Children in the Other America* (Chicago: University of Chicago Press, 1994).

today. But a relative measure would detect no change in the poverty rate. By the same token, if a severe economic downturn decreased the median American wage, the poverty rate would decline, even though the poor might actually be worse off. Thus, "relative poverty" becomes useless as a measuring tool.[20]

Throughout this book, therefore, I reluctantly use the official definition of poverty unless otherwise stated. However, the reader should keep in mind its limitations.

Short- vs. Long-Term Poverty

It is also important to understand the difference between short- and long-term poverty. Many Americans experience brief hard times but recover within a short period of time.

Estimates of the number of poor Americans are "snapshots in time." They tell us nothing about the duration of poverty. A recent Bureau of the Census study examined poverty over a 32-month period from 1990 to 1992 and concluded that, although some Americans remain mired in poverty for long periods, "many more people change poverty status from one year to the next."[21] For example, 19 million Americans were considered poor in 1990 using traditional reporting methods. However, only 10.6 million of those people were poor during every month of 1990. Moreover, of those who were poor throughout 1990, 21 percent were out of poverty in 1991.[22]

Those findings are in line with a 1984 University of Michigan study that found that between one-third and one-half of the poor studied over a 10-year period escaped poverty from one year to the next. The study found that only about 22 percent of the poor were living in poverty during the entire 10-year period.[23]

---

[20]For an excellent discussion of why relative poverty should not be used as a poverty measurement, see Chris Sarlo, "Poverty Update: What Does Poverty Mean?" *Fraser Forum*, January 1996, pp. 1–12.

[21]Bureau of the Census, *Dynamics of Economic Well-Being*, Current Population Reports, Series P70-42 (Washington: Government Printing Office, 1995), p. 10.

[22]Ibid., Table E, p. 9.

[23]Greg Duncan, *Years of Poverty, Years of Plenty: The Changing Fortunes of American Workers and Families* (Ann Arbor: University of Michigan, Institute of Social Research, 1984), pp. 60–80. However, David Ellwood and Mary Jo Bane, who reanalyzed the data, point out that while a substantial number of the poor suffered only very short bouts of poverty, at any point in time 50 percent of the poor were in the midst of a poverty spell that would last eight years or longer. Bane and Ellwood, "Slipping into and Out of Poverty: The Dynamics of Spells," *Journal of Human Resources* 21 (Winter 1986): 1–23.

In fact, poor Americans are more likely to escape poverty than are their counterparts in many European countries with more extensive social welfare systems, including France, the Netherlands, and Sweden.[24] In general, estimates put the number of long-term poor at 6 or 7 percent of the U.S. population.[25]

Who Are the Poor?

As Figure 1.1. shows, the incidence of poverty varies enormously among various demographic groups characterized by such factors as age, race, and gender. Children are far more likely to live in poverty than are adults, and senior citizens are less likely to be poor than is the general population. In 1994 the poverty rate for persons under the age of 18 was 21.8 percent versus 11.9 percent for persons aged 18 to 64.[26] Although children make up just over a quarter of the U.S. population, they account for roughly 40 percent of the poor. In contrast, the elderly are approximately 12 percent of the total population but only 10 percent of the poor.[27] Younger children were even more at risk of being poor. More than 24 percent of children under age six were poor in 1994.[28]

Poor children are also likely to experience a deeper level of poverty than do other poor people. Approximately 44 percent of all poor children live in families with incomes below one-half of the poverty standard.[29]

Poverty rates among both African-Americans and Hispanic Americans are more than triple the rate among whites. In 1994 the poverty rate for blacks was 30.6 percent; for Hispanics, 30.7 percent; and only 9.4 percent for non-Hispanic whites. For Asians and Pacific

[24]Greg Duncan et al., "Poverty and Social-Assistance Dynamics in the United States, Canada, and Europe," Paper presented at the Joint Center for Political and Economic Studies, Washington, September 14, 1991.

[25]Isabel Sawhill, "Poverty in the U.S.: Why Is It So Persistent?" *Journal of Economic Literature* 28 (September 1988): 1080–81; Isabel Sawhill, "The Underclass: An Overview," *Public Interest*, no 96 (Summer 1989): 5; and Lawrence Mead, *The New Politics of Poverty: The Non-Working Poor in America* (New York: Basic Books, 1992), p. 14.

[26]Bureau of the Census, *Income, Poverty, and Valuation of Noncash Benefits: 1994*, Table F, p. xvii.

[27]Ibid.

[28]Ibid.

[29]Bureau of the Census, *Income, Poverty, and Valuation of Noncash Benefits: 1996* (Washington: Government Printing Office, 1996), Table H, p. xx.

Figure 1.1
POVERTY RATES BY DEMOGRAPHIC GROUP, 1994

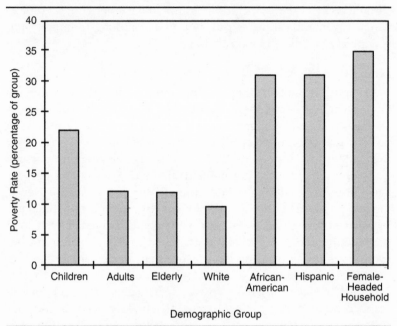

SOURCE: Bureau of the Census, *Income, Poverty, and Valuation of Noncash Benefits: 1994*, Current Population Reports, Series P60-189 (Washington: Government Printing Office, 1996), Table F, p. xvii.

Islanders the poverty rate was 14.6 percent, slightly higher than for whites.[30] However, because whites make up the majority of the population, 48 percent of all poor people were white.[31] The racial disparity among children is even more dramatic. Nearly half (46 percent) of all African-American children are poor, compared to 40 percent of Hispanic children, 22 percent of Asian children, and 12 percent of white children.[32] Black poverty is likely to be of longer duration than white poverty. Among whites, 63.1 percent of all

[30]Bureau of the Census, *Income, Poverty, and Valuation of Noncash Benefits: 1994*, Table F, p. xvii.

[31]Ibid.

[32]William Scarbrough, "Who Are the Poor? A Demographic Perspective," in *Child Poverty and Public Policy*, pp. 66–67.

poverty spells last one year or less. But only 48.4 percent of black poverty spells are that short. At the other end, only 4.3 percent of white poverty spells last seven years or longer. Among African-Americans, 14.9 percent of poverty spells last that long.[33] Again the situation is even more pronounced among children. Only 3 percent of white children will spend 7 to 10 years in poverty, while nearly 34 percent of African-American children will do so.[34]

Women are far more likely to live in poverty than are men.[35] Nearly two-thirds of all poor adults are women.[36] That is even more evident in female-headed households. In 1994, 34.6 percent of all female-headed families were poor.[37] As can be expected, minority women fared even worse: 46.2 percent of households headed by African-American women and 52.1 percent of households headed by Hispanic women were poor in 1994.[38] Indeed, most of the child poverty discussed above is linked to female-headed households.

Changing Trends

There were few accurate measures of poverty in this country before World War II. However, it is safe to say that by many measures a substantial portion of the U.S. population could have been considered poor. More accurate data became available after the war, and in 1949 approximately 34.3 percent of the U.S. population (51 million people) were considered poor.[39]

---

[33]Peter Gottschalk, Sara McLanahan, and Gary Sandefur, "The Dynamics of Intergenerational Transmission of Poverty and Welfare Participation," in *Confronting Poverty: Prescriptions for Change*, ed. Sheldon Danziger, Gary Sandefur, and Daniel Weinberg (Cambridge, Mass.: Harvard University Press, 1994), pp. 88–90.

[34]David Ellwood, *Poverty through the Eyes of Children* (Cambridge, Mass.: Harvard University, Kennedy School of Government, 1989), pp. 200–201.

[35]Sheldon Danziger and Daniel Weinberg, *Fighting Poverty: What Works and What Doesn't* (Cambridge, Mass.: Harvard University Press, 1986), pp. 34–35.

[36]Christopher Pierson, *Beyond the Welfare State?* (University Park: Pennsylvania State University Press, 1991), p. 74.

[37]Bureau of the Census, *Income, Poverty, and Valuation of Noncash Benefits: 1994*, Table F, p. xvii.

[38]Ibid.

[39]The Bureau of the Census provides general population poverty data from 1947. Demographic breakdowns became available in 1959.

Figure 1.2
POVERTY RATES, 1949–95

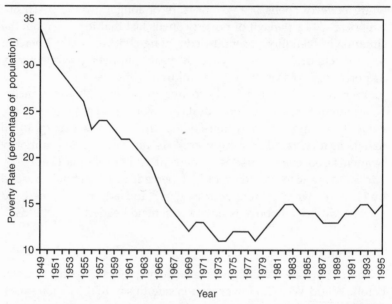

SOURCE: Bureau of the Census, *Current Population Reports*, Series P60, various numbers.

As Figure 1.2 shows, throughout the 1950s and 1960s, before the beginning of the War on Poverty, the poverty rate declined dramatically.[40] However, in the late 1960s the decline began to bottom out, and by 1973 the poverty rate began to rise again. By 1995 the poverty rate had reached pre-1966 levels.

Long-term poverty has also begun to increase. After improving steadily before 1970, and remaining relatively stagnant throughout the 1970s, the proportion of poor moving out of poverty from year to year declined in the 1980s.[41]

[40]Bureau of the Census, *Current Population Reports*, Series P60-124, P60-140, P60-145, P60-149. P60-154, P60-157, P60-161, P60-166, P60-168, P60-174, P60-180, P60-185, P60-188, P60-189.

[41]Terry Adams, Greg Duncan, and Willard Rogers, "The Persistence of Poverty," in *Quiet Riots: Race and Poverty in the United States*, ed. Fred Harris and Roger Wilkins (New York: Pantheon, 1988), Figure 5.2.

Figure 1.3
POVERTY RATES FOR AFRICAN-AMERICANS, 1949–94

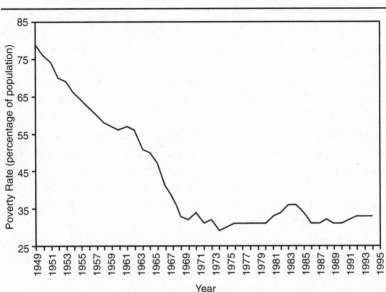

SOURCES: James Tobin, "Macroeconomic Trends, Cycles, and Policies," in *Confronting Poverty: Prescriptions for Change,* ed. Sheldon Danziger, Gary Sandefur, and Daniel Weinberg (Cambridge, Mass.: Harvard University Press, 1994), p. 150; Gerald Jaynes and Robin Williams Jr., eds., *A Common Destiny: Blacks and American Society* (Washington: National Academy Press, 1989), p. 278; and Bureau of the Census, Current Population Reports, Series P60, various numbers.

A look at specific demographic categories shows similar results. Among African-Americans, for example, the decline in poverty through the late 1960s was even more dramatic than the average. In 1949, 75.4 percent of all African-Americans lived in poverty. By 1973 the percentage had declined to 30.5 percent. At that point, it leveled off; it remains virtually unchanged today. Interestingly, not only did the biggest decline in black poverty take place before the advent of the Great Society, it occurred even before the passage of major civil rights legislation. Figure 1.3 illustrates the change in black poverty rates.

However, that fails to tell the whole story. While the overall poverty rate for African-Americans has remained relatively steady since

15

1973, the rate for black men has continued to decline while the rate for black women and children has been increasing since the early 1970s. In 1949, 86.7 percent of African-American children lived in poverty. That declined to a low of 39.4 percent in 1973, but had risen again to 42.4 percent by 1991.[42] Indeed, over the last 30 years the poverty status of African-American children relative to white children has grown worse. In 1960 black children were three times more likely than white children to be poor. Today they are four times more likely to be poor.[43]

The poverty rate for children in general has grown worse in the past 25 years. In 1973, 17 percent of children aged six and under and 15 percent of older children were poor. By 1991 those values had increased to 24 percent and 18 percent, respectively.[44] Moreover, as Figure 1.4 shows, the increase in child poverty after 1973 was steeper than for the general population.

Figure 1.4 also shows that while poverty among the young and working-age populations increased after 1973, poverty among the elderly continued to decline. There is considerable debate about why the elderly have been immune from recent increases in poverty. Liberals argue that decreasing elderly poverty is due to the success of programs such as Medicare and Social Security. However, economists Richard Vedder and Lowell Gallaway point out that the elderly are generally unaffected by the disincentives and other problems of welfare.[45] Sen. Daniel Patrick Moynihan (D-N.Y.) falls somewhere between the two points of view, saying, "[The] period of social reform was most successful . . . where we simply transferred income and services to a stable, settled group like the elderly. It had little success—if you like, it failed—where poverty stemmed from social behavior."[46]

---

[42]Danziger and Gottschalk, *America Unequal*, Table 4.5, p. 90.

[43]Scarbrough, pp. 67–70.

[44]Ibid., pp. 64–66.

[45]Richard Vedder and Lowell Gallaway, "The War on the Poor," Institute for Policy Innovation, Lewisville, Tex., June 1992.

[46]Daniel Patrick Moynihan, "Toward a Post-Industrial Social Policy," *Public Interest* 96 (Summer 1989): 22.

Figure 1.4
POVERTY RATES BY AGE GROUP, 1959–94

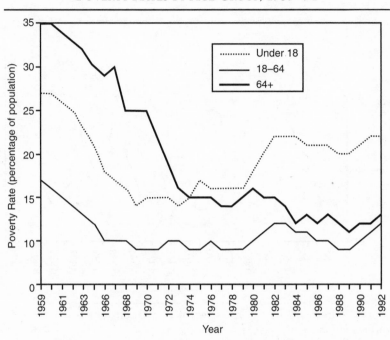

SOURCE: Bureau of the Census, Current Population Reports, Series P60, various numbers.

Causes of Poverty

Senator Moynihan's remarks raise the question of what causes poverty. It has been said that the surest ways to stay out of poverty are to (1) finish school; (2) not get pregnant outside marriage; and (3) get a job, any job, and stick with it. A look at who is poor in America suggests there is something to those suggestions.

For example, the poverty rate for families at least one member of which finished college is just over 2 percent; it is 10.5 percent for high school graduates and 24.2 percent for those who did not finish high school.[47] Nearly half of all poor adults are high school dropouts;

---

[47]William Kelso, *Poverty and the Underclass: Changing Perceptions of the Poor in America* (New York: New York University Press, 1994), p. 67.

Figure 1.5
POVERTY RATES FOR FEMALE-HEADED HOUSEHOLDS, 1959–94

Year

SOURCE: Bureau of the Census, Current Population Reports, Series P60, various numbers.

less than 15 percent are college graduates.[48] Welfare dependency, which could be considered an alternative measure of poverty, also correlates with education. For example, economists Anne Hill and June O'Neill found in a 1993 study that 44.7 percent of women defined as "dependent" on welfare were high school dropouts.[49]

An unmarried woman with children is much more likely to be poor than is a two-parent family. That is true for both divorced women and women with illegitimate children. As mentioned above, nearly 35 percent of female-headed households are poor. As Figure 1.5 shows, that poverty rate has fluctuated between 30 and 40 percent

[48]Vedder and Gallaway, p. 6.

[49]M. Anne Hill and June O'Neill, "Underclass Behaviors in the United States: Measurement and Analysis of Determinants," Baruch College, City University of New York, August 1993, Table 3.5.

since 1965 and in 1994 was actually slightly higher than it was in 1965.[50]

Although all female-headed households suffer a high rate of poverty, the situation is even grimmer for women who give birth out of wedlock. Slightly more than two-thirds (66.1 percent) of female-headed families with never-married mothers are poor, roughly double the rate for divorced women.[51] Only 6.7 percent of children from families with never-married mothers will grow up without experiencing a single year of poverty.[52] Families headed by never-married mothers are more likely to remain poor as well. Nearly 61 percent of children in those families will be poor for seven years or more.[53]

If one uses welfare as a surrogate for poverty, the results are the same. Approximately 30 percent of all welfare recipients go on welfare because they give birth out of wedlock.[54] The trend is even worse among teenage mothers. Half of all unwed teen mothers go on welfare within one year of the birth of their first child; 77 percent are on welfare within five years of the child's birth.[55]

There are several reasons why poverty is worse for unwed mothers than for divorced women. Unwed mothers tend to be younger, have less education and fewer job skills, and be less likely to receive child support.[56]

Of all the ways to avoid poverty, the most obvious—and the most important—is to have a job. Critics often complain that low-wage jobs are insufficient to lift a family out of poverty. In reality, however, very few working people are poor. Only 2.6 percent of full-time workers are poor. The "working poor" are a small minority of the

---

[50]Bureau of the Census, *Income, Poverty, and Valuation of Noncash Benefits: 1994*, Table B-6, p. B19.

[51]Bureau of the Census, *Marital Status and Living Arrangements: 1992*, Current Population Reports, Series P20-468 (Washington: Government Printing Office, 1993), Table 6.

[52]Ellwood, *Poverty through the Eyes of Children*, p. 78.

[53]Ibid.

[54]U.S. House of Representatives, Committee on Ways and Means, *1994 Green Book*, Table 10-50, p. 451.

[55]Douglas Besharov, "Escaping the Dole," American Enterprise Institute, Washington, December 12, 1993.

[56]V. Joseph Hotz et al., *The Costs and Consequences of Teenage Childbearing for Mothers* (Chicago: University of Chicago Press, 1995).

Table 1.2
POVERTY RATES BY WORK LEVEL (percentage)

	All Persons	Female-Headed Household	African-Americans
Overall	15.1	34.8	30.6
Full-time work	2.9	7.3	5.3
Part-time work	13.9	30.9	27.0
Did not work	23.6	55.9	44.7

SOURCE: Bureau of the Census, *Income, Poverty, and Noncash Benefits: 1994,* Current Population Reports, Series P60-189 (Washington: Government Printing Office, 1996), Table 10, pp. 41–44.

poor population. Fewer than 12 percent of poor people work full time. Even part-time work makes a significant difference. Approximately 13.2 percent of part-time workers are poor, compared with 28.7 percent of adults who do not work.[57]

As the data in Table 1.2 indicate, poverty runs higher at all levels of work for female-headed households and for African-Americans. Nevertheless, within each group, poverty declines dramatically for individuals who work.

The three causes of poverty reinforce each other. A woman giving birth out of wedlock is more likely to drop out of school and less likely to work than are other women.[58] For example, only 59 percent of never-married mothers are high school graduates.[59] Only 38 percent are working full time.[60] Likewise, unemployment is much higher among dropouts in general, as is unwed motherhood.

What of other commonly cited causes of poverty? Some liberals have blamed stagnating wages and a declining industrial base for the increase in poverty. Although the extent of poverty is hotly

[57]Bureau of the Census, *Poverty in the United States: 1990,* Current Population Reports, Series P60-175 (Washington: Government Printing Office, 1991), p. 8.

[58]Neil Gilbert, "The Unfinished Business of Welfare Reform," *Society* 24, no. 3 (March–April 1987): 5–11.

[59]Suzanne Bianchi, "Children of Poverty: Why Are They Poor?" in *Child Poverty and Public Policy,* Table 4.2, p. 100.

[60]Ibid.

Table 1.3
PERCENTAGE OF FULL-TIME WORKERS WITH LOW WAGES

	1964	1974	1984	1990
Total	23.1	11.4	14.2	17.8
Men	15.4	6.6	10.1	13.6
Women	44.5	21.8	21.0	24.1
Black men	38.0	13.8	17.5	22.4

SOURCE: Bureau of the Census, "Workers with Low Earnings," Current Population Surveys, Series P60-178, 1992, Table C, p. 4.

debated, there is evidence that real wages have been relatively stagnant over the last 20 years. But stagnant wages are a problem primarily to people who work. As we have seen, the majority of the poor are not full-time workers. Indeed, as Table 1.3 shows, the proportion of full-time workers earning low wages (defined as a wage that would not enable them to live above the poverty level), although rising since the 1970s, is still lower than in 1964.

Since working people are unlikely to be poor, there may be greater reason to argue that lack of jobs is a major cause of poverty. However, as Figure 1.6 illustrates, changes in poverty rates have been only mildly related to changes in the unemployment rate.

Lack of jobs does not appear to be the primary reason why the unemployed poor are not working. In fact, according to a 1990 Bureau of the Census report, when asked the reason for not working, only 4.1 percent of poor people aged 16 and older gave an inability to find work as the reason.[61]

Similarly, lost jobs and declining wages do not appear to be the primary reasons why people go on welfare. Only 15 percent of all people receiving welfare go on the program because of a decline in earnings.[62]

To the degree that stagnant wages and unemployment do increase poverty, they appear to have the greatest impact on two-parent

---

[61]Bureau of the Census, *Poverty in the United States: 1990,* Current Population Reports, Series P60-175 (Washington: Government Printing Office, 1991), Table 15, p. 103.

[62]U.S. House of Representatives, Committee on Ways and Means, *1994 Green Book,* Table 10-50, p. 451.

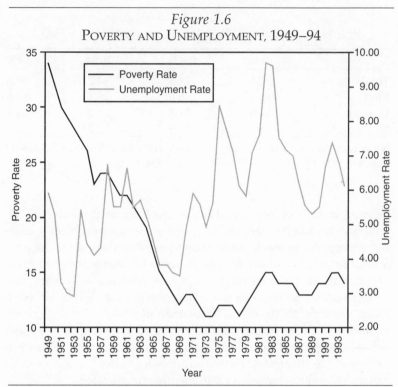

Figure 1.6
POVERTY AND UNEMPLOYMENT, 1949–94

SOURCES: U.S. Department of Labor, Bureau of Labor Statistics, Bulletin 2307; and Bureau of the Census, Current Population Surveys, Series P60, various numbers.

families, essentially those just above the poverty level.[63] Those families may be the most sensitive to temporary economic downturns and recessions, and they may be knocked into poverty for short periods when the economy turns sour. However, it is not among those families that we are seeing the greatest increases in poverty.

Still, one cannot completely disregard economic causes of poverty. The poverty rate's rapid decline during the 1950s and 1960s occurred during a period of relatively sustained economic growth. Economic growth has been relatively sluggish during the period of renewed poverty growth.

[63]David Ellwood, *Poor Support: Poverty in the American Family* (New York: Basic Books, 1988), pp. 96–98.

Changing economic conditions probably have exacerbated some of the problems discussed earlier. For example, the earnings of an individual without a high school education have decreased markedly since the 1970s.[64] There is a substantial body of evidence that links that decline to economic restructuring that has shifted jobs from manufacturing to service and technical occupations.[65] Poor economic conditions also disproportionately affect the availability of, and wages for, low-skilled jobs.[66]

There is also some evidence that economic conditions may lead to an increase in the number of female-headed households; economic conditions may both increase out-of-wedlock births and delay remarriage of divorced women by reducing the supply of employed, "marriageable" men.[67]

Economic conditions worsen the income potential for female-headed families, if for no other reason than that one paycheck brings in less than two. Many two-parent families have coped with economic changes by having a second wage earner in the family. The percentage of women from two-parent families entering the labor force rose steadily, from approximately 28 percent in 1960 to 69 percent in 1994.[68] Female-headed households do not have the option of a second wage earner.

In addition, national economic conditions may not adequately account for local economies. Specifically, economic conditions have deteriorated in inner-city areas regardless of national economic trends. Unemployment is higher in those areas and wages are lower.[69]

[64]Sheldon Danziger and Jonathan Stern, "The Causes and Consequences of Child Poverty in the United States," Innocenti Occasional Paper no. 10, United Nations Child Development Center, Florence, November 1990.

[65]See, for example, Steven Davis and John Haltiwanger, *Wage Dispersion between and within U.S. Manufacturing Plants, 1963–1986,* NBER Working Paper no. 3722 (Cambridge, Mass.: National Bureau of Economic Research, 1991).

[66]Rebecca Blank, "The Employment Strategy: Public Policies to Increase Work and Earnings," in *Confronting Poverty: Prescriptions for Change,* pp. 196–97.

[67]William Julius Wilson, *The Truly Disadvantaged: The Inner City, the Underclass, and Public Policy* (Chicago: University of Chicago Press, 1987), pp. 84–89.

[68]U.S. Department of Labor, Bureau of Labor Statistics, Bulletin 2307 and unpublished data.

[69]Paul Jargowsky and Mary Jo Bane, "Ghetto Poverty: Basic Questions," in *Inner-City Poverty in the United States,* ed. Laurence E. Lynn and Michael McGeary (Washington: National Academy Press, 1990), pp. 28–31.

Perhaps one of the best studies of the interaction between economic conditions and other factors was of the poor in Boston between 1980 and 1988, a period when sustained economic growth reduced the unemployment rate in Massachusetts below 4 percent, a rate generally considered indicative of a "full-employment" economy.[70] The study found that improving economic conditions did reduce poverty. However, the reduction was uneven among different groups. For example, while the poverty rates for both blacks and whites declined at about the same rate, the percentage of African-American families below 125 percent of the poverty level remained a high 22.3 percent.

The situation was even worse for Hispanics, who saw only a slight decline in poverty. Nearly 45 percent of Hispanics remained below the poverty level. Single persons with no children had the greatest decline in poverty for all ethnic groups, while female-headed households had the least. The last point is extremely important, since economic conditions did not seem to change the trend toward single-parent families. Thus, we can say that a growing economy and increased employment are important in reducing poverty but will not by themselves solve the problem.

The high rate and persistence of poverty among African-Americans raise the question of whether racism is a factor in black poverty. No serious observer can deny the continued existence of racism in our society. However, the degree to which racism continues to contribute to black poverty is debatable.

As Table 1.4 shows, poverty rates for African-Americans exceed those for whites in all categories of education, work effort, and family structure.

Wages for African-Americans continue to trail those for similarly educated whites. On average, African-American men earn 73 percent of what similarly situated white men earn, while African-American women earn 89 percent of the wages of white women with similar education levels and job histories.[71] Some studies have suggested

[70]Paul Osterman, "Impact of Full Employment in Boston," in *The Urban Underclass*, ed. Christopher Jencks and Paul Peterson (Washington: Brookings Institution, 1991), pp. 122–34.

[71]Andrew Hacker, *Two Nations, Black and White, Separate, Hostile and Unequal* (New York: Scribners, 1992), p. 98.

Table 1.4
POVERTY RATES BY RACE, 1994 (percentage)

	Black	White
Education		
< High school	44.4	20.6
High school graduate	31.4	8.6
College graduate	5.3	1.8
Work		
Worked full-time	5.3	2.5
Worked part-time	27.0	11.9
Did not work	44.7	31.8
Family Structure		
Two-parent	10.2	6.7
Female-headed	50.2	31.8

SOURCES: Bureau of the Census, *Income, Poverty, and Valuation of Noncash Benefits, 1994*, Current Population Reports, Series P60-188 (Washington: Government Printing Office, 1995), Table 8, pp. 23-24; and Claudette E. Bennett, *The Black Population in the United States: March 1994 and 1993*, Bureau of the Census, Current Population Characteristics Series P20-480 (Washington: Government Printing Office, 1995), Table 7, p. 45.

that 40 to 60 percent of the remaining differential is due to lingering racial bias.[72]

In many cases, African-Americans continue to be the last hired and the first fired, which leaves them more sensitive than whites to changes in economic conditions. There are, however, several important countertrends. For example, the economic well-being of nonelderly, two-parent black families has continued to improve relative to that of similar white families. In 1949 the median income for such a black family was just 44 percent of its white counterpart. That improved to 61 percent by 1969 and to approximately 80 percent

[72]M. Corcoran and G. Duncan, "Work History, Labor Force Attachment, and Earning Differences between the Races and Sexes," *Journal of Human Resources* 14 (Winter 1979): 1–20; Thomas Boston, *Race, Class, and Conservatism* (Boston: Unwin Hyman, 1988), pp. 58–72; and Robert Haveman, *Poverty Policy and Poverty Research: The Great Society and the Social Sciences* (Madison: University of Wisconsin Press, 1987), pp. 142–44.

Figure 1.7
INCOME PER PERSON, BLACK IMMIGRANTS VS. NATIVE BORN

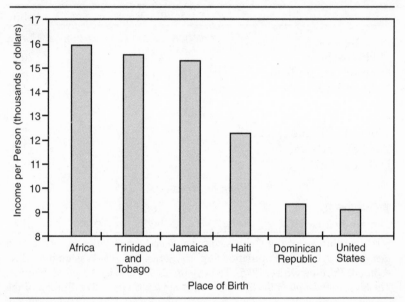

Place of Birth

SOURCE: "Black Like Me," *The Economist*, May 11, 1996, citing Census Bureau data.

by 1994.[73] Black poverty increased at the same time that a large black middle class was developing.

In addition, other ethnic groups—such as Asians and West Indians—that have experienced racial discrimination have much lower rates of poverty. Moreover, as shown in Figure 1.7, black immigrants have higher incomes and lower rates of poverty than do native-born blacks. In some cases, black immigrants have higher incomes than do native-born whites. For example, in New York City more than half of all black immigrant families from the Caribbean have incomes between $25,000 and $75,000 per year, compared with 45 percent of white families and only 39 percent of native-born black families.[74] Finally, as we have seen, the greatest progress in reducing black poverty occurred during a period of overt discrimination.

[73]Danziger and Gottschalk, *America Unequal*, p. 73.
[74]"Black Like Me," *The Economist*, May 11, 1996, pp. 27–28.

Table 1.5
PERCENTAGE OF FEMALE-HEADED FAMILIES

Year	White	Black
1940	10.2	17.9
1950	8.5	17.6
1960	8.1	21.7
1970	9.1	28.3
1980	11.6	40.2
1990	13.2	45.9

SOURCE: William Kelso, *Poverty and the Underclass: Changing Perceptions of the Poor in America* (New York: New York University Press, 1994), Table 9.1.

Why then the overall increase in black poverty? The primary reason appears to be the changing makeup of the black family. As we have seen, female-headed households are much more likely to be poor than are two-parent families. As Table 1.5 shows, the increase in black single-parent families has been much more rapid than in white single-parent families.

We have also seen that poverty is linked to a lack of education. For a variety of reasons, particularly the poor quality of inner-city public schools, African-Americans continue to trail whites in educational achievement. While 85 percent of whites graduate high school, only 73 percent of African-Americans do. Fully 29 percent of whites graduate college, but only 13 percent of blacks do.[75]

Black poverty is also heavily concentrated in urban areas that suffer from a host of social ills, including high crime rates and a deteriorating economic base.[76] Finally, the ill-conceived War on Drugs has severely disadvantaged young black men, leaving one of three in the custody of the criminal justice system.[77] Young men with criminal records are less employable and less marriageable than are young men without criminal records. Therefore, while lingering

[75]Bennett, Table 7, p. 45.

[76]Jargowsky and Bane, p. 33.

[77]That represents a 78 percent increase since 1989. The War on Drugs is responsible for the largest portion of the increase. African-Americans constitute only 13 percent of monthly drug users but account for 35 percent of all those arrested for drug possession, 55 percent of those convicted, and 74 percent of those receiving prison sentences. "Young Black Americans and the Criminal Justice System: Five Years Later," The Sentencing Project, Washington, October 1995.

racism may play a role in black poverty, other factors appear to have a much more significant impact.

Finally, it is important to look at welfare itself as a cause of poverty. Evidence is strong that welfare creates incentives that increase poverty-causing behavior such as unwed motherhood and decrease poverty-avoiding behavior such as work. That will be explored in more detail in subsequent chapters. However, it is worth noting that Vedder and Gallaway found that poor individuals who do not receive welfare are nearly two and a half times more likely to escape poverty within a year than are individuals who receive welfare.[78]

The "Gap" between Rich and Poor

A discussion of poverty in America should include a brief mention of the widely cited growing "gap" between rich and poor. It has become fashionable in recent years to claim that the United States is becoming increasingly stratified in terms of income—that the rich are becoming richer and the poor are becoming poorer.

A recent study by the Organization for Economic Cooperation and Development reported that the United States had the widest gap between rich and poor of any major industrialized nation. According to the report, the poorest 10 percent of the U.S. population had incomes averaging only 35 percent of the median national income, while the richest 10 percent had incomes averaging 206 percent of the median.[79] Other studies have shown that the wealthiest 20 percent of Americans earn 48 percent of the country's income and control the vast majority of its wealth.[80] The gap is said to have grown steadily worse in the last 20 years.

The initial reaction to the inequality between rich and poor is, so what? After all, would the situation be significantly improved if

[78]Vedder and Gallaway, pp. 23–24.

[79]Timothy Smeeding, Lee Rainwater, and Anthony Atkinson, *Income Distribution in OECD Countries* (Paris: Organization for Economic Cooperation and Development, 1995), Table 4.1, p. 40.

[80]Sheldon Danziger and Peter Gottschalk, "Increasing Inequality in the United States: What We Know and What We Don't," *Journal of Post-Keynesian Economics* 11, no. 2 (Winter 1989): 174–95; Gordon Green, John Coder, and Paul Ryscavage, "International Comparisons of Earnings Inequality for Men in the 1980s," *Review of Income and Wealth*, Series 38 (March 1992): 1–15; and Lynn Karoly, "Changes in the Distribution of Individual Earnings in the United States, 1967–1986," *Review of Economics and Statistics* 24, no. 1 (February 1992): 107–15.

Table 1.6
INCREASE IN WEALTH, 1983–89

Family Income	Percent Change in Net Worth
Less than $10,000	+ 2
$10,000–$19,999	+19
$20,000–$29,999	+29
$30,000–$49,999	+28
$50,000 and more	+ 7

SOURCE: Michael Novak, "What Wealth Gap?" *Wall Street Journal*, January 11, 1995.

everyone were equally poor? The question should be whether economic conditions are improving for the poor. As Table 1.6 shows, between 1983 and 1989 all income levels saw an increase in wealth. The gap between rich and poor grew because wealth grew faster for middle- and upper-income groups, but wealth increased for all groups.

Far more important than equality is mobility—do people move easily up and down the income ladder? Income mobility in the United States remains quite significant. As we have already seen, between one-third and one-half of the poor escape poverty from one year to the next.

Moreover, as Table 1.7 shows, of those Americans in the first (lowest) quintile of earnings in 1979, only 14.2 percent remained in the bottom fifth by 1988. Nor were those who moved up grouped at the bottom of the second quintile. While 20.7 percent were in the second quintile, 25 percent had made it into the middle quintile, and even more, 25.3 percent, into the second highest quintile. In fact, 14.7 percent had made it all the way to the highest quintile; they had gone from the lowest fifth of American earners to the highest. The 14.7 percent reaching the highest quintile is a larger group than the 14.2 percent remaining at the bottom. At the same time, 35.2 percent of those in the top quintile in 1979 had fallen out by 1988.[81] The composition of every income group changed over time. Moreover, the general trend in income mobility was up.

[81]U.S. Congress, Joint Economic Committee, *Income Mobility and Economic Opportunity*, 2d ed., Joint Economic Committee Report, August 1995, p. 4.

Table 1.7
INCOME MOBILITY, 1979–88

1979 Quintile	Percent in Quintile in 1979	Percent in Each Quintile in 1988				
		1st	2d	3d	4th	5th
1st	100	14.2	20.7	25.0	25.3	14.7
2d	100	10.9	29.0	29.6	19.5	11.1
3d	100	5.7	14.0	33.0	32.3	15.0
4th	100	3.1	9.3	14.8	37.5	35.4
5th	100	1.1	4.4	9.4	20.3	64.7

SOURCE: U.S. Congress, Joint Economic Committee, *Income Mobility and Economic Opportunity*, 2d ed., Joint Economic Committee Report, August 1995, p. 4.

Two other studies confirm that trend and suggest that it has remained relatively unchanged since the 1970s. Richard Burkhauser, Douglas Holtz-Eakin, and Stephen Rhody of Syracuse University found that of those Americans in the lowest quintile of income, 19 percent would move into a higher quintile within one year, and 36 percent would move up within five years. Those percentages have changed very little over the past 20 years, according to the authors.[82]

A 1995 study for the Federal Reserve Bank of Dallas found that nearly 75 percent of the individuals who had the lowest 20 percent of incomes in 1975 had moved into the top 40 percent of incomes in 1991. In fact, the report concludes that the poor made more dramatic gains in income than any other group.[83]

It seems apparent, therefore, that a person's economic condition is not immutable in America. The poor can become wealthy; the wealthy can become poor. The ability to move out of poverty—for the poor to become wealthy—is far more important than whether the wealthy are getting richer.

[82]Richard Burkhauser, Douglas Holtz-Eakin, and Stephen Rhody, "Labor Earnings Mobility and Inequality in the United States and Germany in the Growth Years of the 1980's," accepted for publication in a forthcoming issue of *International Economic Review*.

[83]W. Michael Cox and Richard Alm, "By Our Own Bootstraps: Economic Opportunity and the Dynamics of Income Distribution," Federal Reserve Bank of Dallas, 1995.

Conclusion

Although the appropriate measure of poverty remains highly controversial, we cannot escape the fact that poverty is far too widespread in the United States. Most poor people do not remain so throughout their lives. However, a small group of hard-core poor remains mired in poverty for long periods. The question, therefore, is, How can we best reduce that poverty? Are government action and social welfare programs the best method? Or is government welfare actually counterproductive? Can private charity be more effective? The following chapters will examine those questions in detail.

2. The Rise of the Welfare State

Poverty in not new in America. Records dating from the 1600s indicate concern for the care of those in need. As one would expect, many of the poor were widows, orphans, and the physically and mentally disabled. Some were victims of fires or storms. However, there were also those who simply lacked work.[1]

Although some conservatives like to portray charity in this country in the early years as a purely private matter, in truth there was some degree of government involvement from the beginning. However, government activity was almost exclusively at the local level. The idea that the federal government should involve itself in charity did occasionally crop up, but it was nearly universally rejected by the Founding Fathers, who considered such action beyond the proper constitutional role of the federal government. In 1794, for example, James Madison, debating a proposed welfare bill, rose on the floor of the House to declare, "I cannot undertake to lay my finger on that article of the Federal Constitution which granted a right to Congress" to pass such a bill.[2]

That was still the attitude in 1854 when President Franklin Pierce vetoed a bill to give land to the states to allow them to build institutions for the insane. In his veto message, Pierce wrote, "I cannot find any authority in the Constitution for making the Federal Government the great almoner of public charity throughout the United States. To do so would . . . be contrary to the letter and spirit of the Constitution and subversive of the whole theory upon which the Union of these States is founded."[3]

---

[1]As early as 1822, records from the Boston Employment Society show a call for assistance for "700 men for whom work cannot be obtained." Cited in Michael Katz, *In the Shadow of the Poorhouse: A Social History of Welfare in America* (New York: Basic Books, 1986), p. 7.

[2]*Annals of the Congress of the United States, 1789–1824* 4 (1794): 179.

[3]Quoted in Charles Warren, *Congress as Santa Claus: Or National Donations and the General Welfare Clause of the Constitution* (1932; reprint, New York: Arno, 1978), pp. 62–63.

Colonial America was influenced by the English Poor Law. That law, passed in 1601, established four basic principles for government charity: (1) care for the poor was a public responsibility; (2) care for the poor was a local matter; (3) public relief was denied to individuals who could be cared for by their families; and (4) children of the poor could be apprenticed to farmers and artisans who would care for them in exchange for work.[4] Those principles would underlie the earliest American welfare programs. The early states also followed English precedent by enacting "settlement laws," which prevented the poor from moving to towns with more generous welfare benefits.

In general, public charity was administered by counties and townships through one of two methods: outdoor relief or poorhouses. Outdoor relief, which most closely resembled today's welfare programs, took a number of forms. In some cases small cash grants were given, in others contributions were "in kind," mainly food. Fuel was generally provided during the winter.[5]

Most recipients of outdoor relief were women, children, elderly, or sick. For example, a census of those receiving outdoor relief in Philadelphia in 1814 revealed that nearly two-thirds of the recipients were sick, disabled, or aged. The remaining third was made up of single mothers, the vast majority of whom were widows.[6] However, a small minority of outdoor relief recipients were able-bodied but unemployed men who engendered a considerable amount of resentment that was often directed toward outdoor relief in general. That led many communities to reduce outdoor relief in favor of poorhouses.

Poorhouses or workhouses were another carryover from England. There were poorhouses from the very earliest days of the colonies. Boston established a poorhouse in 1702, and New York followed suit in 1736. The Philadelphia poorhouse was opened in 1766.[7]

Poorhouses were seen as superior to outdoor relief both because they were less expensive and because they provided a deterrent to able-bodied people's applying for relief. Conditions in poorhouses

---

[4]Katz, *In the Shadow of the Poorhouse*, pp. 13–14.

[5]Ibid., p. 37.

[6]Priscilla Clement, "The Philadelphia Welfare Crisis of the 1820's," *Pennsylvania Magazine of History and Biography* 2 (April 1981): 163.

[7]Eric Monkkonen, "Nineteenth-Century Institutions: Dealing with the Urban Underclass," in *The Underclass Debate: Views from History*, ed. Michael Katz (Princeton, N.J.: Princeton University Press, 1993), p. 344.

were harsh. Long hours of work were mandatory. Whipping and other punishments were common for infractions of the rules.[8] The poor were often housed together with the insane, prostitutes, and petty thieves.[9]

The harshness was intentional, designed to "deter many intemperate wretches and lazy vagrants from seeking admission."[10] Reports of the time indicate that the policy met with some success. Typical was a report from New Bedford, Massachusetts, which said that since the town had switched from outdoor relief to a poorhouse, it had "experienced a diminution of that class of vagrants who have for years annoyed us."[11]

Starting in the 1830s, state governments began to require that cities and counties establish poorhouses.[12] For nearly a century thereafter, they would remain the central feature of government antipoverty policy. During the early part of the 19th century, there was also a brief experimentation with "auctioning" the poor. Poor individuals would be auctioned off to people who agreed to care for them at the lowest cost. However, many bidders saw the auctions as a source of cheap labor, and abuse was rampant. In 1842 a report by Secretary of State J. V. N. Yates of New York warned that "the poor, when farmed out, or sold, are frequently treated with barbarity and neglected by their keepers."[13] As a result of abuses, the practice had largely died out by the middle of the century.

Government welfare was supplemented and generally surpassed by private charitable activities. Alexis de Tocqueville commented on the compassion of ordinary Americans and the widespread activities of private charity, contrasting the United States with European countries, where "the state almost exclusively undertakes to supply

---

[8]Marvin Olasky, *The Tragedy of American Compassion* (Washington: Regnery, 1992), p. 11.

[9]Monkkonen, p. 343.

[10]Charles Burroughs, "A Discourse Delivered in the Chapel of the New Almshouse in Portsmouth, New Hampshire, December 15, 1834, on the Occasion of Its First Being Opened for Religious Service," in *The Jacksonians on the Poor: Collected Pamphlets,* ed. David Rothman (New York: Arno, 1971), pp. 49–50.

[11]Cited in Katz, *In the Shadow of the Poorhouse,* p. 23.

[12]Ibid., p. 341.

[13]J. V. N. Yates, "Report of the Secretary of State of New York on the Relief and Resettlement of the Poor," 1824, p. 952, cited in Olasky, p. 45.

bread to the hungry, assistance and shelter to the sick, work to the idle, and to act as sole reliever of all kinds of misery."[14]

In his seminal work, *The Tragedy of American Compassion*, Marvin Olasky has detailed the astonishing breadth and variety of private charitable efforts throughout the first half of this country's existence. Most were religious in nature—Protestant, Catholic, and Jewish charitable organizations all thrived—and almost all operated on the principle of distinguishing between the "deserving" and the "undeserving" poor.[15]

The deserving poor included those who, although normally self-sufficient, found themselves suddenly in need of help because of sickness, accident, loss of employment during a recession, or similar misfortune. The deserving poor also included the elderly, orphans, and others for whom circumstances made self-sufficiency impossible. The undeserving poor were those who could be self-sufficient but were not because of personal or "moral" failings; that group included drunkards, layabouts, and profligates.[16]

Interestingly, there is evidence that the total amount of charity in a community remained relatively constant regardless of the mix of public and private sources. In 1899 Frederic Almy, secretary of the Buffalo Charity Organization Society, gathered data on public and private charitable activities in 40 cities. Almy ranked the cities in four groups from high to low in both categories of charity. He found that cities in the highest two categories of private charity had the lowest levels of public charity. Those with higher levels of public charity tended to have lower levels of private charity. Almy concluded that "a correspondence or balance between the amounts of public and private relief appears to be established."[17]

The Progressive Era and the Rise of Government Charity

By the closing years of the 19th century, both public and private charity were undergoing profound changes. For public welfare, the

[14]Alexis de Tocqueville, *Democracy in America*, trans. George Lawrence (New York: HarperCollins, 1969), p. 219.

[15]Olasky, pp. 6–24.

[16]Clifford Thies, "Is It Time to End Welfare?" *St. Croix Review* 27, no. 5 (October 1994): 36–37.

[17]Frederic Almy, "The Relation between Public and Private Charities," *Charities Review* 9 (1899): 65–71.

days of purely local control were on the way out. State, and even federal, involvement was rising.

At the same time, a significant change was occurring in Americans' attitude toward government. The rise of "modernism" and "progressivism" caused many Americans to believe that "experts" were required to solve most problems and that only government could provide the needed expertise. Previously, the purpose of government had been seen as protecting individual rights. Now, government was seen as a problem solver.

Reformers admitted that private charities had done a good job so far but thought they were now facing "a problem infinitely bigger than they can handle—a problem so big that no institution short of society itself can hope to cope with it."[18] The problem might be big, but there was no problem that was too big for government experts to fix. Owen Lovejoy, president of the National Conference of Social Work, wrote in a 1920 article of social workers as "social engineers" imposing "a divine order on earth as it is in heaven."[19]

The federal government was taking its first tentative steps into the social welfare arena. The Civil War had left a large number of disabled veterans for whom the federal government provided pensions and other benefits. In addition, the federal government provided emergency relief to victims of floods in 1867, 1874, 1882, and 1884. Farmers devastated by a locust infestation in 1875 received a special appropriation. There was also an 1879 appropriation to establish colleges for the blind.[20]

At the local level, poorhouses were on their way out. A series of reforms had removed many groups—orphans, the mentally ill, the sick—to specialized institutions, leaving the poorhouses to gradually transform themselves into old-age homes. At the same time, outdoor relief was making a resurgence. For example, between 1911 and 1925, the amount of outdoor relief dispensed in the nation's 16 largest cities increased from $1.6 million to $14.7 million.[21]

---

[18]John Haynes Holmes, a Unitarian minister and religious writer, quoted in Paul T. Ringenbach, *Tramps and Reformers, 1873–1916: The Discovery of Unemployment in New York* (Westport, Conn.: Westport, 1973), p. 168.

[19]Owen Lovejoy, "The Faith of a Social Worker," *Survey*, May 18, 1920, p. 209.

[20]Warren, p. 92.

[21]Ann Geddes, *Trends in Relief Expenditures, 1910–1935* (Washington: Government Printing Office, 1937), pp. 8–9.

Not surprisingly, children and the elderly were at the heart of new government programs to help the poor. Certainly many children were living in miserable conditions. What became known as the Child Saving movement developed. The Child Saving movement was a broad, loose social movement that sought better conditions for children. Among the many issues embraced under the general heading of Child Saving were removing children from poorhouses; preventing child abuse and enacting child cruelty laws; replacing institutional care with foster care; juvenile justice reform, including the introduction of juvenile courts and the removal of juveniles from adult prisons; compulsory education; and public health measures to combat infant mortality.[22]

Not all Child Savers favored government action. Many supported traditional charitable activities, with a new emphasis on the problems of children. Many in the Child Saving movement regarded government institutions as corrupt and sought to limit government's role in helping children. That appears to have been particularly true in the East, where big city political machines had corrupted nearly all governmental activities. For example, in New York, the Child Saving movement successfully fought to forbid government regulation of any children's institution that did not receive government money.[23] However, the movement gradually became dominated by pro-government reformers, and the movement's emphasis shifted to government action.

Among the Child Saving movement's greatest successes was moving children out of poorhouses into orphanages. Orphanages had a long history in the United States, as both private and public institutions. Private orphanages were established in New Orleans as early as 1729 and in Savannah in 1738. The first public orphanage was probably the one in Charleston, South Carolina, established in 1794.[24]

But the heyday of the orphanage came in the late 19th and early 20th centuries. Between 1900 and 1904 alone, the number of children

[22]Katz, *In the Shadow of the Poorhouse*, pp. 113–45.

[23]Susan Tiffin, *In Whose Best Interest? Child Welfare in the Progressive Era* (Westport, Conn.: Greenwood, 1983), pp. 204–5.

[24]Homer Folks, *The Care of Destitute, Neglected, and Delinquent Children* (New York: Macmillan, 1902), pp. 7–11.

in public institutions doubled.[25] By 1910 there were at least 1,151 orphanages in the United States. Approximately 90 percent of them were at least nominally private, but nearly all received at least some government funding.[26]

The Child Saving movement continued to drive government to become more involved in social welfare issues. In 1912 Congress established the Children's Bureau to study and report on "all matters pertaining to the welfare of children and child life among all classes of our people."[27] The agency had no authority and an annual budget of only $25,640 but nonetheless represented an important turning point in the growth of the welfare state.[28] The federal government was taking a direct role in social welfare policy.

Among the first state welfare programs were "mothers' pensions," small stipends to widows and other mothers to assist them in caring for their children. In part, those programs were a county-level response to the large number of widows in the aftermath of the Civil War. In part, they were a continuation of the Child Saving movement. Mothers' pensions eventually moved to state government. In 1911 Missouri and Illinois were the first states to enact mothers' pensions. Other states soon followed and, by 1919, 39 states and the territories of Alaska and Hawaii had authorized mothers' pensions. By 1935 every state except Georgia and South Carolina provided widows' pensions.[29]

In many ways mothers' pensions foretokened future welfare programs, particularly Aid to Families with Dependent Children (AFDC). The original recipients of mothers' pensions were intended to be almost exclusively widows. However, the program soon expanded to cover women who for a variety of reasons were "without the support of the normal breadwinner."[30] As a result, the program soon began to provide aid for divorced and abandoned women,

---

[25]Tiffin, pp. 205–10.

[26]Monkkonen, p. 354.

[27]Children's Bureau, *First Annual Report of the Chief*, 1914, p. 2.

[28]Ibid., p. 122.

[29]Ibid., pp. 128–29.

[30]*Proceedings of the Conference on Care of Dependent Children* (Washington: Government Printing Office, 1909), p. 721.

and even unwed mothers.[31] The program grew steadily. By 1930 mothers of more than 200,000 children were receiving funds.[32]

By the 1920s most states had also established a variety of child health programs and clinics. They also provided subsidized milk to mothers with young children and information and referrals to private charities. In 1921, establishing the first federally funded government health care program, Congress passed the Sheppard-Towner Act, which provided matching funds to the states to establish prenatal and child health centers. Among the purposes of those centers was to "teach expectant mothers the rules of personal hygiene and offer advice on how to maintain and improve the health of their children."[33] The program itself was short-lived—Congress stopped funding it in 1929—but the principle of federal government involvement in welfare had been firmly established.

Indeed, in 1921 Warren Harding campaigned on the idea of establishing a federal department of public welfare.[34] His proposal died in Congress, but his attitude shows how far America had come since the days of President Pierce's veto.

States also began to play a role in the care of the aged. In 1914 Arizona passed the first law establishing an old-age pension. By 1933 approximately 30 states had followed suit.[35]

The changing attitude toward government welfare can also be seen in the era's changing terminology. For example, as part of New York's 1929 Public Welfare Law, relief was renamed public welfare, almshouses became county homes, superintendents of the poor became commissioners of public welfare, and the State Board of Charities was renamed the State Board of Social Welfare.[36]

The same reverence for experts and structure was evident in private charities, which became more structured and hierarchical. Volunteers were replaced with paid staff.[37] Social workers became

[31]Olasky, p. 140.

[32]Katz, In the Shadow of the Poorhouse, p. 128.

[33]Sheila Rothman, Woman's Proper Place: A History of Changing Ideals and Practices, 1870 to the Present (New York: Basic Books, 1978), pp. 136–40.

[34]Olasky, pp. 142–43.

[35]Blanche Coll, Safety Net: Welfare and Social Security, 1929–1979 (New Brunswick, N.J.: Rutgers University Press, 1995), p. 4.

[36]Michael Katz, Improving Poor People: The Welfare State, the Underclass, and Urban Schools as History (Princeton, N.J.: Princeton University Press, 1995), p. 44.

[37]Katz, In the Shadow of the Poorhouse, p. 63.

increasingly specialized, styling themselves as medical social workers, visiting teachers, vocational guidance specialists, and psychiatric social workers. Schools of social work sprang up, then proliferated. By 1930 there were 30 schools of social work.[38]

As they became a professional class, social workers began to resent competition from their unschooled counterparts. Increased government regulation of social work and private charitable activities was sought. By 1911 Frederic Almy was led to complain that "social workers, like doctors, will soon have to pass an examination before they are allowed to practice on the poor."[39]

With the changing nature of private charity and the increasing involvement of government at all levels, the stage was set for the next major expansion of the welfare state. The opportunity for that expansion came with the onset of the Great Depression.

African-Americans and Fraternal Organizations

During the 19th and early 20th century, there developed an interesting trend in the African-American community.[40] Most public welfare programs—particularly in the South but throughout the country as well—refused to provide benefits to African-Americans.[41] Many private charities also discriminated. Therefore, African-Americans began to develop their own charitable institutions.

Among them were mutual aid societies and fraternal organizations.[42] Although they provided services to poor whites as well, fraternal organizations were particularly important to the African-American community. Black Bostonians had established the first African-American Masonic Lodge in 1792. Blacks in Philadelphia

---

[38]Ibid., p. 209.

[39]Quoted in Olasky, p. 143.

[40]I am particularly indebted to the pioneering work of David Beito in this field. Much of this section is drawn from his work.

[41]See, for example, Robert Bremner, *Children and Youth in America: A Documentary History* (Cambridge, Mass.: Harvard University Press, 1971), p. 301.

[42]Mutual aid associations have deep historical roots dating back to medieval guilds. For centuries they were a primary source of charity until destroyed by the modern welfare state. For a good discussion of the history of mutual aid, see Otto Friedrich von Gierke, *Community in Historical Perspective*, ed. Antony Black (Cambridge: Cambridge University Press, 1990).

41

followed suit five years later.[43] By the 20th century there were hundreds of black lodges and fraternal groups. Some were segregated black chapters of groups like the Masons, the Elks, and the Loyal Order of Moose. Others were all-black organizations such as the autonomous Grand United Order of Odd Fellows.[44]

Membership in those organizations was enormous. In 1916 the Odd Fellows had more than 304,000 members nationwide. The Knights of Pythias had 250,000 members.[45] In Philadelphia fully 80 percent of the African-American population during the 1800s was said to belong to black fraternal groups and their women's auxiliaries.[46] Nearly 30 percent of all adult black men in southern states were thought to be members of the Prince Hall Masons.[47]

Black fraternal organizations provided a wide variety of social services both to their members and to the African-American community at large. They built orphanages and old-age homes. The Odd Fellows, for example, operated 47 homes for the elderly in 1929.[48] They provided food to the hungry, helped the unemployed find work, and provided shelter for the homeless.

One of the most important services provided by fraternal organizations was the "death benefit," a form of life insurance. Death benefits helped prevent the widows of members from falling into poverty. As a 1910 article in *Everybody's Magazine* put it, "Rich men insure in big companies to create an estate. Poor men insure in the fraternal

---

[43]Joe William Trotter, "Blacks in the Urban North: The Underclass Question in Historical Perspective," in *The Underclass Debate: Views from History*, ed. Michael Katz (Princeton, N.J.: Princeton University Press, 1993), p. 64.

[44]David Beito, "Mutual Aid, State Welfare, and Organized Charity: Fraternal Societies and the Deserving and Undeserving Poor, 1900–1930," *Journal of Policy History* 5, no. 4 (Fall 1993): 419–34.

[45]Monroe Work, *Negro Year Book: Annual Encyclopedia of the Negro, 1916–17* (1918), p. 397, cited in Beito, "Mutual Aid, State Welfare, and Organized Charity," pp. 421–22.

[46]John Hope Franklin and Alfred Moss Jr., *From Slavery to Freedom: A History of Negro Americans* (1947; reprint, New York: Alfred Knopf, 1988), pp. 93–95.

[47]William Muraskin, *Middle-Class Blacks in White Society: Prince Hall Freemasonry in America* (Berkeley: University of California Press, 1975), p. 118, cited in Beito, "Mutual Aid, State Welfare, and Organized Charity," p. 422.

[48]David Beito, "Mutual Aid for Social Welfare: The Case for American Fraternal Societies," *Critical Review* 4, no. 4 (Fall 1990): 712–13.

orders to create bread and meat. It is an insurance against want, the poorhouse, charity, and degradation."[49]

In addition to life insurance, fraternal organizations provided "lodge-practice medicine," an early form of health insurance. Members would pay the lodge a premium of one or two dollars per month. The lodge, in turn, would contract with a doctor who would agree, for a flat monthly or yearly fee, to treat all lodge members. In many ways, lodge-practice medicine resembled health maintenance organizations.[50]

As a result of the widespread influence of black fraternal organizations, African-Americans were more likely to be insured than were whites during the early years of the 20th century.[51] A 1919 survey of African-Americans in Chicago, for instance, found that 93.5 percent of families had at least one member insured.[52] The same year a survey in Philadelphia found that 98 percent of African-American families had at least one insured member.[53]

A strong network of black churches and private organizations such as the National Urban League and the National Association of Colored Women also offered a wide variety of social services, including homes for the aged, women, and children; relief funds for the feeding and care of the unemployed; and job referral services.[54]

Private charitable efforts among African-Americans strongly emphasized the difference between deserving and undeserving poor. Individuals who refused work or engaged in "immoral practices" were routinely denied benefits. Although it may have been making a virtue of necessity, African-American public opinion often appeared contemptuous of public charity. For example, the membership manual of the Colored Knights of Pythias proudly claimed,

[49]Harris Dickson and Isidore Mantz, "Will the Widow Get Her Money? The Weaknesses in Fraternal Life Insurance and How It May Be Cured," *Everybody's Magazine* 22 (June 1910): 776, cited in ibid., p. 713.

[50]Beito, "Mutual Aid, State Welfare, and Organized Charity," p. 423 n. 43.

[51]Beito, "Mutual Aid for Social Welfare," pp. 718–19.

[52]Illinois Health Insurance Commission, *Report of the Health Insurance Commission of the State of Illinois*, 1919, p. 22, cited in ibid., p. 720.

[53]Sadie Tanner Mossell, "The Standard of Living among 100 Negro Migrant Families in Philadelphia," *Annals of the American Academy of Political and Social Sciences* 98 (November 1921): 200, cited in Beito, "Mutual Aid for Social Welfare," p. 719.

[54]Trotter, pp. 65–66.

"The sick among our brethren are not left to the cold hand of public charity; they are visited, and their wants provided for . . . without the humiliation of . . . individual relief—from which the freeborn mind recoils with disdain."[55] In a similar vein, Booker T. Washington argued that "in our ordinary southern communities, we look upon it as a disgrace for an individual to be taken from that community to any institution for dependents."[56]

Immigrants and other groups that were routinely excluded from public charity developed similar private institutions, including Mexican-American Penitente Lodges; Chinese companies and tongs; and organizations in the Polish, Italian, Irish, and Slovak communities.[57]

Fraternal organizations remained a major factor in African-American charity well into the 1930s. However, as the federalization of welfare made government benefits increasingly available to blacks, the mission of the lodges was supplanted. The organizations declined in membership and influence and gave up many of their social service activities.[58]

In addition, the American Medical Association, complaining that lodge-practice medicine was undermining physicians' incomes, launched a campaign against the practice that resulted in its virtual elimination by 1930.[59] As a result, African-Americans moved into the mainstream of the welfare state.

---

[55]*History and Manual of the Colored Knights of Pythias* (Nashville: National Baptist Publishing Board, 1917), pp. 448–49, cited in Beito, "Mutual Aid, State Welfare, and Organized Charity," pp. 429–30.

[56]Booker T. Washington, "Destitute Colored Children of the South," in *Proceedings of the Conference on the Care of Dependent Children*, pp. 114–17.

[57]Beito, "Mutual Aid for Social Welfare." Mutual aid societies were also important sources of charity in other countries. See, for example, David Green, *Reinventing Civil Society: The Rediscovery of Welfare without Politics* (London: Institute for Economic Affairs, 1993); and David Green and Lawrence Cromwell, *Mutual Aid or Welfare State? Australia's Friendly Societies* (Sydney: George Allen & Unwin, 1984).

[58]Beito, "Mutual Aid for Social Welfare," pp. 727–29.

[59]David Beito, "The 'Lodge Practice Evil' Reconsidered," unpublished manuscript, pp. 24–28. Interestingly, the medical establishment in Britain pursued a similar course, attempting to destroy lodge-practice medicine. The ultimate result was the adoption of socialized medicine. David Green, *Working Class Patients and the Medical Establishment: Self-Help in Britain from the Mid-Nineteenth Century to 1948* (New York: St. Martin's, 1985).

The New Deal

The Great Depression was one of the most traumatic events in American history. At its worst point, in 1933, nearly 13 million Americans, 24.9 percent of the labor force, were unemployed. Among nonfarm laborers unemployment was even worse, as high as 37.6 percent. The nation's gross national product declined by half between 1929 and 1933. One-third of the nation's banks suspended operations. Businesses went bankrupt, and there were widespread mortgage foreclosures, particularly on farms.[60] Americans were financially insecure and frightened.

Both public and private charities were unprepared to deal with the sudden massive unemployment and poverty. The burden was huge. For example, a Bureau of the Census survey in 1929 found that an average of 334,000 families were receiving relief nationwide each month. By 1931 that number had risen to more than 1 million per month. By 1933 the number of families on relief each month had increased to 4 million, or nearly 18 million persons.[61] During the first quarter of 1932 public and private relief in New York State totaled more than $15 million compared with less than $4 million in the first quarter of 1929.[62]

Local governments found that providing relief was a serious drain on their resources and created financial crises. Several cities went bankrupt. Detroit and Chicago found themselves without enough money to pay their schoolteachers.[63] Private charities found it equally difficult to cope. In New York City alone nearly 400 private charities went under between 1929 and 1932.[64] A desperate announcement from Silas Strong, president of the U.S. Chamber of Commerce, in 1932 provides a glimpse at how severe the problem was.

> For many months the Illinois Emergency Relief Commission has been taking care of 111,000 families, or about 600,000

[60]Coll, pp. 1–3.

[61]Josephine Chapin Brown, *Public Relief: 1929–1939* (New York: Octagon Books, 1940), p. 126.

[62]James T. Patterson, *The New Deal and the States: Federalism in Transition* (Princeton, N.J.: Princeton University Press, 1969), p. 26.

[63]Coll, p. 8.

[64]William Bremer, *Depression Winters: New York Social Workers and the New Deal* (Philadelphia: Temple University Press, 1984), p. 65.

of the destitute. The $10.5 million fund contributed by the citizens, and the $12.5 million additional, being the proceeds of the State of Illinois notes, in all $23 million are exhausted. Accordingly, the relief stations in Chicago have been notified ... that all available funds having been exhausted, the stations must close tomorrow night.[65]

Local governments, not surprisingly, looked to state governments for assistance. Among the first to respond was New York's governor Franklin Roosevelt, who called a special session of the legislature to pass the Wicks Act, which created the Temporary Emergency Relief Association. TERA, which would later serve as a model for some of Roosevelt's federal anti-poverty programs, provided matching grants to localities for emergency unemployment relief.[66] In the next few months six major industrial states—New Jersey, Pennsylvania, Rhode Island, Wisconsin, Illinois, and Ohio—followed New York's lead and established unemployment relief funds.[67]

Demands for federal action began to mount. There were marches on Washington, protests, even riots. The demands were supported by the now thoroughly "professionalized" social worker class. In 1931, for example, the Rockefeller Foundation gave a $40,000 grant to the American Association of Social Workers to "educate public opinion regarding the fundamental importance of welfare work in the present government."[68]

In Congress Sens. Edward Costigan (D-Colo.), Robert La Follette (D-Wis.), and Robert Wagner (D-N.Y.) pushed hard for the federal government to intervene. In 1931 Congress passed a bill introduced by Senator Wagner that would have established a federally funded public works program, an expanded federal employment service, and unemployment insurance, but the bill was vetoed by President Herbert Hoover.[69]

Hoover was adamantly opposed to federal intervention. In his 1931 message to Congress, he said, "I am opposed to any direct or

[65]Cited in Harry Hopkins, *Spending to Save: The Complete Story of Relief* (New York: W. W. Norton, 1936), p. 77.

[66]David Schneider and Albert Deutsch, *The History of Public Welfare in New York State, 1867–1940* (Chicago: University of Chicago Press, 1941), pp. 307–414.

[67]Coll, p. 9.

[68]Brown, p. 85.

[69]Katz, *In the Shadow of the Poorhouse*, p. 216.

indirect government dole. The breakdown and increased unemployment in Europe is due in part to such practices. Our people are providing against distress from unemployment in true American fashion."[70]

Hoover's opposition to federal government action stemmed from two important experiences. In London in the 1920s he had seen the destructive influence of England's dole on World War I veterans, whom he observed passing up available work in favor of unemployment benefits. Second, Hoover had led the massive private and religious charitable campaign that provided relief to the war's civilian victims. That instilled in him a firm belief in the ability of private charity to meet any crisis.[71]

Hoover repeatedly stressed private charity as an alternative to government action. "This is not an issue as to whether people shall go hungry and cold in the United States," he said. "It is solely a question of how hunger and cold shall be prevented. It is a question of whether the American people on the one hand will maintain the spirit of charity and mutual self-help through voluntary giving and the responsibility of local government as distinguished on the other hand from appropriations from the federal treasury for such purposes."[72]

Private charitable groups were indeed beginning to rally. Americans were contributing more to charity than ever before. In New York City, for example, a group of philanthropists contributed $8.5 million to put the unemployed to work.[73] In 1932, despite worsening economic conditions, the Community Chest set a record for contributions.[74]

Whether Hoover was ultimately correct that private charity would be sufficient to handle the crisis would never be known, because as elections approached and the depression deepened, he began to waver. In 1932 he signed legislation creating the Reconstruction

---

[70]Cited in John McClaughry, *A Better Path: From Welfare to Work* (Concord, Vt.: Ethan Allen Institute, 1990), p. 20.

[71]Coll, p. 2.

[72]Quoted in Katz, *In the Shadow of the Poorhouse*, p. 218.

[73]McClaughry, p. 21.

[74]Coll, p. 13.

Finance Corporation, a $300 million public works highway program.[75] He also supported federal credit guarantees to drought-stricken farmers and other limited federal programs.[76]

In November 1932 Franklin Delano Roosevelt was elected president, and an overwhelming Democratic majority was elected to Congress. Roosevelt wasted no time in expanding the federal welfare role. Just 10 weeks after his inauguration in 1933, he signed the Federal Emergency Relief Act, a $500 million program of grants to state and local governments. Half the funds were to be used as matching grants—$1 of federal money for each $3 of state or local money—for unemployment relief. The other $250 million was set aside in a discretionary fund for states that needed additional assistance in providing relief to a wide variety of needy individuals.[77]

The Federal Emergency Relief Act, the first large-scale entry of the federal government into relief spending, resulted in significant changes in the way state and local governments dispensed relief. For the first time, funds were directed, not narrowly to widows, orphans, and the disabled, but to "all needy unemployed persons and/or their dependents." The measure also covered all "those whose employment or available resources are inadequate to provide the necessities of life for themselves and/or their dependents."[78]

Though it was financed at the federal level, the Federal Emergency Relief Act routed aid through state and local governments. However, Roosevelt quickly began to seek a more direct federal role.

It is impossible within the scope of this book to discuss the whole dizzying array of welfare and employment programs that the Roosevelt administration eventually enacted. However, that administration's plans generally proceeded along three tracks: (1) public works and other programs to provide employment for able-bodied men; (2) direct relief for women, children, and others who could not support themselves; and (3) a broad social insurance system for the middle class.

[75]Katz, In the Shadow of the Poorhouse, pp. 215–16.

[76]Warren, pp. 127–28.

[77]Coll, pp. 15–16.

[78]U.S. Senate Committee on Manufactures, Relief for Unemployed Transients: Hearings on S 5121 before a Subcommittee on Manufactures, 72d Cong., 2d sess. Legislation passed May 12, 1933.

Two of the earliest public works programs were the Civilian Conservation Corps, which provided jobs in the national forests at subsistence wages for 500,000 men, and the Public Works Administration,
which would eventually spend $6 billion on a variety of public
works construction projects.[79] Both programs passed in 1933. Later
that year, the Civil Works Administration, which would become the
greatest public works experiment in American history, was created.
During its brief life, the CWA would employ 4.26 million people.
More than 22 percent of American households had a member working for the CWA.[80] In 1935 Congress created the Works Progress
Administration, which undertook a variety of projects from road
construction to recording the stories of former slaves.[81]

Although they were the most widespread of New Deal welfare
programs, the public works projects were actually short-lived. The
CWA, for example, lasted only four months. By 1939 nearly all were
gone. A few, such as the WPA, limped through World War II with
vastly reduced budgets.[82] Although cash relief was initially much
smaller than the public works projects, it was destined to have a
much greater and longer lasting impact.

Roosevelt claimed to be skeptical of direct relief—in speeches he
warned that the dole could become a narcotic.[83] He nevertheless
continually expanded the programs. By the winter of 1934 there
were already 20 million people on the dole.[84] But the biggest expansion was yet to come. As part of the Social Security Act of 1935,
Roosevelt created Aid to Dependent Children, a program of matching grants to the states, which essentially federalized state mothers'
pensions.[85] Little remarked upon at the time, ADC would eventually
become Aid to Families with Dependent Children, the mainstay of
today's welfare system.

---

[79]Frances Fox Piven and Richard Cloward, *Regulating the Poor: The Functions of
Public Welfare* (New York: Vintage Books, 1971), pp. 72–73.

[80]Katz, *Improving Poor People*, p. 53.

[81]Katz, *In the Shadow of the Poorhouse*, p. 228

[82]Ibid., p. 229.

[83]Olasky, p. 154.

[84]Piven and Cloward, p. 75.

[85]For a discussion of the legislative history of ADC, see Coll, pp. 51–53.

Originally intended as a small program, ADC expanded rapidly. By 1938, 243,000 families with over 600,000 children were participating in the program; the next year the numbers jumped to 298,000 families and 708,000 children. The program's total cost in 1939 exceeded $103 million, of which the federal portion was $34 million.[86] That amount was modest, of course, in comparison with the public works programs, but unlike those programs, ADC was not going to go away. Instead, it would grow inexorably into the future.

Finally, Roosevelt began the construction of a series of social insurance programs to act as a safety net for the middle class. The best known, of course, is Social Security.[87]

President Roosevelt and the New Deal forever changed the face of welfare in America. Between 1932 and 1939 welfare spending at all levels of government—federal, state, and local—increased from $208 million to $4.9 billion. In 1933 welfare programs accounted for only 6.5 percent of all government expenditures; by 1939 that figure had risen to 27.1 percent.[88]

At the same time, the New Deal dramatically increased the federal role in welfare. In 1932, 97.9 percent of all government welfare spending was at the state and local level. By 1939 such spending had declined to just 37.5 percent.[89] The growing government role in charity under the New Deal pushed private charity to the sidelines. As historian William Brock puts it, the New Deal "brought public agencies to the center of the stage and relegated private charities to the wings."[90]

The Great Society

After World War II, during good economic times, the growth in government welfare slowed dramatically but did not stop. The genie was out of the bottle.

The massive public works programs of the New Deal were long gone, leaving direct relief, primarily ADC, as the main vehicle for

---

[86]Ibid., p. 104.

[87]See Michael Tanner, "Social Security: 60 Years of Tinkering," *World & I*, November 1995, pp. 24–29.

[88]Katz, *Improving Poor People*, pp. 55–56.

[89]Ibid., p. 56.

[90]William Brock, *Welfare, Democracy, and the New Deal* (New York: Cambridge University Press, 1986), p. 358.

welfare. ADC's original grants provided only for the needs of children. However, the program was amended in 1950 to provide an additional allowance to support the mother or another adult caretaker relative.[91]

Despite rapid economic growth and declining levels of poverty throughout the 1950s, ADC rolls continued to grow. By 1956, 609,000 families, totaling 2,221,000 people, were receiving benefits.[92] The problems that were to plague the program in the future were fast becoming apparent. As social scientist Charles Murray explained, "By the fifties, it had become embarrassingly, outrageously clear that most of these women were not widows. Many of them had not even been married. Worst of all, they didn't stop having babies after the first lapse."[93]

Indeed, by 1956, 22.7 percent of recipients of aid originally intended for widows were unwed mothers. Widows were only 13 percent of recipients. The rest were divorced, deserted, or disabled.[94]

President John F. Kennedy took office amidst a renewed concern over poverty in America. Several studies in the late 1950s had argued in favor of a theory of "structural poverty." People were poor because they lacked the education, skills, and training necessary to take advantage of good economic conditions.[95]

Kennedy was aware of both those studies and a growing dissatisfaction with ADC. As a result, he proposed remaking welfare programs so that they would no longer provide merely a subsistence living to poor mothers. Instead, they would provide the tools necessary to equip people to lift themselves out of poverty—in Kennedy's words "a hand up, not a hand out."[96]

---

[91]Executive Office of the President, Office of Policy Development, *An Overview of the Current System,* vol. 1 of *The National Public Assistance System,* supplement 1 to *Up from Dependency: A New National Public Assistance Strategy* (Washington: Government Printing Office, 1986), pp. 18–19.

[92]Coll, p. 199.

[93]Charles Murray, *Losing Ground: American Social Policy 1950–1980* (New York: Basic Books, 1984), p. 19.

[94]Coll, p. 199.

[95]See, for example, John Kenneth Galbraith, *The Affluent Society* (Boston: Houghton Mifflin, 1958); and Michael Harrington, *The Other America* (New York: Macmillan, 1962).

[96]Quoted in McClaughry, p. 25.

Beyond renaming ADC Aid to Families with Dependent Children (AFDC) and expanding it to include two-parent families in which the father was unemployed, Kennedy actually took very little action on welfare.[97] But his rhetoric set the stage for Lyndon Johnson's Great Society.

After Kennedy's assassination, Johnson had a free hand in Congress, and he was determined to use it to remake government. In his first state of the union address on January 8, 1964, Johnson announced the War on Poverty. Just eight months later, he signed the Economic Opportunity Act, which created the Office of Economic Opportunity and appropriated $947.7 million for 10 work-training programs, including Job Corps, the Manpower Development and Training Program, the Neighborhood Youth Corps, and the Work Incentive Program.[98] In addition, Johnson greatly enlarged a little-used 1961 food and commodity pilot program, making it permanent and expanding it into the food stamp program we know today.[99]

In 1965 Johnson upped the ante still further, calling for the establishment of the Great Society. Not only would the War on Poverty be waged with double its previous funding, but America's crippled cities would also be rebuilt. America had not seen such an expansion of government or such a proliferation of anti-poverty programs since the New Deal. Among the major Johnson initiatives in 1965 were Medicaid, which would pay for health care for the poor and grow to dwarf all other anti-poverty programs, Head Start, Community Action grants, the Model Cities program, and Legal Services.[100]

Johnson also created the Department of Housing and Urban Development in 1965 and in 1968, at the end of his administration, signed the Housing and Urban Development Act, which authorized HUD to construct 600,000 federally subsidized housing units over the next 10 years.[101]

Finally, Johnson followed in Roosevelt's footsteps by enlarging the social insurance safety net for the middle class, principally through Medicare, a program to provide health care for the elderly.

[97]Executive Office of the President, p. 19.
[98]Coll, p. 241.
[99]Executive Office of the President, p. 23.
[100]McClaughry, pp. 25–26.
[101]Katz, *In the Shadow of the Poorhouse*, p. 265.

52

The proliferation of training and other noncash welfare programs did not mean a reduction in AFDC. On the contrary, its rolls continued to grow. By 1965 the number of people receiving AFDC had risen to 4.3 million.[102] By 1972 that number would more than double to nearly 10 million people. During the 1950s welfare rolls had increased by 17 percent. During the 1960s they increased by 107 percent, and three-quarters of that increase occurred between 1965 and 1968, at a time of relative economic prosperity and low unemployment.[103]

There were warnings. In his famous 1965 report, *The Negro Family: The Case for National Action*, Daniel Patrick Moynihan warned of the increasing breakdown in African-American families and its likely consequences. Introducing themes that would be heard again 20 years later, Moynihan spoke of a growing black underclass and warned that if trends were not reversed welfare would become a way of life.[104] Moynihan's report was highly controversial. Both white liberals and the civil rights establishment loudly and vehemently rejected his analysis.[105]

Other voices on both left and right warned that Johnson's programs were not well thought out, cost too much, and were poorly targeted. Even *Time* magazine noticed that anti-poverty programs did not seem to be working, remarking on "a paradoxical trap: the more the U.S. spends on the poor, the greater the need seems to be to spend more still."[106] However, as Johnson's biographer Doris Kearns Goodwin noted, Johnson's attitude was, "Pass the bill now, worry about its effect and implementation later."[107]

Not only did Johnson greatly increase the size of the welfare state, he increasingly federalized its administration, cutting out state and

---

[102]James T. Patterson, *America's Struggle against Poverty* (Cambridge, Mass.: Harvard University Press, 1989), p. 171.

[103]Olasky, p. 182.

[104]Daniel Patrick Moynihan, *The Negro Family: A Case for National Action* (Washington: U.S. Department of Labor, 1965).

[105]For a discussion of the Moynihan report and its attendant controversy, see Lee Rainwater and William Yancey, *The Moynihan Report and the Politics of Controversy* (Cambridge: Massachusetts Institute of Technology, 1967).

[106]Quoted in Olasky, p. 177.

[107]Doris Kearns Goodwin, *Lyndon Johnson and the American Dream* (New York: Harper & Row, 1976), p. 209.

local governments. Some historians suggest that Johnson's federalization of the welfare state was a deliberate political strategy. For example, historian Frances Fox Piven says that Great Society programs were specifically designed to attract black voters, bypassing local political organizations that were considered too independent or "unreliable." Johnson wanted the federal government to be clearly seen as the source of largesse for the African-American community.[108]

In the years following creation of the Great Society, there was a consensus among both Democrats and Republicans to preserve and even expand Johnson's legacy. Presidents Nixon, Ford, and Carter all added new anti-poverty programs. Nixon even experimented briefly with the idea of a guaranteed national income.

Johnson's legacy was further cemented by a series of court decisions that established the "rights" of welfare recipients. In *King v. Smith* (1968), the Supreme Court struck down state laws denying benefits to mothers with able-bodied men in the house.[109] The same year, a federal appeals court struck down laws against aid to mothers whom AFDC administrators considered "employable."[110] In 1969 the Supreme Court found in *Shapiro v. Thompson* that state residency requirements for welfare were unconstitutional.[111] And, in perhaps the most important welfare rights decision, the Court held in *Goldberg v. Kelly* (1970) that welfare was an "entitlement" that could not be denied without due process.[112]

The real impact of Johnson's programs was not felt until after he had left office. Between 1965 and 1975, measured in constant dollars, spending for cash welfare programs such as AFDC tripled, medical assistance increased nearly fourfold, food aid increased more than fourfold, housing assistance increased sevenfold, and job-training expenditures rose an astounding 15-fold.[113] After 1975 the growth in welfare slowed again but nonetheless continued upward.

---

[108]Richard Cloward and Frances Fox Piven, *The Politics of Turmoil: Poverty, Race, and the Urban Crisis* (New York: Vintage Books, 1975), pp. 271–83.

[109]392 U.S. 309 (1968).

[110]*Anderson v. Burson*, 300 F. Supp. 401 (1968).

[111]394 U.S. 618 (1969).

[112]397 U.S. 354 (1970).

[113]Robert Rector and William Lauber, *America's Failed $5.4 Trillion War on Poverty* (Washington: Heritage Foundation, 1995), p. 11.

Ronald Reagan is often attacked by liberals for cutting welfare programs. There is no doubt that he rode into office with attacks on the welfare system. However, once in office, Reagan did very little to marry his rhetoric to action. In fact, welfare spending grew throughout his two terms. When Reagan took office, federal welfare spending totaled $199 billion. By the time he left office, spending had increased to $230 billion. Spending for cash, food, housing, health care, and energy programs increased under Reagan.[114]

Reagan did shift funding emphasis among programs. Thus funding for AFDC declined by 1 percent (hardly a draconian cut) during his administration, but spending for the Earned Income Tax Credit increased by 102 percent. Food stamp spending declined by 4 percent, but the Women, Infants, and Children Supplemental Food Program (WIC) increased by 58 percent.[115] Reagan also attempted to tighten eligibility requirements on a program-by-program basis in an effort to restrict eligibility to the "truly needy." States were required to set eligibility and income verification standards.[116]

The last major attempt at welfare reform was the Family Support Act of 1988. The centerpiece of that reform effort was the Job Opportunities and Basic Skills (JOBS) Training Program, a combination job-training and job-search program. States were allowed to mandate that individuals participate in job-search programs and could require some participants to perform community service jobs as a prerequisite for receiving benefits. The legislation's chief sponsor, Sen. Daniel Patrick Moynihan (D-N.Y.), said of the legislation, "For 50 years the welfare system has been a maintenance program. It has now become a jobs program."[117]

Despite the work requirements, the percentage of AFDC recipients participating in job search, job training, or community service work ranges from more than 30 percent in Nebraska to a low of less than 1 percent in Hawaii. Nationwide, participation averages only 6.9

---

[114]Ibid., pp. 12–13.

[115]Richard McKenzie, *What Went Right in the 1980s* (San Francisco: Pacific Research Foundation, 1994), Table 8.1, pp. 268–69.

[116]General Accounting Office, "Welfare: Issues to Consider in Assessing Proposals for Reform," February 1987.

[117]Quoted in Bureau of National Affairs, *Daily Labor Report*, March 21, 1988, p. 2.

Figure 2.1
TOTAL FEDERAL, STATE, AND LOCAL WELFARE SPENDING, 1929–93

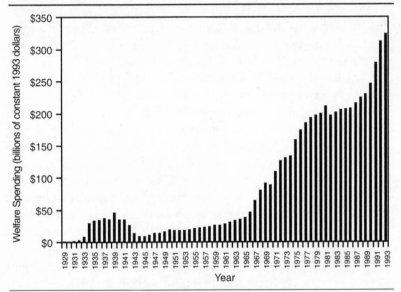

SOURCE: Robert Rector and William Lauber, *America's Failed $5.4 Trillion War on Poverty* (Washington: Heritage Foundation, 1995), Table 1, pp. 92–93.

percent.[118] Predictably, liberals contend that the failure is due to lack of funding, while conservatives claim the work requirements were never sufficiently enforced.[119]

If Reagan slowed the growth in welfare, it exploded again under President Bush. During Bush's four years in office, welfare spending increased by nearly $100 billion to $324 billion per year.[120]

The growth of the welfare state since 1929 can be clearly seen in Figure 2.1. Federal spending on welfare was $28 million in 1929, and total federal, state, and local welfare spending was just $90

[118]Robert Rector, "President Clinton's Commitment to Welfare Reform: The Disturbing Record So Far," Heritage Foundation Backgrounder no. 967, December 17, 1993, citing figures from the Office of Family Assistance, U.S. Department of Health and Human Services.

[119]"The Threat to Welfare Reform," *New York Times*, editorial, May 2, 1994; and Rector.

[120]Rector and Lauber, p. 13.

Figure 2.2
WELFARE SPENDING AS A PERCENTAGE OF GDP, 1929–93

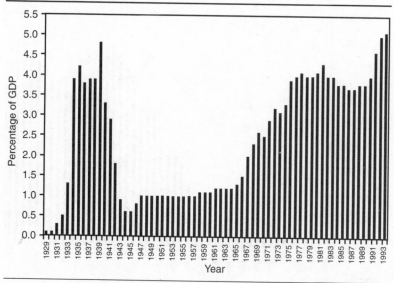

SOURCE: Robert Rector and William Lauber, *America's Failed $5.4 Trillion War on Poverty* (Washington: Heritage Foundation, 1995), Table 2, pp. 94–95.

million. Taking inflation into account, that would equal $813 million today. Welfare spending grew steadily as a result of the Great Depression and the New Deal, peaking in 1939 at $46 billion (1993 dollars). Most of Roosevelt's programs disappeared during World War II and welfare spending remained relatively low during the postwar period. With Lyndon Johnson's War on Poverty, welfare spending quickly reached and then surpassed New Deal spending levels. From there, it has continued steadily upward.[121]

Any way you choose to measure it, welfare spending has skyrocketed since 1965. As Figure 2.2 shows, welfare spending now consumes more than 5 percent of the U.S. gross domestic product, more than at any other time in the country's history.[122]

[121]Ibid., pp. 11–12.
[122]Ibid., pp. 15–16.

Figure 2.3
WELFARE SPENDING PER LOW-INCOME PERSON, 1947–93

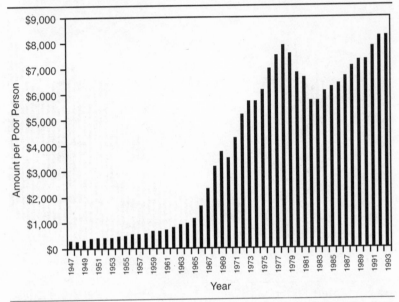

SOURCE: Robert Rector and William Lauber, *America's Failed $5.4 Trillion War on Poverty* (Washington: Heritage Foundation, 1995), Tables 1, 2, pp. 92–95.

The growth in welfare spending is even more dramatic when compared to the number of poor people. Figure 2.3 shows welfare spending per poor person (generously defined as the lowest quarter of incomes). Spending per poor person has increased more than 700 percent since 1965. Indeed, in 1993 we spent more than $8,258 for every poor man, woman, and child in this country. For a poor family of four, that amounts to more than $33,000.[123] If we simply gave poor people the money, we could raise every poor family above the poverty level for less than half of what we are now spending. While that is unrealistic—there would always be some administrative cost involved—something is clearly wrong.

Not only has the welfare state grown steadily since the New Deal; it has also become increasingly federalized. Programs such as food stamps and most of the job-training and education initiatives of the

[123]Ibid., pp. 13–15.

58

Great Society were funded and directed by the federal, not state, government. In addition, the federal government assumed a larger and larger proportion of AFDC costs. The original ADC program was one-third federally funded, with states paying two-thirds of the cost. By 1950 the federal share of AFDC had risen to nearly 44 percent. Today it is approximately 55 percent.[124]

Clinton vs. the Republicans

Such was the welfare state when President Clinton took office in 1993. Bill Clinton had run for president on a platform calling for "ending welfare as we know it," using the issue to cement his credentials as a "New Democrat."

Once in office, however, Clinton quickly found deep divisions in his own administration over how to reform welfare. One Clinton welfare adviser, Bruce Reed, supported substantial changes to welfare, including time limits on benefits, restrictions on benefits to teen mothers, and strict work requirements. Two other welfare experts, Mary Jo Bane and David Ellwood, accepted some restrictions but also called for massive new investment in job training and child care. Finally, others, including Health and Human Services Secretary Donna Shalala and—significantly—Hillary Rodham Clinton, were veterans of the liberal Children's Defense Fund and opposed nearly all reform efforts.[125]

As a result, the Clinton administration never formulated a clear vision of welfare reform. The president's reform plan was repeatedly delayed by internal bickering. When finally released, in June 1994, it called for a two-year time limit for welfare eligibility. During that period, recipients would receive job training and be eligible for other educational programs. At the end of the two years, they would be required to obtain work. If they were not able to find jobs in the private sector, they would be required to work in publicly funded community service jobs. The administration estimated that between 500,000 and 1 million public service jobs might be required. There

[124]Paul Peterson and Mark Rom, *Welfare Magnets: A New Case for a National Standard* (Washington: Brookings Institution, 1990), pp. 100–103.

[125]For an interesting account of the infighting behind development of the Clinton welfare plan, see Ben Wattenberg, *Values Matter Most: How Republicans or Democrats or a Third Party Can Win and Renew the American Way of Life* (New York: Free Press, 1995), pp. 280–90.

would be no limit on the length of time a person could remain in a public service job. In addition, there would be a significant increase in funding for child care. Finally, the president called for a crackdown, including federal sanctions, on fathers who failed to pay child support. Unwed teen mothers would be required to live with their parents in most cases, and the administration would launch a $100 million media and education campaign against teen pregnancy.[126]

The Clinton plan was not an attempt to cut welfare spending. Early versions of the plan were estimated to increase welfare spending by as much as $58 billion over 10 years.[127] That was quickly whittled back, but the final Clinton plan would still have increased spending by $9.3 billion over five years.[128]

For better or for worse, the president's proposal was released at the height of the battle over his plans for health care reform. As a result, it received only cursory public attention and almost no debate in Congress. Thus welfare reform remained a hot political issue going into the 1994 elections.

The centerpiece of the successful Republican effort to capture control of Congress was the "Contract with America," one provision of which called for welfare reform.[129] The Republican plan, dubbed the "personal responsibility act," called for returning responsibility for many welfare programs, including AFDC, to the states and providing them block grants.

Those block grants would not come without strings. States would be prohibited from using federal funds to provide AFDC benefits to unwed teen mothers or to noncitizen immigrants. A lifetime limit of five years of benefits would be established, with states having the option of establishing a limit of two years for any single spell on welfare. A strict and detailed "workfare" requirement was imposed.

Of all the proposals, the most significant was block grants, because they would end welfare's status as an entitlement. Under an entitlement program, every individual who meets the program's eligibility

[126]Jason DeParle, "White House Memo Raises Price Tag of Welfare Plan," *New York Times*, April 5, 1994.

[127]Ibid.

[128]Ron Suskind, "Scaled-Back Welfare-Reform Proposals Are Outlined by Clinton Administration," *Wall Street Journal*, March 3, 1995.

[129]Ed Gillespie and Bob Schellhas, eds., "Contract with America," Times Books, Washington, 1994, pp. 75–76.

criteria is automatically entitled to receive the program's benefits. Spending on the program is not subject to annual appropriation; it rises automatically with the number of people enrolled.

Ending welfare's entitlement status would have two important effects. First, it would allow states to impose a variety of conditions and restrictions on receipt of benefits. Second, it would make welfare spending subject to annual appropriation. Therefore, Congress could assert greater control over the growth in spending.

As did most provisions of the "Contract with America," welfare reform passed the House of Representatives largely intact and was significantly watered down in the Senate. The Senate added a maintenance-of-effort requirement, ordering states to continue at least 80 percent of their previous welfare spending. That would prevent states from dramatically reducing welfare spending or benefits. The Senate also added a new child-care program and other spending increases.

President Clinton initially supported the Senate version and even indicated that he might sign the final compromise. However, he quickly became the target of a withering lobbying campaign by liberal groups, notably the Children's Defense Fund. In the end, Clinton vetoed the welfare reform bill.

However, as the 1996 elections approached, pressure mounted on both the president and Congress to pass some form of welfare reform. Congress wanted to avoid a "do nothing" tag for failing to achieve one of its major goals, and President Clinton wanted to cement his shift to the political center and take another issue away from his rival Robert Dole. Flip-flopping yet again, the president announced that he would support legislation that ended the federal welfare "entitlement." Congressional Republicans responded by dropping plans for Medicaid reform, increasing funding for child care and job training, and eliminating a number of eligibility restrictions that appeared in early versions of the bill.[130]

As a result, in July 1996 Congress passed, and the president indicated that he would sign, the Personal Responsibility and Work Opportunity Reconciliation Act of 1996 that would do the following:

- Convert the federal AFDC program and three other small welfare programs to block grants for Temporary Assistance

[130]Judith Havemann and Barbara Vobejda, "Advancing Welfare Bill Holds Compromises, Radical Changes," *Washington Post*, July 17, 1996.

for Needy Families (TANF) and end the federal entitlement to welfare, giving states increased flexibility to design their own programs and establish their own rules.

● Limit lifetime TANF eligibility to five years and allow states to impose limits as low as two years. However, states could exempt up to 20 percent of recipients from the five-year limit. Individuals who lost eligibility for TANF would still be eligible for other programs.

● Require unmarried teenage mothers under age 18 to remain in school and live with an adult. States may deny benefits to unmarried teens and may prohibit payment of additional benefits to women who conceive additional children while on welfare.

● Impose detailed work requirements for able-bodied recipients of both TANF and food stamps.

● Prohibit legal immigrants from receiving most welfare benefits.

While both sides have hailed the compromise as a "revolutionary" change in the welfare system, the reality is far less dramatic. For example, by allowing states to exempt 20 percent of their welfare population from the five-year lifetime limit, the act would actually apply to few welfare recipients. Most welfare recipients leave the program in far less than five years. The small minority of long-term recipients would be exempt. Thus, the act gives the illusion of forcing people off welfare without actually doing so.

The act also contains a 75 percent "maintenance of effort" provision that prohibits states from significantly reducing welfare spending. Finally, the act affects only a tiny portion of federal welfare programs.

Because it ends the federal entitlement to welfare, the act represents an important first step on the road to welfare reform. But until Congress and the states build on this first step, "welfare as we know it" will not have really changed.

The Welfare State Today

Today there are more than 77 overlapping federal anti-poverty programs, including 59 major means-tested programs. (See appendix for a list and description of those programs.) For example, there are 12 different programs providing food, administered by five separate federal departments and one independent agency. There are seven housing programs, administered by seven separate federal agencies.[131] Those numbers do not include state and local bureaucracies.

In 1993 total welfare spending by state and local governments topped $324.3 billion. Of that total, $234.3 billion (72 percent) came from the federal government, with $90 billion (28 percent) coming from state governments. Approximately 48 percent of total welfare spending goes to medical and health care programs, the largest of which is Medicaid. Cash programs, such as AFDC, take 22.1 percent. Food, housing, and energy programs make up 18.8 percent of the total. The remaining 11.1 percent goes to education, job training, social service, and urban and community aid programs.[132]

Approximately 5 million families receive AFDC.[133] More than one of every seven American children is in a family receiving AFDC.[134] More than 20 percent of all children born in the late 1960s have spent at least one year on welfare; more than 70 percent of African-American children born during those years have done so. And the situation is growing worse. More than 30 percent of children born in 1980 will have spent a year on welfare before they reach age 18; more than 80 percent of African-American children will have done so.[135]

Contrary to stereotypes, 50 percent of welfare recipients are white, 31 percent are African-American, 14 percent are Hispanic, and 5 percent are classified as "other." Ninety-two percent of families on welfare have no father present. The average family size is 2.9 persons, down from 4.0 persons in 1969.[136]

---

[131]Executive Office of the President, pp. 50–54.

[132]Rector and Lauber, pp. 7–10.

[133]Jason DeParle, "Clinton Considers Taxing Aid to Poor to Pay for Reform," *New York Times*, February 13, 1994.

[134]U.S. House of Representatives, Committee on Ways and Means, *1992 Green Book: Background Material and Data on Programs within the Jurisdiction of the Committee on Ways and Means* (Washington: Government Printing Office, 1992), p. 390.

[135]Nicholas Zill and Christine Moore, "The Life Circumstances and Development of Children in Welfare Families: A Profile Based on National Survey Data," Child Trends, Inc., Washington, 1991.

[136]Carrie Teargardin, "Debunking the Welfare Queen Myth: White Women with Children Are Most Typical," *Atlanta Constitution*, December 11, 1992, citing Bureau of the Census data.

Table 2.1
REASONS FOR ENTERING AFDC PROGRAM

Reason	Percentage
Divorce or separation	45
Unwed motherhood	30
Decline in earnings	15
All other	10

SOURCE: Data from U.S. House of Representatives, Committee on Ways and Means, *1992 Green Book: Background Material and Data on Programs within the Jurisdiction of the Committee on Ways and Means* (Washington: Government Printing Office, 1992), Table 43, p. 692.

Table 2.2
LENGTH OF TIME ON AFDC

Expected Time on AFDC	Persons Beginning AFDC Spell (%)	Persons on AFDC at Any Point in Time (%)
2 years or less	30	7
2 to 4 years	20	11
4 to 8 years	19	17
8 years or more	30	65

SOURCE: U.S. House of Representatives, Committee on Ways and Means, *1992 Green Book: Background Material and Data on Programs within the Jurisdiction of the Committee on Ways and Means* (Washington: Government Printing Office, 1992), Table 38, p. 685, citing data from Mary Jo Bane and David Ellwood, *The Dynamics of Dependence: The Route to Self-Sufficiency,* prepared by Urban Systems Research and Engineering, Inc., for the U.S. Department of Health and Human Services, June 1983.

As Table 2.1 shows, divorce is the most common reason a person goes on welfare, followed by an out-of-wedlock birth. Contrary to the rhetoric, relatively few individuals go on welfare because they have lost a job or suffered a decline in wages.[137]

As Table 2.2 shows, although the average length of time spent on welfare is relatively short, generally two years or less, 65 percent of persons enrolled in the program at any one time have been in the program for eight years or longer.

The difference between point-in-time and beginning-spell estimates can be confusing. The probability of being on welfare at any

[137]U.S. House of Representatives, Table 43, p. 692.

given time is necessarily greater for long-term recipients than for those who use the program for a shorter period of time. To better understand that, consider hospitalization. Suppose a hospital has 13 beds. Twelve of those beds are occupied all year by chronically ill patients. The remaining bed is used for one week each by 52 different short-term patients. On any given day, a hospital census would find that about 85 percent of patients (12 of 13) were in the midst of a year-long spell of hospitalization. However, 80 percent of those who enter the hospital (52 of 64) spend only one week there.[138] The same dynamic works for the welfare population.

The most common reason people get off welfare is a change in family structure such as marriage (35 percent) or children reaching the age of 18 (11 percent). Approximately 26 percent of welfare spells end as a result of an increase in earnings—21 percent of those increases are in the earnings of the head of the household, and 5 percent are in the earnings of other household members.[139]

How Much Do Welfare Recipients Receive?

Welfare advocacy groups and the media often portray welfare as a series of frugal programs, barely providing subsistence help to the needy. But that conclusion is based on the faulty assumption that welfare recipients receive only one form of public assistance, AFDC. In reality, most welfare recipients receive assistance from several different government programs.

In 1995 the Cato Institute examined the combined value of benefits for a typical welfare recipient in each of the 50 states and the District of Columbia.[140] That study found that the value of the full package

[138]U.S. House of Representatives, p. 441.

[139]U.S. House of Representatives, pp. 691–92.

[140]Michael Tanner, Stephen Moore, and David Hartman, "The Work vs. Welfare Trade-Off: An Analysis of the Total Level of Welfare Benefits by State," Cato Institute Policy Analysis no. 240, September 19, 1995. The study calculated the value of AFDC; food stamps; Medicaid; housing assistance; Special Supplemental Food Program for Women, Infants, and Children; Low-Income Home Energy Assistance Program; and the free commodities program.

That study has, not surprisingly, been severely criticized by some on the left. For example, the Center for Budget and Policy Priorities has attacked the study for including benefits such as Medicaid, housing, and WIC. Sharon Parrott, "The Cato Institute's Report on Welfare Benefits: Do the Numbers Add Up?" Center for Budget and Policy Priorities, Washington, April 22, 1996. However, the CBPP critique severely understates the value of welfare, asserting, for example, that Medicaid has no economic value to the poor. A reevaluation of the evidence indicates that the Tanner, Moore, and Hartman study accurately reflects the value of welfare benefits. See Michael Tanner and Naomi Lopez, "The Value of Welfare: Cato vs. CBPP," Cato Institute Briefing Paper no. 27, June 12, 1996.

Table 2.3
PRETAX ANNUAL VALUE ($) OF THE WELFARE PACKAGE BY
JURISDICTION, 1995

Rank	Jurisdiction	Value of Benefits	Pretax Equivalent Wage	Hourly Wage Equivalent[a]
1	Hawaii	27,928	36,650	17.62
2	Alaska	26,801	32,150	15.48
3	Massachusetts	24,176	30,500	14.66
4	Connecticut	24,474	29,600	14.23
5	District of Columbia	22,745	29,100	13.99
6	New York	22,124	27,300	13.13
7	New Jersey	21,968	26,500	12.74
8	Rhode Island	21,541	26,100	12.55
9	California	20,591	23,950	11.51
10	Virginia	19,385	23,100	11.11
11	Maryland	19,489	22,800	10.96
12	New Hampshire	19,964	22,800	10.96
13	Maine	19,018	21,600	10.38
14	Delaware	18,486	21,500	10.34
15	Colorado	18,457	20,900	10.05
16	Vermont	18,754	20,900	10.05
17	Minnesota	18,393	20,700	9.95
18	Washington	18,730	20,700	9.95
19	Nevada	18,456	20,200	9.71
20	Michigan	17,560	19,700	9.47
21	Pennsylvania	17,574	19,700	9.47
22	Utah	17,742	19,600	9.42
23	Illinois	17,492	19,400	9.33
24	Oregon	16,959	19,200	9.23
25	Wyoming	17,780	19,100	9.18
26	Indiana	17,192	19,000	9.13
27	Iowa	17,335	19,000	9.13
28	Wisconsin	17,149	18,850	9.06
29	New Mexico	17,368	18,600	8.94
30	Florida	17,268	18,200	8.75
31	Idaho	17,028	18,000	8.65
32	Oklahoma	16,642	17,700	8.51

Rank	Jurisdiction	Value of Benefits	Pretax Equivalent Wage	Hourly Wage Equivalent[a]
33	North Dakota	16,812	17,600	8.46
34	Kansas	16,627	17,500	8.41
35	Georgia	16,405	17,400	8.37
36	Ohio	16,551	17,400	8.37
37	South Dakota	16,688	17,300	8.32
38	Louisiana	16,290	17,000	8.17
39	Kentucky	15,807	16,800	8.08
40	North Carolina	16,007	16,800	8.08
41	Montana	15,814	16,300	7.84
42	South Carolina	15,953	16,200	7.79
43	Nebraska	15,665	15,750	7.57
44	Texas	15,470	15,200	7.31
45	West Virginia	15,202	15,200	7.31
46	Missouri	15,102	14,900	7.16
47	Arizona	14,802	14,100	6.78
48	Tennessee	14,582	13,700	6.59
49	Arkansas	14,088	13,200	6.35
50	Alabama	13,817	13,000	6.25
51	Mississippi	13,033	11,500	5.53

SOURCE: Based on data presented in Michael Tanner and Naomi Lopez, "The Value of Welfare: Cato vs. CBPP," Cato Institute Briefing Paper no. 27, June 12, 1996.

[a]Based on a 2,080-hour work year.

of welfare benefits exceeds the poverty level in all 51 jurisdictions. In addition, because welfare benefits are tax-free, the study compared the value of those benefits with the amount of pretax income that a worker would have to earn to receive an equivalent net income.

According to the study, the value of benefits for a mother and two children ranged from a high of more than $36,000 in Hawaii to a low of $11,500 in Mississippi. In 40 states welfare pays more than an $8.00-an-hour job. In 17 states the welfare package is more generous than a $10.00-an-hour job. In Hawaii, Alaska, Massachusetts, Connecticut, Washington, D.C., New York, and Rhode Island welfare pays more than a $12.00-an-hour job—or two and a half times the minimum wage. Welfare benefits are especially generous in large cities. Welfare has the pretax income equivalent of a $14.75-an-hour job in New York City, a $12.45-an-hour job in Philadelphia, an $11.35-an-hour job in Baltimore, and a $10.90-an-hour job in Detroit.

In 9 states welfare pays more than the average first-year salary for a teacher. In 29 states welfare pays more than the average starting salary for a secretary. In 47 states welfare pays more than a janitor makes. Indeed, in the 6 most generous states, benefits exceed the entry-level salary for a computer programmer. Table 2.3 gives the value of welfare benefits in all 50 states and the District of Columbia.

Conclusion

During much of this country's history, care of the poor was a function of private charity supplemented by local governments. However, beginning with the Progressive Era, those traditional sources of charity began to be pushed aside in favor of first state, then federal government programs. The Great Depression gave new emphasis to the federalization of welfare and established the basic structure for the programs we have today. The final pieces of the welfare state were put in place by President Johnson's War on Poverty. The result is a $350 billion per year welfare state that survives despite the 1996 welfare reform legislation. But has the welfare state worked?

3. The Failure of the Welfare State

As we have seen, America now has a mammoth welfare state. Since the War on Poverty began in 1965, federal, state, and local governments have spent more than $5.4 trillion fighting poverty in this country.[1]

How much money is $5.4 trillion? It is 70 percent more than it cost to fight World War II. For $5.4 trillion you could purchase the assets of all the Fortune 500 corporations *and* all the farmland in the United States.[2] Yet, as Figure 3.1 shows, the poverty rate is actually higher today than it was in 1965. Clearly, welfare has failed to meet the goal of ending poverty. But the real failure of welfare lies not in wasted money but in wasted lives.

Welfare and the Family

Perhaps the gravest social challenge facing America today is the breakup of the American family. As Table 3.1 shows, the number of single-parent families has risen dramatically since 1960. In 1960 more than 80 percent of children lived with their mothers and fathers. An additional 6.7 percent lived with either their mother or father and a stepparent. By 1990 only 57.7 percent of children lived with two biological parents, and an additional 11.3 percent lived with a parent and a stepparent.[3]

---

[1]The figure of $5.4 trillion represents total spending on "anti-poverty programs" since 1965, including all means-tested welfare programs, as well as a small number of federal programs targeted to economically distressed communities. Means-tested programs are those programs available only to low-income Americans. For example, food stamps is a means-tested program. Social Security is not. Testimony of Robert Rector to the U.S. Senate Committee on Finance, "Broad Goals of Welfare Policy," March 9, 1995, p. 77. For a complete list of programs included in this estimate, see appendix.

[2]Robert Rector and William Lauber, *America's Failed $5.4-Trillion War on Poverty* (Washington: Heritage Foundation, 1995), pp. 19–20.

[3]Donald Hernandez, *America's Children: Resources from Family, Government, and the Economy* (New York: Russell Sage Foundation, 1993), p. 65.

Figure 3.1
WELFARE SPENDING VS. POVERTY

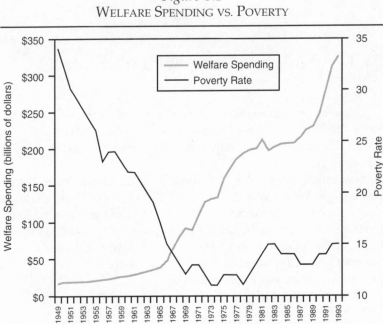

SOURCES: Bureau of the Census, Current Population Surveys, Series P60, various numbers; and Robert Rector and William Lauber, *America's Failed $5.4 Trillion War on Poverty* (Washington: Heritage Foundation, 1995), Table 1, pp. 92–93.

There are many complex reasons for the change. However, welfare is clearly contributing to the problem. Take, for example, the most important reason for the rise in single-parent families—births to unmarried women. As Figure 3.2 shows, out-of-wedlock births have increased by more than 600 percent since 1960. In 1960 only 5.3 percent of all births were out of wedlock. Among whites, only 2.3 percent were out of wedlock, while the out-of-wedlock rate among blacks was 23 percent. By 1990, 28 percent of all births were out of wedlock. The rate among whites had increased to an alarming 21 percent, and among blacks it had skyrocketed to an astonishing 65.2 percent.[4]

[4]National Center for Health Statistics, cited in William Bennett, *The Index of Leading Cultural Indicators* (Washington: Empower America, March 1993), p. 16.

Table 3.1
FAMILY ARRANGEMENTS FOR CHILDREN UNDER AGE 18, 1960–90
(percentage)

Living with	1960	1970	1980	1990
Father and mother	80.6	75.1	62.3	57.7
Mother only	7.7	11.8	18.0	21.6
Never married	3.9	9.3	15.5	31.5
Divorced	24.7	29.7	41.6	36.9
Separated	46.8	39.8	31.6	24.6
Widowed	24.7	21.2	11.3	7.0
Father only	1.0	1.8	1.7	3.1
Father and stepmother	0.8	0.9	1.1	0.9
Mother and stepfather	5.9	6.5	8.4	10.4
Neither parent	3.9	4.1	5.8	4.3

SOURCE: Donald Hernandez, *America's Children: Resources from Family, Government, and the Economy* (New York: Russell Sage Foundation, 1993), p. 65.

The rate of out-of-wedlock births to teenagers has nearly doubled in the past two decades.[5] In fact, as Figure 3.3 shows, the increase in the rate of out-of-wedlock births per 1,000 unmarried women has been greater among women aged 15 to 19 than among any other age group.[6] Teen mothers now account for nearly 30 percent of all out-of-wedlock births. But that figure may understate the severity of the problem. Because women who have out-of-wedlock births as teens frequently go on to have additional out-of-wedlock children, nearly 60 percent of all out-of-wedlock births involve mothers who had their first child as unwed teenagers.[7]

The concern about the increased rate of out-of-wedlock births is not a question of private morality. If Murphy Brown were typical of unwed mothers, objections would be far more muted. However, only 4 percent of out-of-wedlock births to white mothers are to women with a college degree, while 82 percent of such births are

[5]Douglas Besharov and Karen Gardiner, "Teen Sex," *American Enterprise*, January–February 1993, pp. 53–59.

[6]Bureau of the Census, "Births to Unmarried Women and Teenage Mothers," *Statistical Abstract of the United States, 1992* (Washington: Government Printing Office, 1995), Table 88, p. 73.

[7]Douglas Besharov and Karen Gardiner, "Paternalism and Welfare Reform," *Public Interest*, no. 122 (Winter 1996): 72.

Figure 3.2
OUT-OF-WEDLOCK BIRTHS, 1960–94

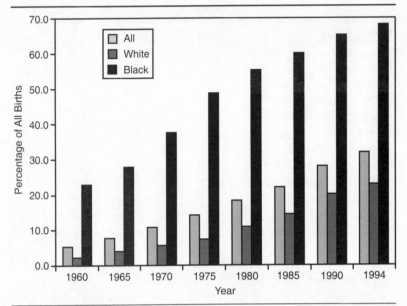

SOURCES: U.S. National Center for Health Statistics, *Vital Statistics of the United States*, various years, *Monthly Vital Statistics Report*, various issues, and unpublished data.

to women with a high school education or less. Women with incomes of $75,000 or more have only 1 percent of illegitimate white children, while women with family incomes under $20,000 give birth to 69 percent.[8]

As we saw in Chapter 1, having a child out of wedlock often means a lifetime in poverty. Approximately 30 percent of all welfare recipients start on welfare because they have an out-of-wedlock birth.[9] The trend is even worse among teenage mothers. Half of all unwed teen mothers go on welfare within one year of the birth of

[8]Charles Murray, "The Coming White Underclass," *Wall Street Journal*, October 29, 1993.

[9]U.S. House of Representatives, Committee on Ways and Means, *1992 Green Book: Background Material and Data on Programs within the Jurisdiction of the Committee on Ways and Means* (Washington: Government Printing Office, 1992), p. 669.

Figure 3.3
INCREASE IN OUT-OF-WEDLOCK BIRTHS BY AGE GROUP, 1966–92

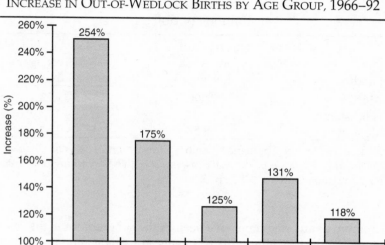

SOURCES: U.S. National Center for Health Statistics, *Vital Statistics of the United States,* various years, *Monthly Vital Statistics Report,* various issues, and unpublished data.

their first child; 77 percent are on welfare within five years of the child's birth.[10] As Table 3.2 shows, nearly 55 percent of Aid to Families with Dependent Children (AFDC), Medicaid, and food stamp expenditures are attributable to families begun by a teen birth.[11] The cost of such other social programs as special education, foster care, and public housing subsidies is not included.

Moreover, once on welfare, women find it very difficult to get off. While the average length of time spent on welfare is relatively short, generally two years or less, 65 percent of persons enrolled in the

[10]Douglas Besharov, "Escaping the Dole," American Enterprise Institute, Washington, December 12, 1993.

[11]Center for Population Options, *Teenage Pregnancy and Too-Early Childbearing: Public Costs, Personal Consequences,* 6th ed. (Washington: Center for Population Options, 1992), p. 5. These figures include expenses for all families begun when the mother was a teenager, even though the mother may now be much older.

Table 3.2
1990 SINGLE-YEAR COST OF WELFARE
(billions of dollars)

Funding Source	Total Outlay for AFDC Recipients	Outlay Attributable to Teenage Childbearing
AFDC	21.20	11.23
Food stamps	7.50	3.98
Medicaid	18.57	9.84

SOURCE: Center for Population Options, *Teenage Pregnancy and Too-Early Childbearing: Public Costs, Personal Consequences,* 6th ed. (Washington: Center for Population Options, 1992), p. 5.

program at any one time have been in the program for eight years or longer.[12] Most long-term recipients are single mothers. Single women average 9.33 years on welfare and are 39.3 percent of all recipients who are on welfare for 10 years or longer.[13]

The noneconomic consequences of out-of-wedlock births are equally stark. There is strong evidence that the absence of a father increases the probability that a child will use drugs and engage in criminal activity. According to one study, children raised in single-parent families are one-third more likely to exhibit anti-social behavior than are children of two-parent families.[14] Yet another study indicated that, holding other variables constant, black children from single-parent households are twice as likely to commit crimes as are black children from families with resident fathers. The likelihood of criminal activity triples if a child lives in a neighborhood with a

[12]Mary Jo Bane and David Ellwood, *The Dynamics of Dependence: The Route to Self-Sufficiency,* prepared by Urban Systems Research and Engineering, Inc., for the U.S. Department of Health and Human Services, June 1983, cited in U.S. House of Representatives, Committee on Ways and Means, *1994 Green Book: Background Material and Data on Programs within the Jurisdiction of the Committee on Ways and Means* (Washington: Government Printing Office, 1994), pp. 440–41.

[13]David Ellwood, *Targeting "Would-Be" Long-Term Recipients of AFDC* (Princeton, N.J.: Mathematica Policy Research, 1986), cited in ibid., Table 10-40, p. 444.

[14]Deborah Dawson, "Family Structure and Children's Health and Well-Being: Data from the 1988 Interview Survey on Child Health," Paper presented at the Annual Meeting of the Population Association of America, Toronto, May 12, 1990.

high concentration of single-parent families.[15] Nearly 70 percent of juveniles in state reform institutions come from fatherless homes.[16]

Children from single-parent homes perform significantly worse in school than do children from two-parent households. They are three times more likely to fail and repeat a year of school and are more likely to be late, have disciplinary problems, and perform poorly on standardized tests, even when studies control for differences in family income. They are twice as likely to drop out of school altogether.[17]

Children from single-parent families are two to three times more likely to experience mental illness and other psychological disorders than are children from two-parent families.[18] Nearly 80 percent of children admitted to psychiatric hospitals come from single-parent homes.[19] There is also evidence that child abuse occurs more frequently in single-parent homes.[20]

The problem perpetuates itself. For example, white women raised in single-parent households are 164 percent more likely to bear children out of wedlock than are white women raised in two-parent homes.[21] Moreover, children raised in single-parent families are three

---

[15]M. Anne Hill and June O'Neill, "Underclass Behaviors in the United States: Measurement and Analysis of Determinants," Baruch College, City University of New York, August 1993.

[16]Barbara Dafoe Whitehead, "Dan Quayle Was Right," *Atlantic Monthly*, April 1993, citing data from National Institutes of Justice, Bureau of Justice Statistics.

[17]Deborah Dawson, *Family Structure and Children's Health: United States, 1988*, data from the National Health Survey, Series 10-178 (Hyattsville, Md.: U.S. Department of Health and Human Services, Centers for Disease Control, National Center for Health Statistics, June 1991); Marybeth Shinn, "Father Absence and Children's Cognitive Development," *Psychological Bulletin* 85, no. 2 (1978): 295–324; and Sheila Krein and Andrea Beller, "Educational Attainment of Children from Single-Parent Families: Differences by Exposure, Gender, and Race," *Demography* 25 (May 1988): 288.

[18]Dawson, *Family Structure and Children's Health: United States, 1988*.

[19]Nicholas Davidson, "The Daddy Dearth," *Policy Review*, no. 51 (Winter 1990): 43.

[20]Selwyn Smith et al., "Social Aspects of the Battered Baby Syndrome," in *Child Abuse: Commission and Omission*, ed. Joanne Cook and Roy Bowles (Toronto: Buttersworth, 1980), pp. 217–20; and A. Walsh, "Illegitimacy, Child Abuse and Neglect, and Cognitive Development," *Journal of Genetic Psychology* 151 (1990): 79–85.

[21]Irwin Garfinkel and Sara McLanahan, *Single Mothers and Their Children: A New American Dilemma* (Washington: Urban Institute Press, 1986), p. 31.

times more likely than are children raised in two-parent homes to become welfare recipients as adults.[22]

This is not to comment on any particular single mother. Millions of single mothers do a tremendous job against difficult odds of raising healthy, happy, and successful children. Still, children growing up in single-parent homes are clearly at higher risk. Obviously, therefore, any public policy that encourages out-of-wedlock births should be viewed as a failure.

Perhaps no issue of welfare reform has been as hotly debated as the link between the availability of welfare and out-of-wedlock births. Since Charles Murray raised the issue in *Losing Ground*, experts have lined up on both sides of the issue. As Figure 3.4 shows, the overall out-of-wedlock birthrate shows at least a surface correlation with welfare receipt.

As early as the 1960s it was recognized that the perverse incentives of welfare were likely to have a negative impact on the family structure of recipients.

> What, after all, was the AFDC program but a family allowance for *broken* families. Generally speaking, one became eligible by dissolving a family or by not forming one.[23]

Of course, women do not get pregnant just to get welfare benefits. It is also true that a wide array of other social factors has contributed to the increase in out-of-wedlock births. But, by removing the economic consequences of out-of-wedlock births, welfare has removed a major incentive to avoid them. A teenager looking around at her friends and neighbors is likely to see several who have given birth out of wedlock. When she sees that they have suffered few visible consequences (the very real consequences of such behavior are often not immediately apparent), she is less inclined to modify her own behavior to prevent pregnancy.

Proof of that can be found in a study by Ellen Freeman of the University of Pennsylvania and others, who surveyed black, never-pregnant females age 17 or younger. Only 40 percent of those surveyed said that they thought becoming pregnant in the next year

---

[22]Ibid.

[23]Daniel Patrick Moynihan, *Family and Nation: The Godkin Lectures* (New York: Harcourt Brace Jovanovich, 1985), p. 8

Figure 3.4
OUT-OF-WEDLOCK BIRTHS VS. WELFARE SPENDING, 1959–94

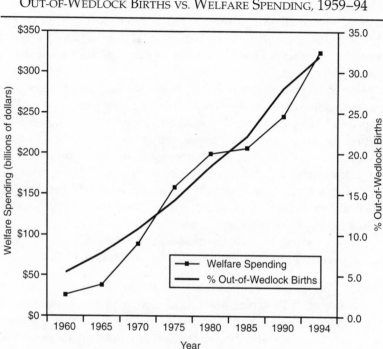

SOURCES: Bureau of the Census, Current Population Surveys, Series P60, various numbers; and Robert Rector and William Lauber, *America's Failed $5.4 Trillion War on Poverty* (Washington: Heritage Foundation, 1995), Table 1, pp. 92–93.

"would make their situation worse."[24] Likewise, a study by Laurie Schwab Zabin and others in the *Journal of Research on Adolescence* found that "in a sample of inner-city black teens presenting for pregnancy tests, we reported that more than 31 percent of those who elected to carry their pregnancy to term told us, before their pregnancy was diagnosed, that they believed a baby would present

---

[24]Ellen Freeman et al., "Adolescent Contraceptive Use: Comparisons of Male and Female Attitudes and Information," *American Journal of Public Health* 70, no. 8 (August 1980): 790–97.

a problem."[25] In other words, 69 percent either did not believe having a baby out of wedlock would present a problem or were unsure.

As Murray explains, "The evil of the modern welfare state is not that it bribes women to have babies—wanting to have babies is natural—but that it enables women to bear children without the natural social restraints."[26]

Until teenage girls, particularly those living in relative poverty, can be made to see the real consequences of pregnancy, it will be impossible to gain control over the problem of out-of-wedlock births.[27] By disguising those consequences, welfare makes it easier for girls to make the decisions that will lead to unwed motherhood.

Current welfare policies seem to be designed with an appalling lack of concern for their impact on out-of-wedlock births. Indeed, Medicaid programs in 11 states actually provide infertility treatments for single women on welfare.[28]

A review of recent studies provides increasing evidence that welfare *does* contribute to rising rates of out-of-wedlock births:

- In a paper presented to the National Academy of Sciences in April 1996, Professor Mark Rosenzweig of the University of Pennsylvania concluded that data from the National Longitudinal Survey of Youth showed that a 10 percent increase in welfare

[25]Laurie Schwab Zabin, Nan Marie Astone, and Mark Emerson, "Do Adolescents Want Babies? The Relationship between Attitudes and Behavior," *Journal of Research on Adolescence* 3 (1993): 77. Zabin et al. report that among teens who chose an abortion, fully 78 percent believed that having a baby would pose a problem. But, as Douglas Besharov of the American Enterprise Institute points out, "that is exactly the point: the more inconvenient unwed parenthood seems to a teenager, the less likely it is that she will become a mother." Douglas Besharov, letter to the editor, *Wall Street Journal*, April 27, 1994.

[26]Charles Murray, "Restore Personal Responsibility," *Future of Welfare* 15, no. 12 (December 1992): 12.

[27]As University of Pennsylvania sociologist Elijah Anderson points out, "Most middle-class youths take a stronger interest in their futures and know what a pregnancy can do to derail it. In contrast many [inner-city] adolescents . . . see little to lose by having a child out-of-wedlock." Quoted in Besharov, "Escaping the Dole," p. 3.

[28]Hawaii, Iowa, Louisiana, Maryland, Minnesota, New Hampshire, New Jersey, New Mexico, New York, Oregon, and Pennsylvania. "The Infertility Trap," *Newsweek*, April 4, 1994.

benefits resulted in a 12 percent increase in out-of-wedlock births among low-income women ages 14 to 22.[29]

- A study by Anne Hill and June O'Neill for the U.S. Department of Health and Human Services found that an increase in monthly welfare benefits led to an increase in out-of-wedlock births. Holding constant a wide range of variables, including income, education, and urban vs. suburban setting, the study found that a 50 percent increase in the value of AFDC and food stamp payments led to a 43 percent increase in the number of out-of-wedlock births.[30]

- Research by Shelley Lundberg and Robert Plotnick of the University of Washington showed that an increase in welfare benefits of $200 per month per family increased the rate of out-of-wedlock births among teenagers by 150 percent.[31]

- C. R. Winegarden of the University of Toledo concluded that half the increase in the out-of-wedlock birthrate since 1965 was due to the perverse incentives of welfare.[32]

- Mikhail Bernstam of the Hoover Institution found that in cities with large African-American populations, the birthrate among single teenage women increased 10 percent for each 10 percent increase in welfare benefits.[33]

- In a 1989 study, Martha Ozawa found a statistically significant correlation between AFDC payments and the illegitimacy rate for adolescents.[34]

[29]Mark Rosenzweig, "Parental Support and AFDC Support of Young Adult Women: Implications for Non-Marital Fertility," Paper presented to the National Academy of Sciences conference on "Welfare and Child Development," Washington, April 11, 1996.

[30]Hill and O'Neill, pp. 76–79.

[31]Shelley Lundberg and Robert Plotnick, "Adolescent Premarital Childbearing: Do Opportunity Costs Matter?" Population Association of America, Ann Arbor, Mich., May 1990.

[32]C. R. Winegarden, "AFDC and Illegitimacy Ratios: A Vector Autogressive Model," *Applied Economics* 20, no. 3 (March 1988): 1589–1601.

[33]Mikhail Bernstam, "Malthus and the Evolution of the Welfare State: An Essay on the Second Invisible Hand," Working Paper E-88-41,42, Hoover Institution, Palo Alto, Calif., 1988.

[34]Martha Ozawa, "Welfare Policies and Illegitimate Birth Rates among Adolescents: Analysis of State-by-State Data," *Social Work Research and Abstracts* 14 (1989): 5–11.

- A 1993 study in the *Journal of Marriage* by Mark Fossett and Jill Kiecolt found a substantial and consistent relationship between the amount of public assistance payments and out-of-wedlock births among black women aged 20 to 24.[35]
- Gregory Acs of the Urban Institute reviewed several major studies and concluded that a 10 percent increase in welfare benefits led to a 5 percent increase in unmarried childbearing among white women.[36]

In all, there have been 14 major studies that have found a statistically significant correlation between welfare and out-of-wedlock births.[37]

Those who dispute any link between welfare and out-of-wedlock births counter with the argument that Louisiana and Mississippi, for example, have approximately the same rate of out-of-wedlock births as does California but have much lower AFDC benefits.[38] That would appear to contradict the argument that high welfare benefits lead to more out-of-wedlock births. But the actual rate of AFDC payments is of far less importance than the value of the entire welfare package within the context of the local economy.[39] In that context,

[35]Mark Fossett and Jill Kiecolt, "Mate Availability and Family Structure among African-Americans in U.S. Metropolitan Areas," *Journal of Marriage and Family* 55, no. 2 (May 1993): 288.

[36]Gregory Acs, "Do Welfare Benefits Promote Out-of-Wedlock Childbearing?" in *Welfare Reform: An Analysis of the Issues*, ed. Isabel Sawhill (Washington: Urban Institute, 1995), pp. 51–54.

[37]In addition to those cited above, other studies showing a correlation between welfare benefits and out-of-wedlock birth are Chong-Bum An, Robert Haveman, and Barbara Wolfe, "Teen Out-of-Wedlock Births and Welfare Receipt: The Role of Childhood Events and Economic Circumstances," *Review of Economics and Statistics*, May 1993; Robert D. Plotnick, "Welfare and Out-of-Wedlock Childbearing: Evidence from the 1980s," *Journal of Marriage and the Family* 52, no. 3 (August 1990): 735–46; Scott J. South and Kim M. Lloyd, "Marriage Markets and Nonmarital Fertility in the United States," *Demography* 29, no. 2 (May 1992): 247–64; Phillip Robins and Paul Fronstin, "Welfare Benefits and Family Size Decisions of Never-Married Women," Institute for Research on Poverty, Discussion Paper no. 1002–93, September 1993; Catherine Jackson, "Welfare, Abortion and Teenage Fertility," RAND Research Paper, August 1994; and Paul Schultz, "Marital Status and Fertility in the United States," *Journal of Human Resources* 29, no. 2 (Spring 1994): 637–59.

[38]David Ellwood and Mary Jo Bane, "The Impact of AFDC on Family Structure and Living Arrangements," *Research in Labor Economics* 6 (1985): 137–207.

[39]Charles Murray notes that a study of total welfare packages in 13 locations across the country by the General Accounting Office found that, taking into account local economies and the combined value of all benefits, there was little actual variation in the value of the benefits package. For example, the welfare package in San Francisco

the welfare packages being compared are essentially equal. It is therefore not surprising that they are correlated with similar rates of out-of-wedlock births.

Critics also contend that the erosion of AFDC benefits since the beginning of the 1980s has failed to reduce out-of-wedlock births. However, concentrating on AFDC ignores the total value of welfare benefits, which include food stamps, Medicaid, public housing subsidies, and other benefits. As a 1995 Cato Institute study showed, the value of the full package of welfare benefits for a mother and two children ranged from a high of more than $36,000 in Hawaii to a low of $11,500 in Mississippi, more than sufficient to provide an incentive for out-of-wedlock childbearing.[40]

Finally, critics note that studies showing a correlation between welfare and out-of-wedlock births generally show a stronger correlation for white women than for African-Americans. They contend that if welfare is responsible for the increase in out-of-wedlock births, the correlation should be consistent across all ethnic groups.

That is not necessarily a correct assumption since many other factors may contribute to the out-of-wedlock birthrate of any particular ethnic group. However, when studies correct for the normally high out-of-wedlock birthrates in areas with large African-American communities, the correlation does remain constant across ethnic groups.

Perhaps as a legacy of slavery, greater tolerance of out-of-wedlock births has become part of African-American culture.[41] Therefore, in

---

provided 66 percent of the median household income, while in New Orleans the package provided 65 percent of the median household income. Murray, "Does Welfare Bring More Babies?" *Public Interest* 115 (Spring 1994): 17–30.

[40]Michael Tanner, Stephen Moore, and David Hartman, "The Work vs. Welfare Trade-Off: An Analysis of the Total Level of Welfare Benefits by State," Cato Institute Policy Analysis no. 240, September 19, 1995.

[41]Out-of-wedlock births have always been higher among African-Americans than among whites at all income and education levels. For example, the out-of-wedlock birthrate among college-educated black women is seven times the rate among college-educated white women. Dinesh D'Souza, *The End of Racism* (New York: Free Press, 1995), p. 515, citing data from the Bureau of Health Statistics. The reasons have been subject to much debate. Robert Park, E. Franklin Frazier, Kenneth Stampp, and others point out that under slavery the only distinction between legitimate and illegitimate children was social, not legal. See, for example, E. Franklin Frazier, *The Negro Family in the United States* (New York: Free Press, 1979); Robert Park, *Race and Culture* (Glencoe, Ill.: Free Press, 1950); and Herbert Gutman, *The Black Family in Slavery and Freedom* (New York: Pantheon Books, 1976). W. E. B. DuBois points out that in 1900, a few decades after emancipation, the black out-of-wedlock birthrate was nearly 25

areas where the black population is densely concentrated, such as the South or urban areas, out-of-wedlock births are relatively high regardless of welfare benefits. The same trend does not hold true for African-Americans in areas where there is no cultural concentration, such as in Idaho or New Hampshire. Reanalyzing the data with that in mind, Murray, among others, notes, "The same data that show no relationship between welfare and illegitimacy among blacks across states suddenly show such a relationship when one controls for the size and density of the black population."[42]

A practical example of the link between welfare and childbearing can be seen in the results from the welfare reform enacted in New Jersey in 1993. The New Jersey law denies additional AFDC benefits to women on welfare who have additional children. The actual financial impact of that "family cap" is quite small, just $44 per month, out of a welfare package that can be as high as $26,500 per year. However, the impact on childbearing by women on welfare appears to be quite significant.[43]

Figure 3.5 shows the birthrate for mothers on AFDC during the months immediately before and immediately after the family cap went into effect. The birthrate shows a better than 10 percent decline following implementation of the family cap, from a precap average of 10.96 births per 1,000 women to a postcap average of 9.72 births per 1,000 women.

The same results can be seen in studies of welfare systems in other countries. For example, a recent study of the impact of Canada's social welfare system on family structure concluded that "providing

---

percent, compared to 2 percent among whites, and strongly argues that this represents a holdover in slave child-bearing patterns. W. E. B. DuBois, *The Negro American Family* (1908; Cambridge, Mass.: MIT Press, 1970), pp. 151–52.

Recently some scholars have suggested additional reasons for the phenomena, including black cultural traditions dating back to the custom of child fostering in Africa. Andrew Miller, "Social Science, Social Policy, and the Heritage of African-American Families," in *The Underclass Debate: Views from History*, ed. Michael Katz (Princeton, N.J.: Princeton University Press, 1993), pp. 252–93. Still others place the emphasis on the lack of economic opportunities for black men throughout much of this country's history. See, for example, William Julius Wilson, *The Truly Disadvantaged: The Inner City, the Underclass, and Public Policy* (Chicago: University of Chicago Press, 1987).

[42]Charles Murray, "Does Welfare Bring More Babies?"

[43]See Robert Rector, "The Impact of New Jersey's Family Cap on Out-of-Wedlock Births and Abortions," Heritage Foundation FYI no. 59, September 6, 1995.

Figure 3.5
BIRTHRATES FOR WOMEN ON AFDC IN NEW JERSEY

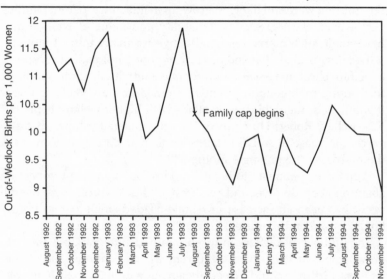

Month

SOURCE: Robert Rector, "The Impact of New Jersey's Family Cap on Out-of-Wedlock Births and Abortions," Heritage Foundation FYI no. 59, September 6, 1995, Figure 2, p. 2.

additional benefits to single parents encourages births of children to unwed women."[44] Studies in Britain have shown similar results.[45] Likewise, an Australian study indicated an increase in out-of-wedlock births as a result of the country's welfare benefits.[46]

In addition, focusing solely on the out-of-wedlock birthrate may actually understate the problem. In the past, women who gave birth out of wedlock frequently married the fathers of their children after the birth. Marvin Olasky, for example, estimates that as many as 85

[44]Douglas Allen, "Welfare and the Family: The Canadian Experience," *Journal of Labor Economics* 7, no. 1 (January 1993): 202.

[45]Charles Murray, *The Emerging British Underclass* (London: Institute for Economic Affairs, 1990).

[46]P. Swan and Mikhail Bernstam, "Brides of the State," *IPA Review* 41 (May–July 1987): 22–25.

percent of unwed mothers in the 1950s ultimately married the fathers of their children.[47] Therefore, while technically born out of wedlock, the children were still likely to grow up in intact two-parent families.

However, the increasing availability and value of welfare may have made such marriages unattractive for many unwed mothers. If the father is unskilled and has few or poor employment prospects, a welfare check may seem a preferable alternative. Studies indicate that young mothers and pregnant women are less likely to marry the fathers of their children in states with higher welfare benefits.[48] Research by Robert Hutchins of Cornell University shows that a 10 percent increase in AFDC benefits leads to an 8 percent decrease in the marriage rate of single mothers.[49]

Welfare also appears to have a modest but significant impact on abandonment, divorce, and remarriage after divorce.[50] The overall result has been an increase in female-headed single-parent households, as shown in Figure 3.6.

The problem of welfare-induced family disintegration is likely to grow worse in the future. If current trends continue, the out-of-wedlock birthrate could exceed 40 percent within the next 10 years.[51]

Because the African-American family was the first to suffer from the anti-family incentives of welfare, much of the larger public has been able to remain indifferent to the consequences of those policies. They have safely watched on television our inner cities decline ever further into poverty, crime, and despair.

But that will not be the case much longer. As Murray has noted, the current 23 percent white out-of-wedlock birthrate is almost

[47]Marvin Olasky, *The Tragedy of American Compassion* (Washington: Regnery, 1992), p. 186.

[48]Shelley Lundberg and Robert Plotnick, "Effects of State Welfare, Abortion, and Family Planning Policies on Premarital Childbearing among White Adolescents," *Family Planning Perspectives* 22, no. 6 (1990): 246–51.

[49]Robert Hutchins, "Welfare, Remarriage and Marital Search," *American Economic Review* 69 (June 1989): 369–79.

[50]Irwin Garfinckel and Sara McLanahan, *Single Mothers and Their Children* (Washington: Urban Institute, 1986); Sheldon Danziger et al., "Work and Welfare as Determinants of Female Poverty and Household Headship," *Quarterly Journal of Economics* 97 (August 1982): 519–34; and Robert Moffitt, "Incentive Effects of the U.S. Welfare System: A Review," *Journal of Economic Literature* 30, no. 1 (March 1992): 1–61.

[51]Lee Rainwater, professor emeritus of sociology, Harvard University, Testimony to Senate Committee on Finance, October 31, 1993.

Figure 3.6
PERCENTAGE OF FEMALE-HEADED HOUSEHOLDS, 1950–93

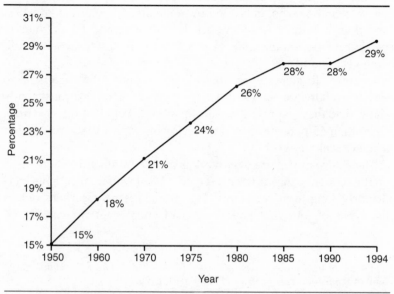

SOURCE: Bureau of the Census, Current Population Surveys, Series P60, various numbers.

exactly what the black rate was in 1965, when Moynihan warned of the destruction of the black family and its consequences. From that point the black out-of-wedlock birthrate escalated sharply. There is no reason to believe that we won't soon see the same thing happen among whites.[52]

That means the problems associated with single-parent families will soon be spilling out of the cities into the suburbs and rural communities. Moreover, since African-Americans make up just over one-tenth of the U.S. population, if white out-of-wedlock birthrates begin to approach those of blacks, the problem will be nine times as large.

[52]Charles Murray, "The Coming White Underclass," American Enterprise Institute On the Issues no. 51, October 1993.

Welfare and the Work Ethic

In 1960 nearly two-thirds of Americans in the lowest income quintile were in households headed by someone who worked.[53] In 1991 less than one-third lived in such households, and fewer than 11 percent were in households headed by a person who worked full-time year round.[54]

Contrary to stereotypes, there is no evidence that people who receive welfare are "lazy." Indeed, surveys of recipients consistently show that they express a desire to work.[55] Yet, at the same time, more than 65 percent of welfare recipients report that they are not actively seeking work.[56]

The choice of welfare over work is often a rational decision based on the economic incentives presented.[57] Most welfare recipients, particularly long-term recipients, lack the skills necessary to obtain the types of jobs that pay more than entry-level wages.[58] Those

---

[53]Bureau of the Census, *Income in 1960 of Families and Persons in the United States*, Current Population Reports, Series P60-80, 1961, p. 26.

[54]Bureau of the Census, "Workers with Low Earnings," Current Population Reports, Series P60-178, 1991.

[55]See, for example, Leonard Goodwin, *Causes and Cures of Welfare* (Lexington, Mass.: Lexington Books, 1983); Marta Tienda and Haya Stier, "Joblessness and Shiftlessness: Labor Force Activity in Chicago's Inner-City," in *The Urban Underclass*, ed. Christopher Jencks and Paul Peterson (Washington: Brookings Institution, 1991), pp. 135–54.

[56]U.S. House of Representatives, Committee on Ways and Means, *1994 Green Book*, Table 1028, p. 404.

[57]Several studies have shown that welfare acts as a disincentive to work. For a good review of the literature, see Sheldon Danziger, Robert Haveman, and Robert Plotnick, "How Transfers Affect Work, Savings, and Income Distribution," *Journal of Economic Literature* 19, no. 3 (September 1981): 975–1028; and Robert Moffitt, "Incentive Effects of the U.S. Welfare System: A Review," *Journal of Economic Literature* 30, no. 1 (March 1992): 1–61.

[58]See, for example, Mary Jo Bane and David Ellwood, "The Dynamics of Dependence: The Routes to Self-Sufficiency," Report prepared for the assistant secretary for planning and evaluation, Office of Evaluation and Technical Analysis, Office of Income Security Policy, U.S. Department of Health and Human Services, Washington, 1983; Greg Duncan, *Years of Poverty, Years of Plenty* (Ann Arbor: University of Michigan, Institute for Social Research, 1984); David Ellwood, "Targeting Would-Be Long-Term Recipients of AFDC," Mathematica Policy Research, Princeton, N.J., 1986; June O'Neill, Laurie Bassi, and Douglas Wolf, "The Duration of Welfare Spells," *Review of Economics and Statistics* 69 (1987): 241–49; and Robert Plotnick, "Turnover in AFDC Population: An Event History Analysis," *Journal of Human Resources* 18 (1983): 65–81.

individuals who do leave welfare for work most often start employment in service or retail trade industries, generally as clerks, secretaries, cleaning persons, sales help, and waitresses.[59] While it would be nice to increase the wages of entry-level workers to the point where work pays better than welfare, government has no ability to do so. (Attempts to mandate wage increases, such as minimum wage legislation, chiefly result in increased unemployment.)[60] For those individuals, welfare simply pays better than work.

As far back as the 1960s experts warned that welfare would discourage work. A panel investigating the Watts riots concluded that welfare was damaging the work ethic. The report noted that a minimum wage job paid about $220 per month in 1965 ($1,063 in 1995 dollars), out of which had to come such work-related expenses as clothing and transportation. In contrast, the average welfare family in the area received from $177 to $238 per month ($855 to $1,150 in 1995 dollars), out of which no work-related expenses had to come.[61]

Studies confirm welfare as a disincentive for work. The Seattle Income Maintenance Experiment and the Denver Income Maintenance Experiment were a series of controlled experiments conducted between 1971 and 1978 to examine the effect of guaranteed income supports on the poor. Researchers concluded that every dollar of

[59]Peter Brandon, "Jobs Taken by Mothers Moving from Welfare to Work and the Effects of Minimum Wages on This Transition," Employment Policies Institute, Washington, February 1995.

[60]A tremendous number of studies have documented the effect of minimum wages on employment opportunities of low-wage workers. See, for example, Edward Gramlich, "Impact of Minimum Wages on Other Wages, Employment, and Family Incomes," Brookings Papers on Economic Activity, Brookings Institution, Washington, 1976, pp. 409–51; Finis Welch and James Cunningham, "Effects of Minimum Wages on the Level and Age Composition of Youth Employment," *Review of Economics and Statistics* 60 (1978): 140–45; David Parsons, *Poverty and the Minimum Wage* (Washington: American Enterprise Institute, 1980); Charles Brown, Curtis Gilroy, and Andrew Kohen, "The Effect of Minimum Wage on Employment and Unemployment," *Journal of Economic Literature* 20 (June 1982): 487–528; Charles Brown, "Minimum Wage Laws: Are They Overrated?" *Journal of Economic Perspectives* 2, no. 3 (1988): 133–46; David Neumark, "Employment Effects of Minimum and Subminimum Wages: Panel Data on State Minimum Wage Laws," *Industrial and Labor Relations Review* 46, no. 1 (1992): 55–81; and Donald Deere, Kevin Murphy, and Finis Welch, "Sense and Nonsense on the Minimum Wage," *Regulation* 18, no. 1 (1995): 47–56.

[61]Governor's Commission on the Los Angeles Riots, *Violence in the City—An End or a Beginning?* (Los Angeles: State of California, 1966), p. 72.

subsidy reduced labor and earnings by 80 cents. The number of hours worked declined by 43 percent for young unmarried males and 33 percent for males who later married. Unmarried women with children reduced work by 25 percent. The length of time spent outside the workforce during unemployment increased by 9 weeks (27 percent) for unmarried men and 56 weeks (60 percent) for single mothers.[62]

An analysis of interstate variation in labor force participation during the 1980s by Richard Vedder, Lowell Gallaway, and Robert Lawson found that such participation declined as welfare benefits increased.[63] Likewise, a study by Sheldon Danziger, Robert Haveman, and Robert Plotnick concluded that the cumulative impact of welfare payments reduced the U.S. labor supply by 4.8 percent.[64]

Robert Moffitt of Brown University reviewed the available literature on welfare and work in 1992 and concluded that welfare does discourage work among recipients. Moffitt found that the work effort of welfare recipients was reduced as much as 30 percent. Moffitt commented that that was "not surprising given that the average benefit is approximately equal to the earnings a woman would receive if she worked full time at a minimum wage job."[65]

Most of the studies probably understate the work disincentive of welfare since they consider only a small portion of the total package of welfare benefits available to recipients. Other studies show that as welfare benefits increase, women are more likely to leave the labor force and enroll in welfare programs. For example, Hill and O'Neill found that a 50 percent increase in monthly AFDC and food stamp benefit levels led to a 75 percent increase both in the number

[62]Gregory Christiansen and Walter Williams, "Welfare Family Cohesiveness and Out-of-Wedlock Births," in *The American Family and the State* (San Francisco: Pacific Research Institute for Public Policy Research, 1986), p. 398.

[63]Richard Vedder, Lowell Gallaway, and Robert Lawson, "Why People Work: An Examination of Interstate Variation in Labor Force Participation," *Journal of Labor Research* 12, no. 1 (Winter 1991): 47–59.

[64]Sheldon Danziger, Robert Haveman, and Robert Plotnick, "How Income Transfers Affect Work, Savings, and Income Distribution: A Critical Review," *Journal of Economic Literature* 19 (September 1981): 996.

[65]Moffitt, p. 17.

of women enrolling in AFDC and in the number of years spent on welfare.[66]

Welfare also appears to have the indirect effect of reducing by as much as 50 percent the work effort of young men in communities with high levels of welfare participation, even though the men themselves do not receive benefits. Hill and O'Neill attribute that to the facts that (1) high benefits reduce the probability of marriage, thereby reducing the necessity for young men to support a family, and (2) many single young men who are boyfriends of single mothers on AFDC are indirectly sharing in the mothers' welfare benefits.[67]

Perhaps most troubling of all is the psychological attitude toward work that appears to be developing among those on welfare. In his excellent book, *The Underclass*, Ken Auletta reports on interviews with a wide variety of inner-city men and women. He found little sense that the poor needed to take charge of their own lives or find work to become self-sufficient. On the contrary, he found that most felt that the government had an obligation to provide for them and their children.[68]

Other reports increasingly show young men and women in the inner city refusing to work for the "chump change" of low-wage jobs. No doubt that attitude stems in part from our general "get it now" culture. But another cause is the realization that there is no *need* to work for low wages. Welfare will always be there as a safety net.

Confirmation can be seen in a study of inner-city poor in Chicago. While nearly all those who were unemployed expressed a desire for work, most also said they expected a job that paid well above the minimum wage. When they were asked how much a job would need to pay for them to take it, answers ranged from $5.50 to $10.20 per hour.[69]

Welfare recipients themselves are not the only ones to develop a prejudice against work. Evidence suggests that anti-work attitudes

---

[66]M. Anne Hill and June O'Neill, "Underclass Behaviors in the United States: Measurement and Analysis of Determinants," Baruch College, City University of New York, March 1993, pp. 82–83.

[67]Ibid., p. 86.

[68]Ken Auletta, *The Underclass* (New York: Random House, 1982).

[69]Tienda and Stier, pp. 141–43.

trickle down to their children. As a recent report by the Maryland NAACP puts it, "A child whose parents draw a welfare check without going to work does not understand that in this society at least one parent is expected to rise five days of each week to go to some type of job."[70]

As a result, children raised on welfare are likely to have lower incomes as adults than children not raised on welfare. The more welfare received by a child's family, the lower that child's earnings as an adult tended to be, even holding constant such other factors as race, family structure, and education.[71] That welfare reduces self-sufficiency and work should hardly come as a surprise. As the Chinese philosopher Lao-Tzu said in 500 B.C., "The more subsidies you have, the less self-reliant people will be."[72]

Welfare and Crime

In 1994 the Maryland NAACP released a report concluding that "the ready access to a lifetime of welfare and free social service programs is a major contributory factor to the crime problems we face today."[73] The NAACP's conclusion is confirmed by additional academic research. For example, M. Anne Hill's and June O'Neill's research showed that a 50 percent increase in the monthly value of combined AFDC and food stamp benefits led to a 117 percent increase in the crime rate among young black men.[74]

Welfare contributes to crime in several ways. First, as already noted, children from single-parent families are more likely to become involved in criminal activity. Recent research indicates a direct correlation between crime rates and the number of single-parent families

[70]John L. Wright, Marge Green, and Leroy Warren Jr., "An Assessment of Crime in Maryland Today," Maryland State Conference of Branches, NAACP, Annapolis, February 1994.

[71]Mary Corcoran et al., "The Association between Men's Economic Status and Their Family and Community Origins," *Journal of Human Resources* 27, no. 4 (Fall 1992): 575–601.

[72]Lao-Tzu, *Tao Te Ching*, trans. Stephen Mitchell (New York: Harper & Row, 1988), p. 57.

[73] Wright, Green, and Warren, p. 7.

[74]Hill and O'Neill, p. 73.

in a neighborhood.[75] As welfare contributes to the rise in out-of-wedlock births, it concomitantly contributes to associated criminal activity.

As Barbara Whitehead noted in her seminal article for the *Atlantic Monthly*,

> The relationship [between single-parent families and crime] is so strong that controlling for family configuration erases the relationship between race and crime and between low income and crime. This conclusion shows up time and again in the literature. The nation's mayors, as well as police officers, social workers, probation officers, and court officials, consistently point to family breakup as the most important source of rising rates of crime.[76]

Second, welfare leads to increased crime by contributing to the marginalization of young black men in society. As George Gilder, author of *Wealth and Poverty*, has noted, "The welfare culture tells the man he is not a necessary part of the family," a process Gilder describes as being "cuckolded by the compassionate state."[77]

The role of marriage and family as civilizing influences on young men has long been discussed. Whether or not strict causation can be proven, it is certainly true that unwed fathers are more likely to use drugs and become involved in criminal behavior than are other men.[78]

Finally, boys growing up in mother-only families naturally seek male influences. Both clinical and anthropological studies agree that boys need adult males to emulate. In his seminal book on the issue, *Fatherless America*, David Blankenhorn explains the "irreplaceable" role of fathers in teaching boys about what it means to be a man in our society.[79] Unfortunately, in many inner-city neighborhoods, desirable male role models may not exist. In *There Are No Children*

[75]Douglas Smith and G. Roger Jarjoura, "Social Structure and Criminal Victimization," *Journal of Research in Crime and Delinquency* 25, no. 1 (February 1988): 27–52.

[76]Whitehead, p. 50.

[77]Cited in Tom Bethell, "They Had a Dream: The Politics of Welfare Reform," *National Review*, August 23, 1993, p. 33.

[78]Robert Lerman, "Unwed Fathers: Who Are they?" *American Enterprise*, September–October 1993, pp. 32–37.

[79]David Blankenhorn, *Fatherless America: Confronting Our Most Urgent Social Problem* (New York: Basic Books, 1995).

Here, one of the most moving books on inner-city poverty, Alex Kotlowitz describes the lives of two brothers, Lafayette and Pharro Rivers, growing up in a Chicago public housing project in the 1980s. He describes a world virtually devoid of responsible adult men. It is also a world of unremitting violence, crime, and murder—a world where mothers purchase funeral insurance for their young children.[80]

It is not an exaggeration to describe some communities as overwhelmingly dominated by single mothers and their children. According to a study by the National Research Council, nearly 70 percent of families with children in high-poverty areas consist of an unmarried mother and her children.[81] Yet we know that when welfare-induced pathologies are concentrated within a single community, the crime problem increases still further. Perhaps Moynihan summarized it best back in 1961 when he warned,

> From the wild Irish slums of the nineteenth century Eastern seaboard, to the riot-torn suburbs of Los Angeles, there is one unmistakable lesson in American history: a community that allows a large number of young men to grow up in broken families, dominated by women, never acquiring any stable relationship to male authority, never acquiring any set of rational expectations about the future—that community asks for and gets chaos. Crime, violence, unrest, disorder—most particularly the furious, unrestrained lashing out at the whole social structure—that is not only to be expected, it is very near to inevitable.[82]

Intergenerational Dependence

If the failures of welfare were not tragic enough today, they are also likely to entrap the next generation as well. Although it is true that the majority of children raised on welfare will not receive welfare themselves, the rate of welfare dependence for children raised on AFDC is far higher than for their nonwelfare counterparts. For example, according to the most commonly cited study, by Greg

---

[80]Alex Kotlowitz, *There Are No Children Here: The Story of Two Boys Growing Up in the Other America* (New York: Anchor Books, 1992).

[81]Laurence Lynn Jr. and Michael McGeary, eds., *Inner-City Poverty in the United States* (Washington: National Academy Press, 1990), p. 26.

[82]Daniel P. Moynihan, *Coping: Essays on the Practice of Government* (New York: Random House, 1961), p. 76.

Duncan and Martha Hill, nearly 20 percent of daughters from families that were "highly dependent" on welfare became "highly dependent" themselves, whereas only 3 percent of daughters from non-AFDC households became "highly dependent" on welfare.[83]

An earlier study by Martha Hill and Michael Ponza showed similar results, although the intergenerational impact was more significant for white children than for black.[84] Studies also show that, if they go on welfare as adults, children who were raised on welfare stay on the program significantly longer than do those who were not raised on welfare.[85]

The degree to which welfare dependency has become an intergenerational problem is brought home vividly in a recent study by scholars at the University of Tennessee. Profiling welfare recipients in that state, the study found that 29.3 percent of recipients had parents who received welfare as children. Even more troubling, 7.5 percent of recipients were actually third-generation recipients. Their parents *and* their grandparents were on welfare.[86]

That should not come as a surprise. We know enough about childhood development to understand that a variety of pathologies, from alcoholism to child abuse, are transmitted from parent to child. Indeed, how a child is raised is one of the most important factors in what that child will be like as an adult. The attitudes and habits that lead to welfare dependency are transmitted the same way other parent-to-child pathologies are. Therefore, unless something is done quickly to change the current welfare system, we can expect to see yet another generation trapped in the system.

Conclusion

Nearly 150 years ago Alexis de Tocqueville called for abolishing government welfare programs, warning that "the number of illegitimate children and criminals grows rapidly and continuously, the

[83]Greg Duncan and Martha Hill, "Welfare Dependence within and across Generations," *Science*, January 29, 1988, pp. 467–71.

[84]Martha Hill and Michael Ponza, "Does Welfare Beget Dependency?" Institute for Social Research, Ann Arbor, Mich., 1984.

[85]Mwangi S. Kimenyi, "Rational Choice, Culture of Poverty, and the Intergenerational Transmission of Welfare Dependency," *Southern Economic Journal* 57, no. 4 (April 1991): 947–60.

[86]William Fox et al., "Aid to Families with Dependent Children: 1995 Case Characteristics Study," University of Tennessee, Center for Business and Economic Research, Knoxville, December 1995, pp. 206–9.

indigent population is endless, the spirit of foresight and of saving becomes more and more alien."[87] Tocqueville could easily have been describing our government welfare system today.

Welfare may have started with the best of intentions, but it has clearly failed. It has failed to meet its stated goal of reducing poverty. But its real failure is even more disastrous. Welfare has torn apart the social fabric of our society. Everyone is worse off. The taxpayers must foot the bill for programs that don't work. The poor are dehumanized, seduced into a system from which it is terribly difficult to escape. Teenage girls give birth to children they will never be able to support. The work ethic is eroded. Crime rates soar. Such is the legacy of welfare.

The failure of welfare is increasingly recognized across political and ideological lines. That is why politicians as disparate as President Clinton and Newt Gingrich cooperated in passing legislation to end "welfare as we know it." But will the solutions proposed by both the left and the right, and embodied in the 1996 welfare reform legislation, solve the problem?

[87]Cited in Gertrude Himmelfarb, "True Charity: Lessons from Victorian England," in *Transforming Welfare: The Revival of American Charity*, ed. Jeffrey Sikkenga (Grand Rapids, Mich.: Acton Institute, 1996), p. 31.

4. Why Liberal Welfare Reform Won't Work

The failures of the welfare state are now generally admitted across the ideological spectrum. But if current programs are not working, what should be done instead? Can welfare be reformed?

A small core of unreconstructed welfare state liberals argues that we have failed to provide sufficient funding to make existing social welfare programs work properly. They call for an expansion of existing programs and new investments in job training and child care. No one can fault their desire to help, but the evidence shows that their proposed solutions will not lift people out of poverty.

Job Training

There is currently a host of government job-training programs. The Department of Education alone runs 59 different job-training programs that cost $13 billion a year. The Department of Labor runs 34 more programs that cost $7 billion a year. Almost every government agency, from the Department of Agriculture to the Appalachian Regional Commission, seems to offer at least one training program.

Unfortunately, there is little evidence that job-training programs actually work. A study by the General Accounting Office of 61 job-training programs in 38 states concluded that the programs "are helping recipients find only dead-end jobs, and are failing to give the poor the education and training they need to advance."[1]

It is difficult to determine the success of various job-training programs because most state officials who administer the programs do not attempt to monitor such things as the proportion of trainees who actually leave welfare, whether they remain off welfare, and whether their incomes actually increase. Another study by the GAO

---

[1]Cited in "Jobs Plan Pays Poorly," *New York Daily News*, February 2, 1987.

found that 75 percent of federal training programs gathered no information with which to evaluate the programs' success.[2]

What little information we have is far from encouraging. The Federal Job Training Partnership Act was designed to boost the earnings of high school dropouts. But the Department of Labor conducted a controlled scientific evaluation of the program and found that it failed to significantly increase the employability of trainees. And it did not significantly increase the wages of those who did find jobs. Female trainees saw their average hourly wage rise by only 3.4 percent after completion of the program. Men saw no increase in wages at all.[3]

A study of the Jobstart training program, which operated in 13 communities across the country, found that the program generated only "statistically insignificant" increases in earnings among participants.[4] As Fred Doolittle, director of Jobstart explains, "Education and training alone, as traditionally offered within the [federal job-training program], are not enough to make a real difference in these young people's lives."[5]

Of 5,000 Baltimore area participants in the Agriculture Department's Food Stamp Employment and Training program, fewer than 1 percent found jobs through the program.[6] Another program in Baltimore, Baltimore Options, which provided basic literacy education, preparation for the general equivalency diploma test, and skills training, produced only a 4.8 percent increase in employment and a $511 per year increase in earnings.[7]

An Urban Institute evaluation of the Massachusetts Employment Training program found that participants had only an 8.2 percent

[2]General Accounting Office, "Youth Job Training: Problems Measuring Attainment of Employment Competencies," GAO/HRD 87-33, February 1987, p. 27.

[3]U.S. Department of Labor, Employment and Training Administration, *The National JTPA Study: Title II-A, Impact on Earnings and Employment at 18 Months*, Research and Evaluation Report 93-C (Washington: Government Printing Office, 1993), pp. 226–28.

[4]The study was conducted by the Manpower Demonstration Research Corporation. Cited in William Claiborne, "Study of 'Jobstart' Participants Shows Little Gain in Earnings, *Washington Post*, December 28, 1993.

[5]Ibid.

[6]Mona Charen, "Job Training Hallucinations," *Washington Times*, December 20, 1993.

[7]Daniel Friedlander, *Supplemental Report on the Baltimore Options Program* (New York: Manpower Demonstration Resource Corporation, 1987), p. 11.

greater increase in employment than did the control group and an average annual increase in earnings of only $360.[8]

The San Diego Saturation Work Initiative Model produced an employment gain of 10.5 percent but an average wage increase of only $352 in the first year. The wage gain declined substantially in subsequent years, and by year five wages of participants were no higher than those of nonparticipants.[9] The Family Independence program in Washington State actually *reduced* both employability and average earnings.[10] In general, the most optimistic evidence from studies of job-training programs, from the 1967 Work Incentive program to the 1988 Job Opportunity and Basic Skills (JOBS) program, indicates that "caseload reductions have not been dramatic and increases in people's standard of living have been limited."[11]

Not only do job-training programs fail to move significant numbers of people from welfare to work, they may actually have the opposite effect—moving people from work to welfare. Since individuals may be eligible for training programs only if they are on welfare, it becomes a rational decision for low-income working people, currently making a marginal living, to quit work and enter the welfare system. A study of a job-training program in Oregon, offered under the 1988 Family Support Act, found that welfare rolls grew significantly after the training program became available. Moreover, the study concluded that the new enrollees were "individuals who previously qualified for AFDC but did not apply for benefits and/or people who reduced their employment to qualify for AFDC."[12] Likewise, when similar training and child-care benefits were introduced in Washington State in 1988, the number of new welfare clients increased by 6 percent.[13]

---

[8]Demetra Smith Nightingale et al., *Evaluation of the Massachusetts Employment and Training (ET) Program* (Washington: Urban Institute, 1991), pp. 91–93.

[9]Daniel Friedlander and Gayle Hamilton, *The Saturation Work Incentive Model in San Diego: A Five-Year Follow-Up Study* (New York: Manpower Demonstration Research Corporation, July 1993), p. xxii.

[10]Sharon Long et al., *The Evaluation of the Washington State Family Independence Program* (Washington: Urban Institute, 1994), pp. 2–3.

[11]Judith Gueron and Edward Pauly, "From Welfare to Work," Russell Sage Foundation, New York, 1991, "Summary," p. 11.

[12]Terry Johnson, Daniel Klepinger, and Fred Dong, "Caseload Impacts of Welfare Reform," *Contemporary Economic Policy* 12, no. 1 (January 1994): 98.

[13]Amitai Etzioni, "Starting Over on Welfare," *Wall Street Journal*, March 31, 1994.

In addition, because people are unlikely to seek work until they have completed their job training, such programs may actually delay departure from the welfare system. The study of Oregon's job-training program concluded that recipients delayed leaving the program until their training eligibility was used up.[14]

The problems with job-training programs lie with both the nature of government programs and the background of welfare recipients. First, government training programs are almost inevitably bureaucratic, arbitrary, and inflexible.

They also have a history of being oddly detached from the realities of the job market. For example, Atlanta, Georgia, was once the headquarters of Eastern Airlines. Logically, therefore, the state offered programs to train airline mechanics. Eastern Airlines is no longer in business, but Georgia continues to train thousands of airline mechanics each year. Likewise, one federal program provides loans to train 81,000 cosmetology students each year, but the labor market can absorb fewer than 18,000 cosmetologists a year.[15]

The second problem lies with the recipients themselves. Welfare recipients can essentially be divided into two groups. The largest group consists primarily of women who enter the system as a result of divorce, along with the small number who enter because of the loss of a job. As noted earlier, that group tends to spend two years or less in the program. Not only do those recipients appear not to need job training, but most would not be in the welfare system long enough to benefit from the programs. Indeed, studies of job-training programs have found that they had no impact on that group of recipients.[16]

In contrast, the small core of long-term recipients, made up primarily of those who go on welfare because of an out-of-wedlock birth, presents an entirely different set of problems. One study found that women in that group had aptitude and achievement scores well below the mean of even the lowest occupational classes. Both verbal and math abilities were in the lowest 20 percent of scores for the

[14]Johnson, Klepinger, and Dong, p. 97.

[15]"How Many Bureaucrats Does It Take . . . ?" editorial, *Washington Times*, July 31, 1995.

[16]Gueron and Pauly, p. 31.

U.S. population.[17] Other studies have found that 80 percent of teen mothers are high school dropouts.[18] They are likely to have been out of the job market for a longer period of time than the first group and may never even have held a job at all. They have high levels of substance abuse problems, and domestic violence is common.[19]

A job-training program is unlikely to be sufficient to prepare them to support their families in a competitive economy. The only real solution that will have a widespread impact on that group is to reduce out-of-wedlock births. Job training does nothing to address that problem.

Child Care

Liberal approaches to welfare reform also call for a heavy investment in child-care services. Generally, it is argued that (1) there is a significant shortage of child-care facilities, and (2) what facilities do exist are too expensive for poor mothers to afford. However, a careful examination of the facts suggests that neither claim is true.

The most comprehensive survey of regulated child-care services yet conducted was the 1991 "Profile of Child Care Settings" by the U.S. Department of Education.[20] The survey found approximately 80,000 center-based early education and child-care programs nationwide. The centers had space for about 5.3 million children (4.2 million preschool age and 1.1 million school age). An additional 118,000 licensed non-center-based family day care providers were identified, with a capacity to care for 860,000 children. At the time of the survey, there was an average of four full-time vacancies in each center-based facility and one vacancy in each family day care home, a total of roughly 440,000 available spaces.

[17]Nicholas Zill et al., *Welfare Mothers as Potential Employees: A Statistical Profile Based on National Survey Data* (Washington: Child Trends, 1991), pp. 13–17.

[18]D. M. Upchurch and Joseph McCarthy, "Adolescent Childbearing and High School Completion in the 1980's: Have Things Changed?" *Family Planning Perspectives*, September–October 1989, pp. 199–202.

[19]See Valerie Polakow, *Lives on the Edge: Single Mothers and Their Children in the Other America* (Chicago: University of Chicago Press, 1994).

[20]Ellen Eliason Kisker et al., "A Profile of Child Care Settings: Early Education and Care in 1990," Study conducted for U.S. Department of Education by Mathematica Policy Research, Princeton, N.J., 1991.

The survey did not include the nearly 1.75 million unlicensed day care providers in the United States.[21] Contrary to media imagery, there is no evidence that unlicensed day care providers are in any way less safe or healthful than licensed facilities or large group care centers. A study by the U.S. Department of Health and Human Services found that over half of the parents of children in unlicensed day care facilities had known the caregiver for six months or longer before placing their children in the provider's care. Indeed, one-third of the parents claimed to have a close personal friendship with the caregiver. Over half the children in unlicensed day care lived within a few blocks of the caregiver's home.[22]

Unlicensed day care providers are more likely than licensed providers to be caring for their own children and, on average, have a lower adult/child ratio. When asked directly, parents of children in unlicensed day care reported a high degree of satisfaction with their children's care.[23]

However, even including unlicensed providers does not give the full story because the vast majority of working mothers does not use outside providers at all, relying instead on informal arrangements with relatives, friends, neighbors, and baby sitters. Such informal arrangements are even more common among the poor than among the public at large. Table 4.1 shows the type of child-care arrangements being used by working parents. Approximately 57.5 percent of the children of all working mothers and 68.2 percent of the children of poor working mothers are cared for by a relative or baby sitter. An additional 8.7 percent of all children and 9.5 percent of poor children are cared for by the mother at work.[24]

[21]Sandra Hofferth and Donna Phillips, "Child Care in the United States, 1980–1995," *Journal of Marriage and Family* 49, no. 3 (1987): 559–71. See also "The Demand and Supply of Child Care in 1990: Joint Findings from the National Child Care Survey, 1990, and the Profile of Child Care Settings," National Association for the Education of Young Children, Washington, 1991.

[22]Patricia Divine-Hawkins, "Final Report of the National Day Care Home Study, Family Day Care in the United States: Executive Summary," U.S. Department of Health and Human Services, Office of Human Development Services, Administration for Children, Youth, and Families, Day Care Division, OHDS 80-30287, 1981, p. 4.

[23]Ibid., p. 22.

[24]Bureau of the Census, *Who's Minding the Kids? Child Care Arrangements: Fall 1991*, Current Population Reports, Series P70 (Washington: Government Printing Office, 1994), p. 1.

Table 4.1

CHILD-CARE ARRANGEMENTS OF WORKING MOTHERS WITH
CHILDREN UNDER AGE FIVE, 1991 (percentage)

Type of Care	Total	Poor	Nonpoor
Care in child's home	15.7	19.0	15.4
Grandparent	7.2	8.1	7.1
Other relative	3.2	6.7	2.8
Baby sitter	5.3	4.2	5.5
Care in another home	13.1	12.9	13.0
Grandparent	8.6	8.2	8.5
Other relative	4.5	4.7	4.5
Parental care	28.7	36.2	27.9
Father	20.0	26.7	19.4
Mother (at work)	8.7	9.5	8.5
Outside day care	42.5	31.8	43.8
Family day care	17.9	10.8	18.7
Group care center	15.8	14.8	16.0
Preschool	7.3	3.6	7.6
Other school	1.6	2.6	1.5

SOURCE: U.S. House of Representatives, Committee on Ways and Means, *1994 Green Book: Overview of Entitlement Programs* (Washington: Government Printing Office, 1994), Table 12.7, p. 540.

All of this has led Sandra Hofferth, one of the nation's leading authorities on child care, to conclude that "analysis of the number of centers and family day-care homes . . . over the past 15 years does not suggest any evidence of a shortage."[25]

There clearly appears to be sufficient child care available, so the next question is, Is it affordable? Approximately one-third of all full-time working mothers and nearly 58 percent of poor working mothers actually pay *nothing* for child care. For other mothers, child care may actually be less expensive than is commonly believed. The average weekly payment for child care is approximately $63. However, the amount paid for child care actually rises with income, meaning that poor mothers pay less. For families with incomes under

---

[25]Quoted in Rick Santorum, "Welfare: Faking Reform," *Washington Post*, December 12, 1993.

$15,000 per year, the average child-care payment was only $38 per week in 1990.[26]

Child care, therefore, appears to be both available and affordable. Certainly it has become more available than it was 30 years ago. Yet the percentage of poor women working full-time has declined by nearly 50 percent over that period.[27] Therefore, lack of affordable child care cannot be the primary reason why poor women are not working.

Nevertheless, both federal and state governments have made major investments in child care in recent years. The 1990 Act for Better Child Care created a vast new federal child-care program at a cost of nearly $10 billion over five years.[28] In addition, the Aid to Families with Dependent Children program has an open-ended entitlement that provides child care to recipients, including transitional assistance to mothers who lose AFDC eligibility because they have accepted work. Federal spending for child care under that program totaled more than $470 million in 1993.[29] Roughly 37 percent of the nonworking poor and 30 percent of the working poor receive some government child-care assistance.[30] Table 4.2 details the major current federal government child-care programs. In addition, nearly all states also provide child-care assistance.

However, welfare rolls have continued to grow despite the massive government investment in child care. There is no reason to suppose, therefore, that additional spending on child care will lead to welfare reductions, when previous expenditures have failed to do so.

[26]Sandra Hofferth et al., *National Child Care Survey, 1990* (Washington: Administration for Children and Families and the National Association for the Education of Young Children, 1991), p. 167.

[27]William Kelso, *Poverty and the Underclass: Changing Perceptions of the Poor in America* (New York: New York University Press, 1994), p. 130.

[28]Frank Swoboda, "Congress Passes $22 Billion Child Care Package," *Washington Post*, October 28, 1990. Only $10 billion was direct child-care subsidies. The remainder was an expansion of the Earned Income Tax Credit.

[29]U.S. House of Representatives, Committee on Ways and Means, *1994 Green Book: Background Material and Data on Programs within the Jurisdiction of the Committee on Ways and Means* (Washington: Government Printing Office, 1994), p. 541.

[30]Sandra Hofferth, "The Impact of Welfare Reform and Work Requirements on the Demand for Child Care," Testimony before the Senate Committee on Labor and Human Resources, March 1, 1995.

Table 4.2
MAJOR FEDERAL CHILD-CARE PROGRAMS, 1995

Program	Cost ($ millions)	Children Served
AFDC child care	470.4	339,244/month
Transitional child care	112.7	84,682/month
At-risk child care	269.8	219,017/month
Child-care and developmental block grant	890.6	62,991/month
Total	1,743.5	705,935/month

SOURCE: Derived from Sandra Clark and Sharon Long, "Child Care Block Grants and Welfare Reform," in *Welfare Reform: An Analysis of the Issues,* ed. Isabel Sawhill (Washington: Urban Institute, 1995), p. 25.

It is also worth noting that, even when government-funded child care is available, many otherwise eligible welfare recipients choose not to take advantage of the program, preferring relatives and other informal alternatives. For example, Ohio's Learning, Earning and Parenting (LEAP) program offered subsidized day care to teen mothers while they attended school or other education programs. But fewer than 20 percent of eligible mothers reported using LEAP-funded child care.[31]

Other programs have had similar results. In Massachusetts only 14 percent of eligible mothers took advantage of child care available under the Employment Training program. In California only 10 percent of eligible mothers took advantage of state-provided day care under the Greater Avenues to Independence (GAIN) program. Just 8 percent of eligible mothers nationwide enrolled their children in organized day care centers under the Work Incentive program.[32]

Finally, we should note that poor women themselves do not blame lack of child care for their lack of work. In one survey, only about 14 percent of welfare mothers said that lack of child care was the

---

[31]Robert G. Wood et al., "Encouraging School Enrollment and Attendance among Teenage Parents on Welfare: Early Impacts of Ohio's LEAP Program," *Children and Youth Services Review* 17 (January–February 1995): 277–307.

[32]Lawrence M. Mead, *The New Politics of Poverty: The Nonworking Poor in America* (New York: Basic Books, 1992), pp. 169–70.

primary reason for not taking a job.[33] Likewise, surveys of women who left welfare for work under California's GAIN program but later returned to the welfare rolls revealed that only about 5 percent said that lack of child care was the reason for returning to the dole.[34]

Child Support Enforcement

Liberals and conservatives agree on the need for tougher enforcement of child support requirements. There is little doubt that the failure of noncustodial fathers to pay child support is a serious problem. Only 51.4 percent of women who are supposed to receive child support payments actually receive full payment. An additional 23.8 percent receive partial payment.[35]

Both federal and state governments have taken action in recent years to strengthen enforcement of child support. In 1975 Congress established the Office of Child Support Enforcement, described as the "federal government's first step towards paying for and overseeing enforcement of private child support."[36] In 1984 Congress passed additional child support legislation establishing uniform national standards for the size of child support awards, requiring states to withhold wages from fathers who fail to pay child support, and stepping up efforts to identify delinquent fathers. The 1988 Family Support Act provided additional resources to states for monitoring and enforcing child support payments.[37] Both President Clinton and Congress have called for federal legislation to suspend the professional and driver's licenses of deadbeat fathers.[38] Several states have already enacted similar legislation.[39]

[33]Kelso, p. 130.

[34]Cited in Mead, p. 170.

[35]David Blankenhorn, *Fatherless America: Confronting Our Most Urgent Social Problem* (New York: Basic Books, 1995), Table 7.2, p. 131.

[36]Irwin Garfinkel, *Assuring Child Support: An Extension of Social Security* (New York: Russell Sage Foundation, 1992), p. 22.

[37]Blankenhorn, pp. 129–47.

[38]See Executive Office of the President, Office of Communications, "Remarks by President Bill Clinton to the National Governors' Association Meeting," Burlington, Vt., July 31, 1995.

[39]As of March 1, 1996, the states that had passed legislation suspending professional licenses were Arizona, Arkansas, California, Connecticut, Florida, Illinois, Indiana, Iowa, Kansas, Louisiana, Maine, Massachusetts, Minnesota, Montana, Nevada, New Hampshire, New Mexico, New York, North Carolina, North Dakota, Ohio, Oklahoma, Oregon, Pennsylvania, Rhode Island, South Dakota, Texas, Vermont, and Virginia. States suspending driver's licenses included Arizona, Arkansas, California, Colorado,

Today there are at least 230 federal and 38,000 state employees involved in child support enforcement. Total expenditures on child support enforcement programs topped $1.6 billion in 1990.[40]

Although the concept of requiring fathers to support their children has broad support, there is considerable question about whether such action will significantly reduce the welfare rolls. Clearly, despite the increased enforcement of recent years, welfare rolls have not declined. The primary reason is that many unwed fathers are "poorly educated, lack job skills, and earn little or no regular income, especially when their children are young."[41] Roughly one-quarter of the fathers are under age 18, and 29 percent are either dropouts or at least two years behind in school.[42] Approximately 26 percent of all noncustodial fathers are themselves living below the poverty level. The situation is even worse among black noncustodial fathers, of whom 56 percent are classified as poor.[43] In fact, a 1992 study from the University of Wisconsin found that 52 percent of fathers who were delinquent in their child support payments earned less than $6,155 per year.[44]

Even if every deadbeat dad paid all the child support ordered, the amount of support would fall far short of the money necessary to lift poor women out of poverty. According to the federal government's *Annual Child Support Report*, about $4.9 billion in child support goes unpaid each year.[45] That amounts to less than $1,300 for every

---

Connecticut, Florida, Illinois, Indiana, Iowa, Kentucky, Louisiana, Maine, Maryland, Massachusetts, Minnesota, Montana, Nevada, New Hampshire, New Mexico, New York, North Carolina, North Dakota, Oklahoma, Oregon, Rhode Island, South Dakota, Texas, Vermont, and Virginia. U.S. Department of Health and Human Services, Administration for Children and Families, Office of Child Support Enforcement, *State Licensing Suspension/Revocation Legislation* (Washington: U.S. Department of Health and Human Services, 1996), pp. 1–27.

[40]Blankenhorn, pp. 129–30.

[41]Robert Lerman and Theodora Ooms, "Unwed Fathers: Complex Dilemmas for Policy Makers," *American Enterprise*, September–October 1993, p. 36.

[42]Freya Sonenstein and Gregory Acs, "Teenage Childbearing: The Trends and Their Implications," in *Welfare Reform: An Analysis of the Issues*, p. 49.

[43]Elaine Sorensen, "The Benefits of Child Support Enforcement," in ibid., pp. 55–56.

[44]Cited in Stuart Miller, "Dead-Broke Dads," *Playboy*, February 1996.

[45]Cited in Stuart Miller, "The Myth of Deadbeat Dads," *Wall Street Journal*, March 2, 1995.

mother on welfare, hardly enough to end poverty. (Of course, many of the owed mothers are not on welfare or even poor.)

Thus, while vigorous child support enforcement should be encouraged and will certainly help some women, it is unlikely to significantly affect the problem of long-term welfare dependence. The Urban Institute estimates that if every noncustodial father met his child support obligations in full, total welfare costs would be reduced by about 9 percent, AFDC participation would also decline by approximately 9 percent, and the number of women living in poverty would be reduced by about 5 percent.[46]

Earned Income Tax Credit

The federal Earned Income Tax Credit (EITC) is a refundable tax credit available to lower income working families and individuals.[47] The EITC is intended to provide lower income working families and families in transition from welfare to work with a financial incentive to work. The maximum available credit in 1995 was $3,110. The credit is phased in when annual income is below $8,400 and is phased out starting at $11,290 and stopped completely at $26,673 for a family of four.

The program has historically enjoyed broad bipartisan support as one of the most effective available federal tools for combating poverty. The EITC was originally established in 1975 to encourage work by offsetting employee payroll taxes. However, since its inception, the original tax credit program has evolved into a tax rebate program under which workers can obtain tax refunds that actually exceed their payroll tax and income tax liability. In 1996 four of every five dollars spent on that program will be disbursed as cash payments.[48]

As a result of numerous revisions and expansions since the program was enacted 20 years ago, the EITC is currently used by over 18 million households—half of which fall above the poverty line and up to one-third of which earn more than $20,000 per year. In fact, loopholes in the program allowed nearly 2 million households

---

[46]Sorensen, pp. 56–57.

[47]For a complete discussion of the Earned Income Tax Credit, see U.S. Department of the Treasury, Internal Revenue Service, "Earned Income Credit," Catalog no. 15173A, Publication 596, 1994.

[48]John Merline, "The Democrats' Taxing Rhetoric, Claims on Working-Poor Tax Credit Strain Belief," *Investor's Business Daily*, October 24, 1995.

Figure 4.1
EITC PROGRAM COSTS

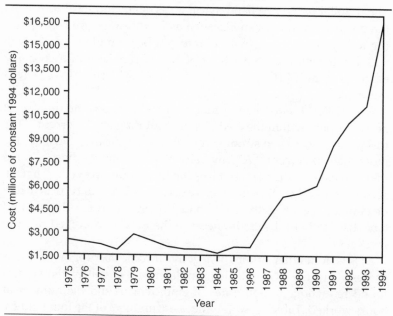

SOURCE: U.S. House of Representatives, Committee on Ways and Means, *1994 Green Book: Overview of Entitlement Programs* (Washington: Government Printing Office, 1994), Table 16-13, p. 704.

with earnings over $30,000 per year and 3,000 households with earnings over $75,000 per year to obtain EITC money in 1994.[49]

The program's expansion has caused its annual cost to taxpayers to skyrocket.[50] In fact, EITC is now the fastest growing federal welfare program. Figure 4.1 shows the rapid growth in EITC costs.

Despite the program's popularity, it has several significant problems. First, EITC may be a disincentive to work. Under the program, once poverty level income has been obtained, EITC support begins to phase out. For example, between $11,600 and $28,500 in income for a family of four, the credit declines by 21 cents for each dollar

---

[49]U.S. House of Representatives, Table 16-12, p. 703.
[50]Ibid., Table 16-13, p. 704.

of additional income. That, in effect, establishes an incentive equivalent to an additional marginal tax rate of 21 percent on every additional dollar earned. When payroll taxes, state and local taxes, and
the phaseout of other benefits such as food stamps are considered,
the total effective marginal tax rate can be as high as 65 percent.
Faced with return on their labor of just 35 cents out of each dollar
earned, some EITC recipients may find additional work less
attractive.[51]

A 1993 GAO report found that the EITC reduced the number of
hours worked within the credit's phaseout range by 7 percent.[52] The
disincentive was even stronger for second wage earners in a family,
more than 10 percent.[53] A University of Wisconsin study concluded
that "on balance the EITC reduces the total hours worked."[54] In fact,
according to Edgar Browning of Texas A&M University, nearly half
of families receiving the EITC had less income than they would
have had without the credit, because the EITC encouraged them to
work less.[55]

At least four other studies of negative income tax programs similar
in design to the EITC yielded similar results.[56] All of the studies
found reductions in both rates of employment and the number of
hours worked. Table 4.3 summarizes the findings of the four studies,
with results translated into common denominators.

The impact on youths and wives may be overstated since they
generally worked only part-time and, therefore, had a smaller statistical base to start with (e.g., a one-hour reduction from a two-hour
base is a 50 percent reduction). However, there is no doubt that the
negative income tax reduced work effort.

[51]Edgar Browning, "Effects of Earned Income Tax Credit on Income and Welfare,"
National Tax Journal 45, no. 1 (March 1995): 23–43.

[52]General Accounting Office, "Earned Income Tax Credit: Design and Administration Could Be Improved," GAO/GGD-93-145, September 1993, pp. 51–52. However,
the report did find a positive work incentive among the lowest income recipients.
Among all recipients, the average work reduction was 3.6 percent.

[53]Ibid.

[54]Cited in James Glassman, "A Program Gone Bonkers," *Washington Post*, October
12, 1995.

[55]Browning, pp. 23–43.

[56]Philip K. Robins, "A Comparison of the Labor Supply Findings from the Four
Negative Income Tax Experiments," *Journal of Human Resources* 20, no. 4 (Fall
1985): 567–82.

Table 4.3
IMPACT OF NEGATIVE INCOME TAX ON WORK EFFORT

	Hours Worked (%)	Employment Rate (%)
Husbands	− 5.0	− 3.5
Wives	− 21.1	− 22.5
Single female heads of household	− 13.2	− 15.7
Youths	− 22.2	− 20.0

SOURCE: Philip K. Robins, "A Comparison of the Labor Supply Findings from the Four Negative Income Tax Experiments," *Journal of Human Resources* 20, no. 4 (Fall 1985): 577.

Second, the EITC may discourage marriage. The federal tax system already penalizes married individuals. The EITC magnifies that marriage discrimination, and recent program expansions tend to intensify the effect. In fact, in the most adverse circumstances, the marriage penalty can be as high as $5,000 per year, or about 25 percent of the married couple's annual income.[57]

Finally, the EITC program has an extremely high fraud and error rate. A crude Internal Revenue Service survey conducted in 1994 estimated that 29 percent of 1.3 million EITC returns filed during a two-week period claimed too large a refund, and about 13 percent of the 1.3 million returns were classified as intentionally in error.[58]

As a way to offset payroll taxes for the working poor, the EITC was probably originally a good idea. As the guaranteed income transfer program it has evolved into, it has significant problems. EITC is unlikely to prove a solution to our welfare problems.

Conclusion

Liberals have belatedly come to the realization that something is wrong with the welfare system. They are now willing to see the program "reformed." However, they remain captives of the idea that there is a programmatic response to poverty. Most liberal proposals for welfare reform involve additional government spending

[57]General Accounting Office, "Tax Policy: Earned Income Tax Credit: Design and Administration Could Be Improved."

[58]General Accounting Office, "Earned Income Credit: Noncompliance and Potential Eligibility Revisions," GAO/T-GGD-95-179, June 8, 1995.

and new government programs—for job training, child care, education, and many other initiatives.

That approach seems to reflect a stubborn refusal to learn from past results. Nearly all such programmatic responses have been tried before—and failed miserably. For example, more than 150 job-training programs have failed to move large numbers of welfare recipients into the job market. Is there any reason—except blind faith in government—to believe that another one will work?

Liberals must understand that solving the problem of poverty is beyond the power of government programs. Liberal approaches to fighting poverty have the best of intentions. But they have been tried before and have almost inevitably made the situation worse. The next question is whether conservative reforms are any better.

5. Why Conservative Welfare Reform Won't Work

Some people object that criticism of the welfare system is a "new paternalism," a form of "behavioral modification measure aimed at eliminating immorality among poor women."[1] Certainly, some conservatives are more than a little paternalistic. For example, Robert Rector of the Heritage Foundation calls for "legislation requir[ing] responsible behavior as a condition of receiving welfare benefits."[2]

Many conservative approaches to welfare reform do tend to be punitive in nature or designed to micromanage the behavior of poor people. Michael Schwartz of the Free Congress Center for Family Policy explains it this way: "Responsible behavior (marriage) should be rewarded, irresponsible behavior (out-of-wedlock childbearing) should not."[3] Some conservatives would extend the system of reward and punishment far beyond marriage and childbearing. For example, the LEARNfare proposals of Wisconsin's governor Tommy Thompson require that the children of welfare recipients attend school as a condition of their parents' receiving benefits.[4] And Rector has called for conditioning welfare benefits on childhood immunization.[5] Nearly all conservative welfare reform proposals link benefits to some form of work requirement.

---

[1]Martha Davis, "The New Paternalism: War on Poverty or War on Women?" *Georgetown Journal on Fighting Poverty* 1, no. 1 (1993): 88–94.

[2]Robert Rector, "A Comprehensive Urban Policy: How to Fix Welfare and Revitalize America's Inner Cities," Heritage Foundation Memo to President-Elect Clinton, no. 12, January 18, 1993, p. 9.

[3]Michael Schwartz, "Families First," in *Breaking the Chain: From Dependency to Opportunity,* ed. Samuel Brunelli (Washington: American Legislative Exchange Council, 1992), p. 5.

[4]Tommy Thompson, "Getting into the Game: Welfare Reform in Wisconsin," in ibid., pp. 9–11.

[5]Rector, "A Comprehensive Urban Policy," p. 9.

Clearly, women who cannot afford to care for children should not have children. People who can work should do so. Young people should remain in school. Conservatives are correct that welfare has distorted behavior in ways that are generally damaging to recipients and their children. But, oddly, many conservatives then turn to government to solve the problem. The conservative conceit is that government can devise a mix of incentives and disincentives, rewards and punishments, that can cause poor people to act in some preconceived manner.

Some conservatives have even suggested that welfare programs can be a good thing if correctly used to manipulate the behavior of the poor. For example, Paul Weyrich says that conservatives should favor providing "the financial support welfare recipients require" in exchange for behavior that would "restore functional, traditional values," which he defines as "delayed gratification, work and saving, commitment to the family . . . and rejection of . . . casual sex." Weyrich calls that combination of welfare payments and behavioral control "cultural welfare."[6]

Proposals that use as examples of "welfare reform" massive government programs to teach abstinence or greatly restrict the availability of divorce reveal the larger conservative agenda.[7] Thus does welfare reform become merely a building block in the conservative call for a "moral and cultural renewal."[8]

It is not necessary to resolve the philosophical issue of whether it is proper for government to be attempting to mold citizens' behavior to show that the government has been remarkably unsuccessful in developing programs to change underclass behavior.

Workfare

One program very popular among conservatives is "workfare," the requirement that welfare recipients perform public service jobs

---

[6]Paul Weyrich, *Cultural Conservatism: Toward a New National Agenda* (Washington: Institute for Cultural Conservatism and Free Congress Research and Education Foundation, 1987), p. 83.

[7]Robert Rector, "Combatting Family Disintegration, Crime, and Dependence: Welfare Reform and Beyond," Heritage Foundation Backgrounder no. 983, April 8, 1994, p. 19.

[8]Ibid., p. 23.

in exchange for benefits. The belief is that such jobs will give recipients both work experience and incentives to get off welfare. In fact, requiring work for welfare is a central part of the 1996 welfare reform bill.

One difficulty in evaluating the effectiveness of workfare is sorting out what is meant by the term. Many studies of the issue have rather indiscriminately lumped together all forms of welfare-to-work programs, including those that rely heavily on training rather than actual work requirements, job search programs, subsidized private-sector jobs, and public service jobs. Some workfare programs have been voluntary, and participation in others has been mandatory.

The 1996 welfare reform legislation contains a mandatory requirement that welfare recipients either take jobs in the private sector (with their wages supplemented by welfare benefits) or perform public service jobs. Unlike previous programs, the current legislation focuses exclusively on work rather than training and a much more vigorous enforcement of participation. For that reason, this legislation cannot be strictly compared with programs of the past. Even so, the history of workfare suggests little reason to believe that such a program would be successful in reducing either poverty or welfare dependence.

The first work requirement for welfare was the 1967 Work Incentive (WIN) program, which was supposed to require that all welfare recipients be placed in jobs or training programs. However, "according to state and local welfare officials, of the 2.5 million exempt adult AFDC recipients, between 60 and 65 percent are exempt from WIN because they are caring for a child under 6 years of age."[9] Earnings of those who did participate increased by less than $1,000 per year, and no decrease in welfare dependency was produced.[10] In 1981, recognizing the failure of WIN, the Reagan administration allowed states to opt out of the program if they had their own workfare requirements. In 1990 the program was reorganized out of existence as part of the new Job Opportunities and Basic Skills (JOBS) program.

[9]Comptroller General of the United States, *An Overview of the WIN Program: Its Objectives, Problems, and Accomplishments* (Washington: General Accounting Office, 1982), p. 12.

[10]Ronald Ehrenberg and James Hewlitt, "The Impact of WIN 2 Programs on Welfare Costs and Recipient Rates," *Journal of Human Resources* 11 (Spring 1976): 219–32.

JOBS appears to have been no more successful than its predecessor. After seven years and more than $13 billion in additional spending, JOBS has increased employment of welfare recipients less than 1 percent.[11]

In fairness, it should be pointed out that meeting the JOBS work-fare requirement has been far from universal. As pointed out in Chapter 2, the percentage of recipients of Aid to Families with Dependent Children (AFDC) participating in any of the job search, job-training, or community service programs ranges from a high of 31.5 percent in Nebraska to a low of less than 1 percent in Hawaii. Nationwide, participation averages only 6.9 percent.[12] Table 5.1 shows the state-by-state participation rates.

Low participation rates are typical of workfare programs. Because of concerns about mothers with young children, a lack of funds for public service jobs, and many other reasons, there are always large numbers of exceptions built into workfare programs. However, there is no reason to believe that a higher participation rate would lead to a significant improvement in the program's performance.

Workfare programs are likely to fail for many of the same reasons as job-training programs. As previously discussed, most long-term welfare recipients have few skills and severe sociological and educational problems. Since welfare benefits are far more generous than the low-wage jobs they could expect to find, they are unlikely to take private-sector jobs that will remove them from the welfare system.

The types of jobs envisioned under most workfare programs are unlikely to give recipients the work experience or job skills necessary to find work in the private sector. For example, New York mayor Rudolph Giuliani wants welfare recipients to perform such jobs as scrubbing graffiti and picking up trash from city streets.[13] It is difficult to imagine graffiti scrubbers learning the skills needed to put them in demand by private employers. As Charles Hobbs, who

---

[11]Karl Zinsmeister, "Chance of a Lifetime," *American Enterprise*, January–February 1995, p. 5.

[12]Robert Rector, "President Clinton's Commitment to Welfare Reform: The Disturbing Record So Far," Heritage Foundation Backgrounder no. 967, December 17, 1993, citing figures from the U.S. Department of Health and Human Services, Office of Family Assistance.

[13]Jonathan Hicks, "Giuliani Plan to Put Welfare Recipients to Work," *New York Times*, March 15, 1994.

Table 5.1
PERCENTAGE OF WELFARE RECIPIENTS PARTICIPATING IN JOBS

Jurisdiction	Participation (%)	Jurisdiction	Participation (%)
Alabama	7.2	Montana	15.1
Alaska	3.8	Nebraska	31.5
Arizona	2.8	Nevada	9.0
Arkansas	9.6	New Hampshire	9.8
California	4.8	New Jersey	8.9
Colorado	11.1	New Mexico	7.6
Connecticut	14.6	New York	6.8
Delaware	8.0	North Carolina	5.1
District of Columbia	6.0	North Dakota	13.0
Florida	3.8	Ohio	9.6
Georgia	4.7	Oklahoma	24.6
Hawaii	0.7	Oregon	10.4
Idaho	8.4	Pennsylvania	5.9
Illinois	6.6	Rhode Island	10.9
Indiana	1.2	South Carolina	5.4
Iowa	3.8	South Dakota	8.6
Kansas	9.2	Tennessee	4.2
Kentucky	5.1	Texas	5.2
Louisiana	4.0	Utah	30.0
Maine	5.2	Vermont	7.4
Maryland	4.6	Virginia	6.7
Massachusetts	16.5	Washington	11.2
Michigan	6.9	West Virginia	6.9
Minnesota	5.1	Wisconsin	18.1
Mississippi	2.5	Wyoming	11.7
Missouri	3.8		

SOURCE: Robert Rector, "President Clinton's Commitment to Welfare Reform: The Disturbing Record So Far," Heritage Foundation Backgrounder no. 967, December 17, 1993, Table 1, p. 2.

headed Ronald Reagan's task force on welfare dependency, warns, "Too often workfare has been a buzzword for the kind of government make-work jobs that don't lift people out of poverty."[14]

---

[14]Quoted in Carl Horowitz, "The Dismal Record of Workfare," *Investor's Business Daily*, December 21, 1994.

If welfare recipients do not move into the private sector, they will simply remain in public-sector jobs indefinitely. There seems to be little difference, therefore, between this type of work program and the type of government-guaranteed jobs program traditionally decried by conservatives.

Indeed, there is ample experience with government-created public service jobs. The Comprehensive Employment Training Program (CETA) is perhaps the best example. CETA was established in 1973 to provide public service jobs for the economically disadvantaged. At its zenith as many 750,000 Americans were working in CETA jobs, approximately 12.6 percent of the unemployed population at the time.[15] Jobs were funded by the federal government, but the program was administered by state and local governments. The program quickly became one of the most wasteful and scandal-ridden government efforts in recent years.[16] Make-work projects and political patronage were the norm. CETA's effect on earnings was marginal, and few participants moved to employment in the private sector.[17] In the end, a study for the Department of Labor concluded that "all the program activities have a negative effect."[18] The program was finally eliminated in 1982. Would a conservative CETA really be better?

The idea of providing an incentive for recipients to get off welfare is based on the belief that welfare recipients are essentially lazy, looking for a free ride. But, as discussed previously, choosing to go on welfare is more likely a result of a rational conclusion that welfare pays better than low-wage work. Since public service jobs do little to change the earning differential, they are unlikely to entice many people to leave welfare.

The Manpower Demonstration Research Corporation conducted a review of workfare programs across the country and found few, if any, employment gains among welfare recipients.[19] Several other

[15]William Mirengoff et al., *CETA: Assessment of Public Service Employment Programs* (Washington: National Academy of Sciences, 1980), pp. 40–41.

[16]For a detailed discussion of CETA's failure, see James Bovard, "The Failure of Federal Job Training," Cato Institute Policy Analysis no. 77, August 28, 1986, pp. 4–5.

[17]Lawrence M. Mead, *The New Politics of Poverty: The Nonworking Poor in America* (New York: Basic Books, 1992), pp. 165–66.

[18]Cited in ibid., p. 164.

[19]Kevin Hopkins, "A New Deal for America's Poor," *Policy Review*, no. 45 (Summer 1988): 70–73.

studies support that conclusion. For example, a study by the Center on Budget and Policy Priorities, admittedly an anti-workfare organization, found that only a tiny number of workfare recipients found employment that could support them and their families.[20] The Urban Institute estimates that strict workfare requirements will move 5 to 8 percent of welfare recipients into the private-sector workforce and increase earnings by $500 to $1,000 per year.[21] A Brookings Institution study found that no workfare program raised the yearly earnings of welfare mothers by more than $2,000.[22] Studies of workfare programs in San Diego, Arkansas, Baltimore, and Virginia found that 82 percent of participants were still receiving welfare after 18 months in the program.[23] James Heckman, Rebecca Roselius, and Jeffrey Smith reviewed the available literature on the issue for the American Enterprise Institute and found a general consensus that "mandatory work experience programs produce little long-term gain."[24] Even Lawrence Mead, one of workfare's most outspoken advocates, concedes that workfare "has not yet shown much power to reduce welfare rolls."[25]

Supporters of workfare generally counter with three examples. The program most commonly cited as demonstrating the success of workfare is the Riverside, California, portion of California's GAIN program. Unlike other counties participating in GAIN, which stress job training and education, Riverside emphasizes work.

Any review of the Riverside program should recognize the program's unique circumstances. The Riverside program was run by

[20]Kathryn Porter, "Making JOBS Work: What Research Says about Effective Employment Programs for AFDC Recipients," Center on Budget and Policy Priorities, Washington, March 1990, p. 5.

[21]Robert Lerman, "Increasing the Employment and Earnings of Welfare Recipients," in *Welfare Reform: An Analysis of the Issues*, ed. Isabel Sawhill (Washington: Urban Institute, 1995), p. 19.

[22]Gary Burtless, "The Effect of Reform on Employment, Earnings, and Income," in *Welfare Policy for the 1990s*, ed. Phoebe Cottingham and David Ellwood (Cambridge, Mass.: Harvard University Press, 1989), pp. 103–40.

[23]Zinsmeister, p. 6.

[24]James Heckman, Rebecca Roselius, and Jeffrey Smith, "U.S. Education and Training Policy: A Reevaluation of the Underlying Assumptions behind the 'New Consensus,'" American Enterprise Institute for Public Policy Research, Washington, March 7, 1994, p. 28.

[25]Mead, p. 183.

an energetic, decisive administrator who was given extraordinary freedom to define work rules, replace staff who did not perform, and enforce sanctions against welfare recipients who did not cooperate.[26] Does anyone seriously believe that those characteristics could be replicated nationwide?

Yet, even under extraordinarily propitious conditions, Riverside's results were modest. The program increased participants' chances of escaping poverty by about 4 percent, from 15.7 percent to 19.4 percent. Earnings increased only slightly, approximately $1,000 per year. Most participants continued to be dependent on government programs. In fact, per person welfare payments decreased by only 14 percent.[27]

Proponents of workfare also point to the efforts of Wisconsin's governor Tommy Thompson. Thompson was among the first to adopt many of the proposed conservative reforms. In 1987 he established the Work Experience and Jobs Training program, which combined job-training and workfare requirements, that became one of the inspirations for the federal JOBS program. Subsequently, the program was updated and strengthened several times.[28]

While welfare caseloads have climbed in nearly every other state, Wisconsin has reduced the number of families receiving welfare by 23 percent since 1987. That is clearly an impressive achievement, but no study has ever shown the decline to be linked to workfare requirements. In fact, the largest portion of the decline occurred before widespread implementation of the most stringent aspects of the workfare program, indicating that the decline may be due to two other important factors: a 6 percent benefit reduction in 1987 and one of the nation's highest economic growth rates. A University of Wisconsin evaluation of the state's reforms concludes that the workfare program has had no impact on welfare participation.[29]

---

[26]Charles Murray, "What to Do about Welfare," American Enterprise Institute On the Issues no. 52, December 1994, p. 3.

[27]Daniel Friedlander and Gary Burtless, *Five Years After: The Long-Term Effects of Welfare-to-Work Programs* (New York: Russell Sage Foundation, 1995), pp. 28–29.

[28]Thompson, "Getting into the Game," pp. 9–12.

[29]John Pawasarat and Lois M. Quinn, "Evaluation of the Wisconsin WEJT/CWEP Welfare Employment Programs," University of Wisconsin, Employment and Training Institute, Milwaukee, April 1993.

In fact, a study by the Wisconsin Department of Health and Social Services found that participants in workfare were actually somewhat less likely to leave welfare than were nonparticipants.[30] Roughly 40 percent of workfare participants were off welfare at the end of one year, while 47 percent of cases in the control group were closed. However, average payments to those remaining on the rolls were lower for program participants than for nonparticipants.

The work requirement has not had a significant impact on employment or earnings of participants. The Health and Social Services evaluation found that individuals who participated in the program increased the number of hours worked per week by only 1.9 hours after two years. Monthly earnings increased by between $29 and $75.

Finally, workfare supporters point to the success of America Works, a private job placement firm that has been hired by New York City to find jobs for welfare recipients. No one can deny that America Works has done extremely well at placing welfare recipients in jobs.[31] Nearly 60 percent of program participants are placed in private-sector jobs, and nearly two-thirds of those are hired permanently by private-sector employers at an average wage of $15,000. A recent evaluation by the New York Department of Social Services found that 75 percent of America Works' placements were still off welfare 18 months after being placed in a job.[32]

However, America Works is not really a workfare program. A purely voluntary effort, it attracts those welfare recipients who most desire work. Those people are likely to be the recipients who use welfare as a temporary safety net, have skills that make them readily employable, and are likely to find jobs regardless of whether they use America Works. Hard-core, long-term welfare recipients with few skills and a multitude of other social problems are unlikely to participate. At any rate, there has been no scientific evaluation of

[30]Wisconsin Department of Health and Human Services, Office of Policy and Budget, Evaluation Section, "Evaluation of the Second Year of the Wisconsin Work Experience and Job Training Program," Madison, March 1989.

[31]See Steve Cohen and William Eimicke, "Assessing the Cost-Effectiveness of Welfare-to-Work Programs: A Comparison of America Works and Other Job Training and Partnership Act Programs," Columbia University, School of International and Public Affairs, New York, April 19, 1996.

[32]Cited in Will Marshall, "Replacing Welfare with Work," Progressive Policy Institute Policy Briefing, July 1994, p. 11.

whether the program would be successful if applied across the entire welfare population.

Thus, workfare's success appears to be more theoretical than practical. Regardless, it clearly cannot be successful unless nearly all welfare recipients are forced to participate. But full participation soon runs headlong into the desire expressed by some conservatives that women with young children stay home rather than enter the workforce. Rector, for example, opposes workfare requirements for women with children under the age of five, saying, "Great caution should be exercised toward any policy that separates young children from their mothers."[33] But, since approximately three-quarters of welfare recipients are unmarried women with children under the age of five, exempting the mothers of young children eviscerates any workfare requirement.[34] Rector attempts to get around that by expanding the work requirement to those mothers who have been on welfare for five years or more regardless of the age of their children, but that still would not cover more than half of welfare recipients.[35]

Martin Anderson, former senior economic adviser to President Reagan, sums up the simple illogic of workfare:

> If people are on welfare then, by definition, those people should be unable to care for themselves. They can't work, or the private sector can't provide jobs enough. That is supposed to be the reason they are on welfare. What sense does it make to require someone to work who cannot work?
>
> The idea of making people work for welfare is wrongheaded. If a person is capable of working, he should be ineligible for welfare payments. Instead of requiring men and women who are receiving fraudulent welfare payments to work, we should simply cease all payments.[36]

---

[33]Robert Rector, "Rethinking Welfare after the LA Riots," in *The Future of Welfare* (Washington: Youth Policy Institute, 1992), p. 20.

[34]U.S. House of Representatives, Committee on Ways and Means, *1994 Green Book: Background Material and Data on Programs within the Jurisdiction of the Committee on Ways and Means* (Washington: Government Printing Office, 1994), Table 10-31, p. 410.

[35]Rector, "Rethinking Welfare after the LA Riots."

[36]Martin Anderson, "A Two-Year Wink at Welfare," *Wall Street Journal*, November 28, 1993.

Ultimately, the justification for workfare comes down to an emotional appeal to an innate sense of justice, a feeling that no one should get something for nothing. But public service jobs are not free. The Congressional Budget Office estimates that each public service job created costs as much as $6,000 to $8,000 over and above the cost of welfare benefits.[37] That is a great deal of money to spend for psychic satisfaction.

Workfare does not address the most serious social consequence of welfare—children growing up in single-parent families. In fact, not only does workfare not deter out-of-wedlock births, it doesn't even prevent additional births to program participants. The Manpower Demonstration Research Corporation found that more than half of all welfare mothers became pregnant again after enrolling in workfare.[38] The social pathologies associated with out-of-wedlock births will not disappear simply because the mothers are put to work in public service jobs.

Subsidized Jobs

A different, but still untested, approach to work requirements was pioneered by the Oregon Full Employment program.[39] The plan, enacted through a 1990 ballot initiative, would eliminate AFDC, food stamps, and unemployment insurance. Funds that would have been used to finance those benefits would instead be used to subsidize jobs in the private sector. Rather than draw a check from the government, individuals would be paid by employers in exchange for work. The jobs would pay 90 percent of the minimum wage, which would give recipients a strong incentive to move off the program into regular jobs.

That approach seems superior to other forms of workfare. At the very least it avoids the type of make-work jobs likely in the public sector. However, the program is far too new to know what the results will be.

---

[37]Cited in Douglas Besharov, "Escaping the Dole," American Enterprise Institute On the Issues no. 3, Washington, 1994, p. 3.

[38]Zinsmeister, p. 6.

[39]For a detailed discussion of Oregon's Full Employment program, see John McClaughry, *A Better Path: From Welfare to Work* (Concord, Vt.: Ethan Allen Institute, 1993).

One potential problem is "substitution." Employers given the option of hiring a person who is not eligible for welfare, for example, a person working today in a low-wage job, and receiving no subsidy may instead choose to hire a welfare recipient in order to receive a subsidy and reduce labor costs. There is evidence that that has occurred in the past in the case of public service jobs. For example, a Brookings Institution study found that states, municipalities, and nonprofit organizations that received federal subsidies to provide public service jobs gradually substituted subsidized jobs for unsubsidized jobs on their payroll. As a result, there was no net increase in employment.[40]

LEARNfare

A second welfare reform much ballyhooed by conservatives is LEARNfare, a requirement that the children of welfare recipients attend school as a condition of their parents' receiving benefits. Gov. Tommy Thompson, who pioneered LEARNfare in Wisconsin, says he did so to "keep teenagers in school and make welfare recipients more responsible parents."[41]

As is the case with other conservative reforms, while the theory is admirable, LEARNfare appears to have little impact in actual practice. To start with, the program may have been unnecessary. Children of parents receiving AFDC are *not* more likely to miss school than are other children.[42] Nor does LEARNfare appear to increase the likelihood that such children will stay in school. A multiyear evaluation of Wisconsin's LEARNfare program by the University of Wisconsin showed no improvement in either attendance or graduation rates of children covered by the program.[43]

---

[40]George Johnson, "Structural Unemployment Consequences of Job Creation Policies," in *Creating Jobs: Public Employment Programs and Wage Subsidies*, ed. John Palmer (Washington: Brookings Institution, 1978), pp. 20–26.

[41]Tommy Thompson, "Land of Milk and Money," *Policy Review*, no. 60 (Spring 1991): 34.

[42]*Do School Attendance Rates Vary between AFDC and Non-AFDC Supported Children?* (Milwaukee: University of Wisconsin, Urban Research Center, 1989), p. 9.

[43]John Pawasarat et al., "Evaluation of the Impact of Wisconsin's Learnfare Experiment on the School Attendance of Children Receiving AFDC," University of Wisconsin, Milwaukee, 1992.

Block Grants

At the heart of the 1996 welfare reform legislation is a plan for returning many welfare programs, especially AFDC, to the control of state governments and funding them through block grants. The theory is that, while the federal government will continue to provide funding, states will be free to experiment more widely.

Block grants are not new. The federal government has been providing funds to the states since at least 1862, when the Morrill Act provided money for the support of higher education. There followed a number of grants for such things as agricultural research, forestry promotion, merchant marine schools, highways, and education. Federal entanglement with state government increased throughout the first half of the 20th century and exploded during the New Deal and its aftermath.[44]

Today, there are two basic types of federal grants to state and local governments. The first is categorical grants, money provided to the states for specific, narrowly defined purposes. There are generally a great deal of accountability to the federal government and strict controls over how the money is spent. As of 1993 there were 578 federal categorical grant programs, totaling $182 billion per year in federal spending. The largest of those is a welfare program— Medicaid.[45]

The second type of federal grant to state and local governments is the block grant. Block grants apply to much broader areas, such as health or education. Money can be spent on a wide range of activities within the broadly defined function area. Recipients have substantial discretion to identify problems, design programs, and allocate resources. Administrative rules, reporting, and other federal requirements are reduced.[46]

While some minor block grant programs existed early in this century, the two programs most often identified as the quintessential prototypes of block grants were created by the 1966 Partnership for Health Act and the 1968 Omnibus Crime Control and Safe Streets

[44]Carole Cox, *Block Grants: An Overview of Where We've Been and Where We're Going* (Washington: National Academy on Aging, 1995), pp. 1–4.

[45]General Accounting Office, *Block Grants: Characteristics, Experience, and Lessons Learned* (Washington: Government Printing Office, 1995).

[46]Ibid.

Act. There are 15 major block grants today in such areas as community services, substance abuse and mental health, primary health care, social services, maternal and child health, preventive health care and health services, education, low-income home energy assistance, and community development. Together, they account for only 7.5 percent of all federal aid to the states.[47]

Block grants are certainly not the ideal answer to the need to remove the federal government from welfare. They are almost certain to have numerous strings attached. Further, there is something less than clear logic in the idea of sending money from the states to Washington, having Washington take a cut off the top, then sending the money back to the states. The only reason for the federal government's involvement is to redistribute monies among the states—a less than equitable procedure.

Finally, we should acknowledge that the history of block grants is not a pretty one. Tales of mismanagement, waste, and abuse in past or existing block grant programs are legion. Most audits have shown little or no increase in administrative efficiency. Although supporters of block granting welfare have suggested that administrative savings could be as high as 20 percent of program costs, past block grant programs have seldom achieved savings of more than 5 percent.[48] And the tensions between state and federal governments were often merely shifted to a battle between local and state governments.

Block grants reduce accountability by separating the revenue collector from the spender of the money—never a wise practice. Congress can blame the states for not spending the money wisely, while the states can blame Congress for failing to provide enough money to do the job.

Moreover, as Norman Ornstein of the American Enterprise Institute has pointed out, from Richard Nixon's "New Federalism" to Ronald Reagan's "New New Federalism" to Newt Gingrich's "New New New Federalism," the federal government has talked about shifting power to the states, giving them more money and more

[47]George Peterson, "A Block Grant Approach to Welfare Reform," in *Welfare Reform: An Analysis of the Issues,* p. 4.

[48]Ibid., p. 6.

flexibility. But reality has seldom matched the rhetoric. Reality has usually meant less money *and* less flexibility.[49]

If Congress is serious about returning control over welfare to the states, it should revive a Reagan-era reform known as "turn-backs," in which specific federal aid programs (in this case welfare programs) are terminated and specific federal taxes are repealed. Responsibility for both collecting the revenue and spending the money is turned back to state and local governments. Turn-backs would eliminate the federal middleman altogether.

However, it should be noted that, at least so far, states have not been particularly bold in experimenting with welfare reform. While 35 states have received federal waivers for welfare experiments since 1992, and several other states have waivers pending, most state reforms have been relatively timid. Among the most popular reforms so far are family caps, job training, child-care programs, and work requirements.[50]

Fraud, Waste, and Abuse

Fraud, waste, and abuse have traditionally been targets of conservative critics of welfare. Certainly the public has been outraged at high-profile cases such as that of Shirley Simmons, the Brooklyn, New York, woman convicted of using 15 names to collect $450,000 for herself and her 73 fictitious children.[51]

But, in reality, that type of welfare fraud is not as widespread as commonly believed. Pilot fingerprint identification studies in New York and Los Angeles indicate a fraud rate of about 4.3 percent.[52] It is also estimated that approximately 4.1 percent of recipients overclaim the amount of benefits they are entitled to.[53]

The amount of welfare fraud varies widely from program to program. AFDC has a relatively low rate of fraud. A random audit of

[49]Norman Ornstein, "Medicaid, the Immovable Force, Meets the Balanced Budget, the Irresistible Object," in *Three Perspectives on Block Granting Federal Programs* (Washington: National Academy on Aging, 1995), pp. 5–9.

[50]Barbara Vobejda, "Most States Are Shaping Their Own Welfare Reform," *Washington Post*, February 3, 1996.

[51]John Tierney, "Cheats Like Us," *New York Times Magazine*, July 2, 1995.

[52]Roger Kuhns, "Food Stamp Fraud Analysis: Scope and Solution," Avant, Inc, Concord, Mass., 1995, p. 1.

[53]Ibid.

recipients in California, for example, revealed that about 4 percent of cases involved some form of fraud.[54] Other programs, notably food stamps and Supplemental Security Income (SSI), have much higher fraud rates.[55] Medicaid is another program with relatively high fraud rates. However, in that program the fraud is much more likely to be committed by the providers than by the recipients.[56]

Still, in dollar terms, the amount of fraud in welfare is fairly small.[57] Most fraud is of the petty variety—claiming an extra child, failing to report outside income. That represents a problem, not a crisis.

Fraud is endemic to nearly all government programs, from defense contracting to Medicare billing. Welfare is no exception. However, in may ways focusing on fraud, waste, and abuse is a distraction from the real evils of the welfare system. Wherever possible, we should strive to eliminate welfare fraud. However, the real problem of welfare lies, not with people cheating the system, but with what welfare does to people who are receiving it legitimately. Even if welfare could be made the most efficient and least expensive government program, it would still be unacceptable.

Welfare and Immigration

One of the most disturbing aspects of recent conservative welfare proposals has been a tendency to make immigrants—legal and illegal—scapegoats for America's welfare problems. There is no evidence that immigrants contribute significantly to our welfare problems.

Although some conservatives suggest that immigrants are flooding the welfare system, in reality, as shown in Table 5.2, legal immigrants use welfare at approximately the same rate as do native-born Americans.[58] However, even those figures may overstate actual

[54]General Accounting Office, *Welfare Programs: Opportunities to Consolidate and Increase Program Efficiencies* (Washington: Government Printing Office, May 1995), p. 20.

[55]See, for example, Christopher M. Wright, "SSI: The Black Hole of the Welfare State," Cato Institute Policy Analysis no. 224, April 27, 1995.

[56]William Cohen, "Gaming the System: Billions of Dollars Lost to Fraud and Abuse Each Year," Senate Special Committee on Aging, July 7, 1994.

[57]General Accounting Office, *Welfare Programs*, p. 2.

[58]Jeffrey Passel and Michael Fix, "How Much Do Immigrants Really Cost? A Reappraisal of Huddle's 'Cost of Immigrants,'" Urban Institute, Washington, January 1994.

Table 5.2
PERCENTAGE OF POPULATION RECEIVING WELFARE, 1989

Population Group	Percentage Receiving Welfare
Aged 15 and younger	
Native born	4.2
Immigrants	4.7
Refugees	15.6
Aged 15–64	
Native born	3.7
Immigrants	3.3
Refugees	13.4
Aged 65+	
Native born	6.9
Immigrants	13.1
Refugees	49.6

SOURCE: Derived from Jeffrey Passel and Michael Fix, "Setting the Record Straight," Urban Institute, Washington, January 1994, Figure 21, p. 65.

NOTE: Refugees are from Albania, Afghanistan, Cambodia, Cuba, Ethiopia, Laos, Iraq, Poland, the Soviet Union, and Romania.

welfare use by immigrants, because most immigrant welfare use is by either refugees (who of necessity come to this country with few assets) or the elderly (who frequently use SSI as a substitute for Social Security, to which they are not entitled).[59] Those two groups represent only 21 percent of the immigrant population but make up 40 percent of immigrant welfare users.[60] With the exception of those groups, immigrants use welfare slightly less than do native-born Americans.[61] Moreover, immigrants as a group pay more in taxes than they consume in government services.[62]

[59]Rebecca Clark, "The Cost of Providing Public Assistance and Education to Immigrants," Urban Institute, Washington, May 1994, revised August 1994.

[60]Michael Fix and Wendy Zimmerman, "When Should Immigrants Receive Public Benefits?" in *Welfare Reform: An Analysis of the Issues*, p. 69.

[61]Ibid.

[62]Julian Simon, *The Economic Consequences of Immigration* (Washington: Cato Institute, 1989).

Illegal immigrants actually use welfare less than legal immigrants, both because they are ineligible for many programs and because they fear that applying for services means they will be detected and deported.[63] Illegal immigrants from Mexico, for example, are often portrayed as a drain on welfare. But studies have shown that only about 2 percent of Mexican illegals use Medicaid or AFDC. Use of food stamps is only slightly higher, while use of most other welfare programs is even lower.[64] Moreover, approximately half of illegal immigrants are not the poor slipping across the border but middle-class workers who have overstayed their visas and can be expected to have much lower rates of welfare use.

Welfare for immigrants is a bad idea for the same reason that it is a bad idea for native-born Americans—because of the harm it does to society and the recipients themselves. Immigrants would be better off without welfare. But making immigrants scapegoats for our welfare problems flies in the face of the facts and does little to advance the welfare reform debate.

Conclusion

Conservatives have traditionally expressed little faith in government—and justifiably so. But when it comes to welfare reform, many conservatives suddenly believe that government is capable of devising precisely the right set of incentives and disincentives to deal with the deep-rooted social, cultural, and spiritual problems of the underclass. Workfare, LEARNfare, and other "cultural welfare" programs are all based on the idea that government knows best.

Conservatives should realize that government programs are far less capable of changing human behavior than is simple economic reality. A more realistic approach is stated by Mickey Kaus in *The End of Equality*: "Instead of attempting to somehow teach mainstream culture to people who spend most of their day immersed in ghetto culture, we should make ghetto culture economically unsustainable."[65]

---

[63]Julian Simon, *Immigration: The Demographic and Economic Facts* (Washington: Cato Institute and the National Immigration Forum, 1995), p. 32.

[64]Marta Tienda and Zai Liang, "Poverty and Immigration in Policy Perspective," in *Confronting Poverty: Prescriptions for Change*, ed. Sheldon Danziger, Gary Sandefur, and Daniel Weinberg (Cambridge, Mass.: Harvard University Press, 1994), pp. 352–53.

[65]Mickey Kaus, *The End of Equality* (New York: Basic Books, 1989), p. 41.

Welfare reform is not a simple matter of eliminating fraud, waste, and abuse. The destructiveness of welfare lies in the nature of the programs themselves, not in their abuse. Even if all fraud, waste, and mismanagement could be eliminated (something no government program has ever achieved), the fundamental problems of the welfare state would remain.

Immigrants are not driving up the cost of welfare. But even if they were, that would have little to do with welfare's real problems. Welfare reform is not a question of money. If welfare cost only one dollar of federal spending but produced the results it does today, it would still be a disaster.

Conservatives have correctly diagnosed many of the problems with today's welfare state. Unfortunately, their proposed solutions fall far short of the radical changes needed.

6. Replacing Welfare

Detailing the failures of the current welfare system and proposed liberal and conservative reforms is easy. However, critics of welfare have an obligation to go beyond attacking the system to provide an effective, compassionate alternative.

The first step is to recognize that the 1996 welfare reform legislation falls far short of what is needed to fix the system. Welfare cannot be reformed. Instead, we should eliminate the entire social welfare system for individuals able to work. That means eliminating not just Aid to Families with Dependent Children (AFDC) but also food stamps, subsidized housing, and all the rest. Individuals unwilling to support themselves through the job market should have to fall back on the resources of family, church, community, or private charity.

As both a practical matter and a question of fairness, no child currently on welfare should be thrown off. However, a date should be set (for symbolic reasons, I like nine months and one day from now), after which no one new would be allowed into the welfare system. As we have already seen, there are two distinct populations of welfare recipients. Those who currently use the system as a temporary safety net will be out of the system relatively soon. Immediately ending their eligibility would have only a minor impact on the system but would risk flooding the job market and private charities without allowing for a transition.

We have seen that there are serious problems with expecting hard-core, long-term welfare recipients to be able to find sufficient employment to support themselves and their families. When we established the incentives of the current system, we may have made a Faustian bargain with those recipients. Now it may be too late to change the rules of the game. We should do whatever we can to move those people out of the system but recognize that success may be limited. It is far more important to prevent anyone new from becoming trapped in the system. That will be possible only if the trap is no longer there.

What would happen to the poor if welfare were eliminated? First, without the incentives of the welfare state, fewer people would be poor. For one thing, there would probably be far fewer children born into poverty. We have seen that the availability of welfare leads to an increase in out-of-wedlock births and that giving birth out of wedlock leads to poverty. If welfare were eliminated, the number of out-of-wedlock births would almost certainly decline. How much is a matter of conjecture. Some social scientists suggest as little as 15 to 20 percent; others say as much as 50 percent.[1] Whatever the number, it would be smaller.

In addition, some poor women who did still bear children out of wedlock would put the children up for adoption. The civil society should encourage that by eliminating the present regulatory and bureaucratic barriers to adoption.[2] Other unmarried women who gave birth would not be able to afford to live independently; they would choose to live with their families or with their boyfriends. Some might even choose to marry the fathers of their children.

Poor people would also be more likely to go to work, starting to climb the ladder that will lead out of poverty. A General Accounting Office report on women who lost their welfare benefits after the Reagan administration tightened eligibility requirements in 1981 found that, on average, the women increased the number of hours they worked and their hourly wage and had a significantly higher overall earned income. Two years after losing their eligibility, a significant minority of the women (43 percent in Boston, for example) had incomes as high as or higher than they did while receiving benefits.[3]

Similarly, in 1991 Michigan abolished its General Assistance program, which provided cash assistance for poor adults without children. Two years later, a survey for the University of Michigan found

[1]Charles Murray, "Does Welfare Bring More Babies?" *Public Interest*, no. 115 (Spring 1994): 17–30.

[2]Chief among the needed changes is the removal of all restrictions on transracial adoptions. Nearly every state prohibits or delays the adoption of minority children on the basis of the race of the adoptive parents. Yet there is no evidence that transracial adoption has any adverse impact on a child's development. See Rita J. Simon, Howard Altstein, and Marygold Melli, *The Case for Transracial Adoption* (Washington: American University Press, 1994).

[3]General Accounting Office, *An Evaluation of the 1981 AFDC Changes: Initial Analysis* (Washington: Government Printing Office, 1984), p. 48.

that 36.7 percent of those people were working in the month before the survey. Of those with at least a high school education, 45.6 percent were working. Two-thirds of former General Assistance recipients, regardless of education, had held a job at some point during the two years before the survey.[4]

It is important to recognize that job opportunities do exist for individuals willing to accept them. That can be seen in the experience of unskilled immigrants who enter this country with disadvantages at least as significant as those of welfare recipients. Many have less schooling than the average welfare recipient and many cannot even speak English. Yet the vast majority finds jobs, and most eventually prosper.[5]

Of course, it may be necessary for people to move where the jobs are. In some ways, the availability of welfare disrupts normal labor migration patterns by allowing people to remain in areas with low employment. If welfare had been in place at the beginning of the century, the great migration of black sharecroppers and farm workers from southern farms to northern factories would never have taken place.

People forced to rely on themselves will find a variety of ways to get out of poverty. Richard Vedder and Lowell Gallaway of the University of Ohio examined the movement of poor individuals out of poverty. They found that 18.3 percent of poor people receiving welfare moved out of poverty within one year. However, 45 percent of poor people who did not receive welfare were able to escape poverty.[6]

Even many liberals understand that without welfare many poor people would find other options. As Gary Burtless of the Brookings Institution says, "My guess is that if welfare recipients realize their

---

[4]Sandra Danziger and Sherrie Kossoudji, "When Welfare Ends: Subsistence Strategies of Former GA Recipients," University of Michigan School of Social Work, Ann Arbor, 1995. Approximately 27 percent of former General Assistance recipients were on disability; 9 percent were on other welfare programs; and 16 percent were relying on families, friends, or spouses. Only 12 percent reported no income in the month before the survey.

[5]R. Kent Weaver and William Dickens, eds., *Looking Before We Leap: Social Science and Welfare Reform* (Washington: Brookings Institution, 1995), pp. 60–61.

[6]Richard Vedder and Lowell Gallaway, *The War on the Poor* (Lewisville, Tex.: Institute for Policy Innovation, June 1992), pp. 21–24.

benefits are going to stop ... it will cause them to search much, much harder for alternatives."[7]

Of course, many people will still need help. As the Bible says, "The poor always you will have with you."[8] The civil society will not turn its back on those people. Instead, they will be helped through a newly invigorated system of private charity.

Replacing Welfare with Private Charity

Private efforts have been much more successful than the federal government's failed attempt at charity. America is the most generous nation on earth. Americans already contribute more than $125 billion annually to charity.[9] In fact, more than 85 percent of all adult Americans make some charitable contribution each year.[10] In addition, about half of all American adults perform volunteer work; more than 20 billion hours were worked in 1991.[11] The dollar value of that volunteer work was more than $176 billion.[12] Volunteer work and cash donations combined bring American charitable contributions to more than $300 billion per year, not including the countless dollars and time given informally to family members, neighbors, and others outside the formal charity system.

Private charities have been more successful than government welfare for several reasons. First, private charities are able to individualize their approach to the circumstances of poor people in ways that governments can never do. Government regulations must be designed to treat all similarly situated recipients alike. Glenn C. Loury of Boston University explains the difference between welfare

---

[7]Quoted in Barbara Vobejda, "Finding a Way Out Proves No Easy Task," *Washington Post*, March 5, 1995. However, in fairness, it should be noted that Burtless does not advocate abolishing welfare.

[8]John 12:8.

[9]According to the American Association of Fund Raising Council Trust for Philanthropy, the figure was $124.3 billion in 1992, of which the vast majority, $101.8 billion, was contributed by individuals. American Association of Fund Raising Council Trust for Philanthropy, "Giving USA, 1995," 1995 data series, New York.

[10]Based on a Gallup poll cited in John Goodman, Gerald Reed, and Peter Ferrara, "Why Not Abolish the Welfare State?" National Center for Policy Analysis Policy Report no. 187, Dallas, Tex., October 1994.

[11]American Association of Fund Raising Council Trust for Philanthropy.

[12]Ibid.

and private charities on that point. "Because citizens have due process rights which cannot be fully abrogated ... public judgments must be made in a manner that can be defended after the fact, sometimes even in court."[13] The result is that most government programs rely on the simple provision of cash or other goods and services without any attempt to differentiate between the needs of recipients.

Take, for example, the case of a poor person who has a job offer. But she can't get to the job because her car battery is dead. A government welfare program can do nothing but tell her to wait two weeks until her welfare check arrives. Of course, by that time the job will be gone. A private charity can simply go out and buy a car battery (or even jump-start the dead battery).

The sheer size of government programs works against individualization. As one welfare case worker lamented, "With 125 cases it's hard to remember that they're all human beings. Sometimes they're just a number."[14] Bureaucracy is a major factor in government welfare programs. For example, a report on welfare in Illinois found procedures requiring "nine forms to process an address change, at least six forms to add or delete a member of a household, and a minimum of six forms to report a change in earnings or employment." All that for just one program.[15]

In her excellent book *Tyranny of Kindness*, Theresa Funiciello, a former welfare mother, describes the dehumanizing world of the government welfare system—a system in which regulations and bureaucracy rule all else. It is a system in which illiterate homeless people with mental illnesses are handed 17-page forms to fill out, women nine months pregnant are told to verify their pregnancies, a woman who was raped is told she is ineligible for benefits because she can't list the baby's father on the required form. It is a world

---

[13]Glenn C. Loury, "Values and Judgments: Creating Social Incentives for Good Behavior," in *Transforming Welfare: The Revival of American Charity*, ed. Jeffrey Sikkenga (Grand Rapids, Mich.: Acton Institute, 1996), p. 24.

[14]Quoted in Marvin Olasky, *The Tragedy of American Compassion* (Washington: Regnery, 1992), p. 191.

[15]M. Bateman, "Administration of AFDC in Illinois: A Description of Three Local Efforts," Apt Associates, Cambridge, Mass., July 1990.

totally unable to adjust to the slightest deviation from the bureaucratic norm.[16]

In addition to being better able to target individual needs, private charities are much better able to target assistance to those who really need help. Because eligibility requirements for government welfare programs are arbitrary and cannot be changed to fit individual circumstances, many people in genuine need do not receive assistance, while benefits often go to people who do not really need them. More than 40 percent of all families living below the poverty level receive no government assistance. Yet more than half of the families receiving means-tested benefits are not poor.[17] Thus, a student may receive food stamps, while a homeless man with no mailing address goes without. Private charities are not bound by such bureaucratic restrictions.

Private charity also has a better record of actually delivering aid to recipients. Surprisingly little of the money being spent on federal and state social welfare programs actually reaches recipients. In 1965, 70 cents of every dollar spent by the government to fight poverty went directly to poor people. Today, 70 cents of every dollar goes, not to poor people, but to government bureaucrats and others who serve the poor.[18] Few private charities have the bureaucratic overhead and inefficiency of government programs.

---

[16]Theresa Funiciello, *Tyranny of Kindness: Dismantling the Welfare System to End Poverty in America* (New York: Atlantic Monthly Press, 1993). Funiciello reaches some unfortunate conclusions regarding welfare reform, notably her call for a guaranteed national income. However, her book remains must reading for anyone interested in the failures of today's welfare system.

[17]Bureau of the Census data cited in Goodman, Reed, and Ferrara, p. 25.

[18]Cited in Robert Woodson, "Is the Black Community a Casualty of the War on Poverty?" Heritage Foundation Lecture, February 6, 1990. It is important to note that the 70 percent figure is not solely government administrative overhead. That figure also includes government payments to the nonpoor on behalf of the poor. For example, Medicaid payments go to doctors. Housing subsidies are frequently paid directly to landlords. Woodson bases his estimate on figures provided in Executive Office of the President, Office of Policy Development, *An Overview of the Current System*, vol. 1 of *The National Public Assistance System,* supplement 1 to *Up from Dependency: A New National Public Assistance Strategy* (Washington, Government Printing Office, 1986). Several local studies have shown a similar 70/30 split. See, for example, "New York's Poverty Budget," Community Service Society of New York, 1984, and "The Cook County, Illinois, Welfare System," Northwestern University, Center for Urban Affairs and Policy Research, Evanston, Ill., 1991.

Second, in general, private charity is much more likely to be targeted to short-term emergency assistance than to long-term dependence. Thus, private charity provides a safety net, not a way of life.

Moreover, private charities may demand that the poor change their behavior in exchange for assistance. For example, a private charity may reduce or withhold benefits if a recipient does not stop using alcohol or drugs, look for a job, or avoid pregnancy. Private charities are much more likely than government programs to offer counseling and one-on-one follow-up rather than simply provide a check.

By the same token, because of the separation of church and state, government welfare programs are not able to support programs that promote religious values as a way out of poverty. Yet church and other religious charities have a history of success in dealing with the problems that often lead to poverty.[19]

Finally, and perhaps most important, private charity requires a different attitude on the part of both recipients and donors. For recipients, private charity is not an entitlement but a gift carrying reciprocal obligations. As Father Robert Sirico of the Acton Institute describes it, "An impersonal check given without any expectations for responsible behavior leads to a damaged sense of self-worth. The beauty of local [private charitable] efforts to help the needy is that . . . they make the individual receiving the aid realize that he must work to live up to the expectations of those helping him out."[20]

Private charity demands that donors become directly involved. Former Yale University political science professor James Payne notes how little citizen involvement there is in government charity:

> We know now that in most cases of government policy making, decisions are not made according to the democratic ideal of control by ordinary citizens. Policy is made by elites, through special interest politics, bureaucratic pressures, and legislative manipulations. Insiders decide what happens, shaping the outcome according to their own preferences and their political pull. The citizens are simply bystanders.[21]

[19]For an excellent discussion of the religious and spiritual dimensions of fighting poverty, see Marvin Olasky, *Renewing American Compassion* (New York: Free Press, 1996).

[20]Robert Sirico, "Restoring Charity," in *Transforming Welfare*, p. 6.

[21]James Payne, *The Promise of Community* (Indianapolis: Philanthropy Roundtable, 1994), p. 13.

Private charity, in contrast, is based on "having individuals vote with their own time, money, and energy."[22]

There is no compassion in spending someone else's money—even for a good cause. True compassion means giving of yourself. As historian and social commentator Gertrude Himmelfarb puts it, "Compassion is a moral sentiment, not a political principle."[23] Welfare allows individuals to escape their obligation to be truly charitable. As Robert Thompson of the University of Pennsylvania said a century ago, government charity is a "rough contrivance to lift from the social conscience a burden that should not be either lifted or lightened in that way."[24]

That is the essence of the civil society. When George Washington contrasted government to civil society in his farewell address, warning that "government is not reason, it is not eloquence—it is force," he was making an important distinction. Government relies on force and coercion to achieve its objectives, including charity. In contrast, the civil society relies on persuasion—reason and eloquence—to motivate voluntary giving. In the civil society people give because they are committed to helping, because they believe in what they are doing.

Thus private charity is ennobling of everyone involved, both those who give and those who receive. Government welfare is ennobling of no one. Alexis de Tocqueville recognized that 150 years ago. Calling for the abolition of public relief, Tocqueville lauded private charity for establishing a "moral tie" between giver and receiver. In contrast, impersonal government relief destroys any sense of morality. The donor (read taxpayer) resents his involuntary contribution, while the recipient feels no gratitude for what he receives and inevitably believes that what he receives is insufficient.[25]

Perhaps the entire question of government welfare versus private charity was best summed up by Pope John Paul II in his recent encyclical *Centesimus Annus*.

[22]Ibid., p. 15.

[23]Gertrude Himmelfarb, *Poverty and Compassion* (New York: Alfred Knopf, 1991), p. 3.

[24]Robert Thompson, *Manual for Visitors among the Poor* (Philadelphia: Lippincott, 1879), p. 246, cited in Olasky, *The Tragedy of American Compassion*, p. 224.

[25]Cited in Gertrude Himmelfarb, "True Charity: Lessons from Victorian England," in *Transforming Welfare*, pp. 31–32.

By intervening directly and depriving society of its responsibility, the welfare state leads to a loss of human energies and an inordinate increase in public agencies, which are dominated more by bureaucratic ways of thinking than by concern for serving their clients, and which are accompanied by an enormous increase in spending. In fact, it would appear that needs are best understood and satisfied by people who are closest to them and who act as neighbors to those in need. It should be added that certain kinds of demands often call for a response which is not material but which is capable of perceiving the deeper human need.[26]

Better yet, consider this simple thought experiment: If you had $10,000 available that you wanted to use to help the poor, would you give it to the government to help fund welfare or would you donate it to the private charity of your choice?

Big Charity and Big Government

Interestingly, some of the biggest critics of replacing welfare with private charity are some of the country's biggest charitable organizations. Their attitude has been summed up by Brian O'Connell, president of Independent Sector, an organization that represents most of the large charitable groups. "We lose our perspective on the voluntary sector and society when we exaggerate the importance of private philanthropy and volunteer organizations, particularly when we put them ahead of our responsibility to democratic government."[27]

At first, such an attitude seems surprising for organizations that should be cheerleading for private charity. But a closer look shows that large charitable foundations are no longer private charities; they have become virtual arms of the government.

Most large nationwide charities now derive most of their income, not from private donations, but from government itself. For example, federal, state, and local governments provide nearly two-thirds of the funding Catholic Charities USA uses to operate its nearly 1,400 programs. The Jewish Board of Family and Children Services

---

[26]Quoted in Sirico, "Restoring Charity," p. 7.

[27]Brian O'Connell, "Private Philanthropy and the Preservation of a Free and Democratic Society," in *Philanthropy: Four Views*, ed. Robert L. Payton (New Brunswick, N.J.: Transaction Books, 1988), p. 32.

receives 75 percent of its funding from the government. Many other prominent charities receive similar levels of government funding.[28]

A recent newspaper investigative report described those organizations as "transformed from charitable groups run essentially on private donations into government vendors—big businesses wielding jobs and amassing clout to further their own agendas."[29]

Not only does government provide most of the funding for those organizations, but in terms of their bureaucratic structure and lack of accountability, they frequently resemble government agencies. Writing for the Philanthropy Roundtable, Payne compares large, bureaucratic charities with small, community-based organizations.[30] According to Payne, the large organizations are generally managed and directed by a class of permanent, professional social workers. That is the final result of the professionalization of social work that began in the early part of the century.

Payne says that the big charities "are best understood as commercial charities, entities that rely on mass-marketing techniques to sell a charitable concept to distant, rather uninformed donors."[31] As a result, there is little or no direct donor supervision and a lack of volunteers in supervisory roles. In contrast, Payne notes,

> In the task-oriented local voluntary organizations, those who supply cash and labor are well-informed about its problem-solving activities. The group is run by an inner core of several dozen volunteers who carry out operational duties. They are the managers and policy makers of the group. If the organization has paid employees, the active volunteers work with them, and are in a position to observe and evaluate their performances. Beyond this core group, the organization has several hundred less active supporters, individuals who occasionally volunteer, and who also provide financial support.[32]

[28]Laurie Goodstein, "Churches May Not Be Able to Patch Welfare Cuts," *Washington Post*, February 22, 1995.

[29]Robin Kamen and Steve Malanga, "Nonprofits: NY's New Tammany Hall," *Crain's*, October 31, 1994.

[30]Payne, pp. 11–12.

[31]Ibid., p. 11.

[32]Ibid.

Like government, big charities have become an instrument of the elites. Professional social workers prescribe the correct policies. Direct citizen involvement is unneeded and unwanted.

That situation produces three results. First, an increasing amount of the charitable dollar is eaten up by bureaucratic overhead and salaries. Less and less reaches the poor. Before his conviction for embezzling funds from the organization, William Aramony of the United Way had a salary of $390,000, a $4.4 million pension, an apartment in New York paid for by the charity, and a personal chauffeur and car.[33] His successor earns $195,000 plus benefits.[34]

Second, the organizations become more and more distant from the poor they serve. The United Way, for example, does not even operate anti-poverty programs of its own. It simply collects funds and then farms them out to other organizations, such as the National Council of Churches and the Council of Jewish Federations, that, in turn, farm the money out to other agencies.[35]

Third, it becomes extremely important for the organizations to protect their flow of money from the government. As Kimberly Dennis, executive director of the Philanthropy Roundtable, complains, the big foundations "have been more interested in expanding government's responsibilities than in strengthening private institutions to address social concerns."[36]

Many charities actually maintain lobbyists on Capitol Hill to seek more of the taxpayers' money. Private donors may be surprised to find that their contributions go, not to help the poor, but to influence votes in Washington.

Private Charity in Action

The type of charity that will make a difference in the civil society will not be the large bureaucratic monsters described above. Rather, it will be local, individually based operations, capable of close interaction between donors and recipients. For example, the Center for

---

[33]For a discussion of Aramony's tenure at United Way, see John S. Glaser, *The United Way Scandal: An Insider's Account of What Went Wrong and Why* (New York: John Wiley & Sons, 1994).

[34]Payne, p. 39.

[35]Ibid.

[36]Kimberly Dennis, "Some Philanthropists Turn Their Backs on Voluntarism," *The Freeman*, October 1994, p. 565.

the Homeless in South Bend, Indiana, provided shelter for approximately 2,500 homeless men, women, and families in 1994.[37] Its three dormitory rooms hold beds for 72 men and 20 women. In addition, there are 13 apartments for families with children.

Throughout the center, the approach is one of "tough love." As Louis Nanni, the center's executive director, explains, "I realized that providing free food, material goods, and a place to sleep was not enough. In fact, simply doing that would be counterproductive. Unconditional handouts would sustain bad habits and allow people to put off facing their real problems."[38]

When homeless people decide to stay at the center, they are presented with a set of strict rules that must be read and signed. The rules are reviewed in daily orientation sessions. All guests receiving income (either government benefits or wages) must save at least 75 percent of it after deducting obligations such as child support. Alcohol and drugs are strictly forbidden, and guests may be randomly tested for their use.

A case manager works individually with each homeless person to develop a plan to address his or her problems and work toward self-sufficiency, whether that involves job search, education, literacy classes, or drug and alcohol therapy. Peer monitoring and mentorship programs assist the person to complete his or her program.

The shelter's goal is to provide not just a temporary roof and food but self-sufficiency, which Nanni defines as "having the knowledge, discipline, and skills necessary to secure one's own shelter, maintain a healthy livelihood, and establish the relationships necessary to flourish personally and in a community."[39]

Another private charity assisting the homeless is the St. Martin de Porres House of Hope in Chicago. The program is run by Sister Connie Driscoll, who specializes in helping homeless women. Women staying at the shelter are required to be drug free. Those who don't work must perform chores around the shelter.[40] Sister

[37]Louis Nanni, "Not by Bread Alone," *American Enterprise*, January–February 1994, pp. 56–60.

[38]Ibid., p. 58.

[39]Ibid., p. 59.

[40]Robert Sirico, "Putting Private Charity Back into Welfare," *Detroit News*, May 28, 1995.

Connie describes the program's philosophy: "Giving people a bag of food and a pat on the head is not the answer anymore. Once people stop thinking of help as a right, they'll understand they have to work."[41]

The shelter is not a big-budget charity. It spends less than $7 per person per day, compared to an average of more than $22 per person per day in government-funded homeless shelters. Yet it has a phenomenal success rate. Fewer than 6 percent of women who go through its program end up back on the street.[42]

Kid-Care, Inc., provides food to poor children in inner-city Houston. Operating as a sort of "meals on wheels" for children, Kid-Care delivers nearly 20,000 meals per month to more than 300 needy families. When there are extra funds, Kid-Care also provides shoes and clothing. Kid-Care workers are nearly all volunteers, and the operation spends more than 80 percent of its budget directly on food.[43]

Kid-Care demands that the people it helps be taking steps to help themselves. As the organization's founder, Carol Doe Porter, says, "Kid-Care is not an entitlement. It's a privilege. I'll withdraw in an instant if you're a user or abuser. Instead of giving a hand-out, we should be giving a hand up."[44]

One of the most successful private charities in Washington, D.C., is the Gospel Mission, which has been operating since 1906. The mission operates a homeless shelter for 150 men, a soup kitchen and food bank, and a drug treatment center. The mission operates on the principle that no one should receive something for nothing. Therefore, the homeless must pay $3 a night or agree to perform one hour of work around the mission in exchange for their lodging.[45]

The mission tries to address the full range of its clients' needs, providing not only food and shelter but also education classes, job placement assistance, and spiritual advice. Recipients must demonstrate their desire to improve their lives.

---

[41]Quoted in ibid.

[42]Robert Sirico, "Charities on the Dole," *Wall Street Journal*, March 31, 1995.

[43]Gregg Vanourek, Scott Hamilton, and Chester Finn Jr., *Is There Life after Big Government?* (Indianapolis: Hudson Institute, 1996), pp. 23–26.

[44]Quoted in ibid., p. 25.

[45]Ibid., pp. 40–43.

"Sometimes we have to put a time limit on a guy, " says Rev. John Woods, the mission's director. "I had one guy tell me, 'Reverend, the best thing you ever did for me was kick me out.' He was using the mission for a crutch. Compassion is lifting people out of the gutter, not getting down there with them and sympathizing. These people need responsibility."[46]

The Gospel Mission has had extraordinary success at helping its clients put their lives together and return to mainstream society. For example, nearly two-thirds of the addicts completing its drug treatment program remain drug free. By comparison, a government-run drug treatment center just three blocks away has only a 10 percent success rate yet spends nearly 20 times as much per client.[47]

In Grand Rapids, Michigan, an organization called Faith, Inc., provides job training to the homeless and others without jobs. Faith, Inc., operates a small assembly and packaging operation to provide its clients with training and work skills. As clients gain skills, they are subcontracted to other area firms for a fee. Counseling and education are also provided. Eventually, clients are assisted in finding full-time jobs with outside companies. About 50 percent of those who enter the program eventually complete it and find employment. The program has been so successful that it has become self-financing and even earns a small profit.[48]

A similar approach is used by St. Paul's Community Baptist Church in one of the most poverty-stricken sections of Brooklyn. The church has purchased a number of small businesses that it uses to provide jobs for neighborhood poor people. If people are willing to work—and only if they are willing to work—St. Paul's will help them get a job at one of the church-run enterprises.[49]

The church has also purchased and refurbished a number of houses and is offering them to poor families for mortgages as low as $400 per month. Still, the poor are always required to pay at least something. As the church's pastor, Rev. Johnny Ray Youngblood,

[46]Quoted in ibid, p. 41.

[47]Sen. Daniel Coats, *Congressional Record* 141, no. 123 (July 27, 1995): 510823.

[48]Amber Veverka, "Self-Dependence Aided by Faith, Inc., Success," *Grand Rapids Business Journal*, February 3, 1992.

[49]Thomas McArdle, "Tools of Success for the Poor," *Investor's Business Daily*, November 11, 1993.

explains, St. Paul's philosophy is, "Never do unto others what they can do for themselves."[50]

All across America tens of thousands of small local charities like those are achieving real results in helping the poor. Those charities will form the vanguard of the civil society's fight against poverty.

Will There Be Enough Charity?

Those who oppose replacing welfare with private charity often argue that there will not be enough charitable giving to make up for the loss of government benefits. That criticism is based on some serious misunderstandings. First, it assumes that existing government programs would simply be transferred intact to private charity. All that would change would be the funding source. But the government programs have failed. Why would private charities want to replicate them? All the charities described above have far smaller budgets and operate far more efficiently than do their government counterparts.

Second, it assumes that private charity would have to care for the same number of poor as the government does today. However, as discussed above, without the incentives of today's welfare system there would actually be fewer people requiring assistance.

Finally, there is every reason to assume that charitable giving will increase in the absence of welfare. As we have already seen, welfare crowds out private charitable giving. A number of studies have demonstrated that "displacement effect."[51] That effect can be seen in Figure 6.1, which shows per capita charitable giving since 1950. Giving, which had been rising steadily throughout the 1950s and early 1960s, declined dramatically in the wake of the Great Society. In the 1980s, as the rise in welfare spending began to flatten out, the public was deluged with media stories warning of cutbacks in government programs (although, as we have seen, such cutbacks were more in the minds of the public and the media than in reality). The public responded by increasing private giving.[52]

[50]Quoted in ibid., p. 2.

[51]See, for example, Russell Roberts, "A Positive Model of Private Charity and Public Transfers," *Journal of Political Economy* 92 (1984): 136–48; and B. A. Abrams and M. D. Schmitz, "The Crowding Out Effect of Governmental Transfers on Private Charitable Contributions," *Public Choice*, no. 1 (1978): 28–40.

[52]Charles Murray, *In Pursuit of Happiness and Good Government* (New York: Simon & Schuster, 1988), pp. 275–76.

Figure 6.1
CHARITABLE GIVING, 1950–94

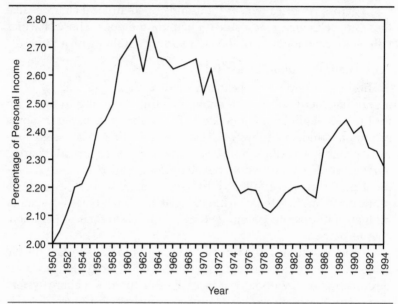

Year

SOURCE: American Association of Fund Raising Council Trust for Philanthropy, "Giving USA, 1995," 1995 data series, New York.

It important to note that Figure 6.1 shows all private charitable giving, only a portion of which goes to social welfare programs. But, if anything, social welfare charity was affected even more. For example, in the wake of the Great Society, the proportion of philanthropic giving devoted to social welfare declined from 15 percent to 6 percent.[53] Following the pattern of overall giving, during the Reagan years social welfare giving increased, peaking at 11.6 percent of total giving in 1985. Following the Reagan years, as people again became convinced that government programs would take care of the poor, the proportion of charity dedicated to such purposes again declined, reaching 9.9 percent in 1993.[54]

[53]Ralph Kramer, *Voluntary Agencies in the Welfare State* (Berkeley: University of California Press, 1981), pp. 57–76.

[54]American Association of Fund Raising Council Trust for Philanthropy.

146

That is a natural reaction. If people believe that their contributions are not needed to help the poor, they will contribute instead to the symphony or the Friends of the Earth. When convinced that their contributions are needed, they give more to the poor.

That is not a new phenomenon. There is evidence from Frederic Almy's study of outdoor relief in the 1890s (see Chapter 2) that private giving increased as government programs decreased and decreased as government programs grew more generous, leaving the overall amount of charity in society (both public and private) relatively constant.[55] If government welfare disappears, there is no reason to believe that Americans will not respond, as they have in the past, with increased giving.

If worst-case scenarios do come true, and private charities initially lack sufficient funds, there are ways for the government to spur charitable giving. One method, strongly promoted by the National Center for Policy Analysis, would be to provide taxpayers with a dollar-for-dollar tax credit for private charitable contributions.[56] That is to say, if an individual gives a dollar to charity, he should be able to reduce his tax liability by a dollar. Since current federal welfare spending is equivalent to 41 percent of the revenues generated from personal income taxes (for all major means-tested programs), the credit could be capped at 41 percent of tax liability.[57]

Such an approach is not perfect. It is a coercive method of financing charity, but it does give individuals greater control over where their charitable dollar goes, and it puts day-to-day operation of charity in private hands. Unlike government grants to private charitable organizations, there are no strings attached or other government controls. Nor does government decide which charities are worthy of funding.

That is quite different, it should be pointed out, from proposals by some conservatives, such as Sen. Dan Coats (R-Ind.), to provide federal government grants to the type of small private charitable

---

[55]Frederic Almy, "The Relation between Public and Private Charities," *Charities Review* 9 (1899): 65–71.

[56]Goodman, Reed, and Ferrara, pp. 28–31.

[57]Ibid., p. 30.

organizations described above.[58] Allowing the federal government to get involved in funding local charities risks destroying exactly what makes those charities so effective. In a very brief time they would be transformed into smaller clones of the large, national government-dependent charities. Richard Cornuelle, founder of the Center for Independent Action, a private charitable organization, warned about the dangers of a Coats-style approach 30 years ago in *Reclaiming the American Dream*.

> Those who are succeeding with the poor, helping them climb out of poverty—like the Y.M.C.A., Urban League, community welfare councils—are independent institutions. It seems logical then to subsidize the independent institutions. And, just as logically, that is how to kill them. You can almost see the work slow down and the "co-ordination" begin, the substitutions of administrators for workers. And then the paper blizzard. The tragedy is that the final effect of the poverty program may be to destroy the agencies which could eliminate poverty.[59]

Therefore, any direct government subsidy of private charity should be avoided. But that is not what is envisioned by a tax credit. Under the National Center for Policy Analysis approach, individuals are contributing their own funds to the charity of their—not the government's—choice. Government policy simply serves as an encouragement for them to do so. As an interim measure, that would certainly be preferable to the current welfare system.

Conclusion

Welfare has failed and cannot be reformed. It is time to end it. In its place, the civil society would rely on a reinvigorated network of private charity.

An enormous amount of evidence and experience shows that private charities are far more effective than government welfare

---

[58]For details of Coats's proposal, see Dan Coats, "Can Congress Revive Civil Society?" *Policy Review*, January–February 1996, pp. 25–28. For an excellent critique of the Coats plan, see David Boaz, "Conservative Social Engineering," *Policy Review*, January–February 1996, pp. 32–33.

[59]Richard C. Cornuelle, *Reclaiming the American Dream: The Role of Private Individuals and Voluntary Associations* (1965; New Brunswick, N.J.: Transaction Publishers, 1993), p. 161.

programs. While welfare provides incentives for counterproductive behavior, private charities can use their aid to encourage self-sufficiency, self-improvement, and independence. Private charities can individualize their approaches and target the specific problems that are holding people in poverty. They are also much better at targeting assistance to those who need it most and at getting the most benefit out of every dollar.

Most important, private charity is given out of a true sense of compassion, which forms a moral bond between giver and receiver. Private charity enriches the lives of everyone involved and helps to nurture the true tendrils of community.

Eliminating welfare does not mean turning our backs on the poor. It does mean finding a more effective and compassionate way to help them.

7. Creating Opportunity

In her classic 1969 book, *The Economy of Cities*, Jane Jacobs wrote, "Poverty has no causes. Only prosperity has causes." She then went on to say that the only real way to fight poverty is through economic development. The way for individuals to escape poverty is to enter the labor market and earn enough money to afford what they need.[1]

Jacobs was right. Far too much of our anti-poverty policy has been devoted to making poverty comfortable and not enough to creating the conditions necessary for people to get out of poverty. The search for widespread and general prosperity should proceed along two tracks. Our primary goal should be to create prosperity for the population at large. The desirability of general prosperity is self-evident. However, numerous studies have also shown that the chief beneficiaries of economic growth and prosperity are the poor. Reviewing the available literature on the subject, Bruce Bartlett concluded, "Rapid economic growth based on free markets and low taxes has narrowed the distribution of income between the highest and lowest income classes."[2] And, while pursuing growth and prosperity for society at large, we should also attempt to remove the barriers that particularly limit prosperity for the poor.

Experience has shown that government can do very little to create prosperity. Attempts at central economic planning have been a dismal failure—as Eastern Europe can attest. Government cannot really create jobs through public works. Not only are such jobs usually only temporary, but the government's efforts to finance them may destroy more jobs than are created. Richard Vedder of the University of Ohio estimates that for every additional 1 percent of gross domestic product devoted to government employment programs, unemployment *increases* by 1.3 percent.[3]

[1]Jane Jacobs, *The Economy of Cities* (New York: Vintage Books, 1969), p. 11.

[2]Bruce Bartlett, "Supply-Side Sparkplug: The Case for Tax Cuts in the Third World," *Policy Review*, no. 37 (Summer 1986): 52.

[3]Richard Vedder, "Why Government Job Training Fails," *Investor's Business Daily*, January 10, 1996.

Government is unable to create prosperity for several reasons. First, the taxation or borrowing, or both, necessary to finance government programs tends to reduce the pool of funds needed for private investment and job creation. Second, because they are not market driven, government programs are not able to respond to the actual needs of the economy as they develop and change. Third, because they lack the discipline imposed by competition and markets, government programs tend to be less efficient than their private-sector counterparts.[4]

In addition, whatever the intention of government programs, they are soon captured by special interests. The nature of government is such that programs are almost always implemented in a way to benefit those with a vested interest in them rather than to actually achieve the programs' stated goals.

As economists Dwight Lee and Richard McKenzie point out, the political power necessary to transfer income to the poor is power that can be used to transfer income to the nonpoor, and the nonpoor are usually better organized politically and more capable of using political power to achieve their purposes.[5] Among the nonpoor with a vital interest in anti-poverty programs are social workers and government employees who administer the programs and businesspeople, such as landlords and physicians, who are paid to provide services to the poor. Thus, anti-poverty programs are usually more concerned with protecting the prerogatives of the bureaucracy than with fighting poverty.

Both theory and experience show that government attempts to fight poverty or create prosperity will fail.[6] Although government cannot *create* prosperity, wrongheaded government policies can inhibit economic growth. For example, almost everyone agrees that a job is better than any welfare program. Yet for years this country has pursued tax and regulatory policies that seem almost perversely designed to discourage economic growth and reduce entrepreneurial

[4]James Gwartney and Richard Stroup, *What Everyone Should Know about Economics and Prosperity* (Tallahassee, Fla.: James Madison Institute, 1993).

[5]Dwight R. Lee and Richard B. McKenzie, *Failure and Progress: The Bright Side of the Dismal Science* (Washington: Cato Institute, 1993), pp. 120–22.

[6]This is not necessarily to say that there is no role for government. Government can and should defend people's rights, including property rights, so that people can coordinate their behavior in ways that will create wealth and prosperity.

opportunities. Government regulations and taxes are steadily cutting the bottom rungs off the economic ladder, throwing more and more poor Americans into dependency.

Taxes

America's tax burden has both diverted capital from the productive economy and discouraged job-creating investment. As Figure 7.1 shows, federal, state, and local taxes take 39 percent of the national income, the largest tax burden in the nation's history.

The high tax burden is hurting the American economy. Economist Robert Genetski has demonstrated that high marginal tax rates are inversely related to growth of productivity.[7] As shown in Figure 7.2, productivity increases when marginal income tax rates are low and declines when marginal tax rates are high, as they are today.

Economists Dale Jorgenson and Kun-Young Yun estimate that every dollar of taxes raised by the federal government results in a net loss to the economy of 18 cents,[8] an annual loss of $200 billion per year from our gross national product.

Those figures do not include the estimated $600 billion that the American economy loses every year because of the cost of complying with our dizzyingly complex tax system. In 1990 American workers and businesses were forced to spend more than 5.4 billion man-hours figuring out their taxes and filing the paperwork. That was more man-hours than were used to build every car, truck, and van manufactured in the United States.[9]

In addition to their negative impact on the economy, taxes also have a negative impact directly on the individual. After all, money paid in taxes is money no longer available for other purposes— whether for helping oneself or for helping others. As Frederic Bastiat wrote in his essay "What Is Seen and Not Seen" more than 200 years ago,

[7]Robert Genetski, *Taking the Voodoo Out of Economics* (Chicago: Regnery Gateway, 1986).

[8]Dale W. Jorgenson and Kun-Young Yun, "The Excess Burden of Taxation in the United States," in *Taxation in the United States and Europe: Theory and Practice*, ed. Anthonie Knoester (New York: St. Martin's, 1993), pp. 117–18.

[9]James L. Payne, *Costly Returns: The Burdens of the U.S. Tax System* (San Francisco: Institute for Contemporary Studies Press, 1993), pp. 150–52.

Figure 7.1
FEDERAL, STATE, AND LOCAL TAXES AS A SHARE OF NATIONAL INCOME

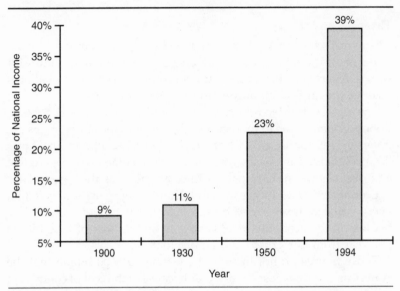

SOURCES: Stephen Moore, *Government: America's #1 Growth Industry* (Lewisville, Tex.: Institute for Policy Innovation, 1995), p. 68; and Robert Rector and William Lauber, *America's Failed $5.4 Trillion War on Poverty* (Washington: Heritage Foundation, 1995), Table 2, pp. 94–95.

[Money] spent by the state can no longer be spent as [it] would have been spent by the taxpayers. From all the benefits attributed to public spending we must deduct all the harm caused by preventing private spending. . . . [The taxpayer] would be better fed, better clothed; he would have had his sons better educated; he would have increased the dowry of his daughter, and he can no longer do so: *this is what is not seen. He would have joined a mutual aid society and can no longer do so.*[10]

[10]Frederic Bastiat, *Selected Essays on Political Economy*, trans. Seymour Cain (Irvington-on-Hudson, N.Y.: Foundation for Economic Education, 1964), p. 39. Emphasis added.

Figure 7.2
MARGINAL TAX RATES VS. PRODUCTIVITY

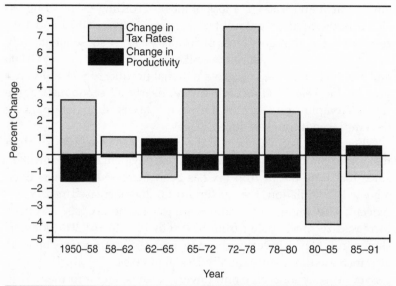

SOURCE: Robert Genetski, *Taking the Voodoo Out of Economics* (Chicago: Regnery Gateway, 1986), cited in *The Cato Handbook for Congress: 104th Congress* (Washington: Cato Institute, 1995), p. 111.

NOTE: Tax changes are differences in marginal income tax rates from beginning to end of the period. Productivity changes are differences in the annualized underlying trend from the previous period.

Several alternatives have been suggested for making our income tax system fairer and simpler, including a flat tax and a national retail sales tax.[11] Regardless of the nature of tax reform, however, economic growth and prosperity require taxes to be one thing— lower.

As bad as income taxes are, two other taxes have an even worse impact on the poor. After all, most poor people do not pay income taxes. They do, however, pay payroll taxes. In fact, 76 percent of Americans pay more in payroll taxes than they do in federal income

[11]For a discussion of the national sales tax, see Laurence J. Kotlikoff, "The Economic Impact of Replacing Federal Income Taxes with a Sales Tax," Cato Institute Policy Analysis no. 193, April 15, 1993. For a discussion of the flat tax, see Robert Hall and Alvin Rabushka, *The Flat Tax* (Stanford, Calif.: Hoover Institution Press, 1995).

taxes. The payroll tax paid directly by individuals is matched by a payment from employers. That adds significantly to the cost of employment and leads to a loss of jobs. According to the Congressional Budget Office, payroll tax increases between 1979 and 1982 resulted in the permanent loss of 500,000 jobs.[12] A subsequent study of the 1988 and 1990 payroll tax hikes estimated lost jobs at 50,000 and a reduction of the U.S. gross national product of $30 billion per year by the year 2000.[13] Furthermore, nearly all economists agree that the employer's share of the payroll tax is ultimately paid by the employee through reduced wages.

When Social Security began, the payroll tax was quite small, a maximum combined employer-employee payment of $60. However, since that time the payroll tax has been increased 13 times. Even adjusted for inflation, the maximum tax has increased nearly 900 percent. The amount of earnings subject to the tax has also been increased 26 times, rising from $3,000 in 1937 to $61,200 today, as shown in Table 7.1.[14] During the same period, Social Security benefits also increased, but substantially less than taxes.

Sam Beard, a long-time anti-poverty activist and a former aid to Sen. Robert F. Kennedy, warns that the Social Security payroll tax drains capital out of the inner city. Beard points out that not only do the poor have to pay a regressively high proportion of their income in payroll taxes, money that flows out of poor communities, but they receive disproportionately fewer benefits. Therefore less money flows back into the community.[15]

That is because the amount of benefits received from Social Security and Medicare is largely dependent on longevity. The longer people live, the more they get back in benefits. For example, a person

---

[12]Congressional Budget Office, "Aggregate Economic Effects of Changes in Social Security Taxes," August 1982, p. 30.

[13]Aldona Robbins and Gary Robbins, "The Effect of the 1988 and 1990 Social Security Tax Increases," Institute for Research on the Economics of Taxation, Washington, 1991, pp. 14–15.

[14]*1995 Annual Report of the Board of Trustees of the Federal Old-Age and Survivors Insurance and Disability Insurance Trust Funds* (Washington: Government Printing Office, 1995), Table II.b.1, pp. 35–36.

[15]Sam Beard, *Restoring Hope in America: The Social Security Solution* (San Francisco: Institute for Contemporary Studies, 1996), pp. 41–81.

Table 7.1
Payroll Taxes, 1937–95
Tax Rates and Taxable Income in Nominal Dollars

Year	Tax Rate (%)	Taxable Income ($)
1937	2.00	3,000
1950	3.00	3,600
1960	6.00	4,800
1970	9.60	7,800
1980	12.26	25,900
1990	15.30	53,400
1995	15.30	61,200

Source: *1995 Annual Report of the Board of Trustees of the Federal Old-Age and Survivors Insurance and Disability Insurance Trust Funds* (Washington: Government Printing Office, 1995), Table II.b.1, pp. 35–36.

who dies the day after he turns 65 clearly receives less money from Social Security than an individual who lives to be 100.

For a variety of reasons, there is a close relationship in this country between wealth and longevity.[16] Put simply, wealthy people live longer than poor people. Therefore, wealthy retirees will probably receive Social Security for a longer period of time than will their poorer counterparts. Daniel Garrett, writing last year in *Economic Inquiry*, demonstrated that when mortality differentials are considered, slightly more than half (53.7 percent) of single-earner couples receive a negative return from Social Security. Because single-earner couples receive the highest return on their Social Security payments, the impact on other types of households is likely to be even greater.

[16]See, for example, Harriet Duleep, "Measuring the Effect of Income on Adult Mortality Using Longitudinal Administrative Record Data," *Journal of Human Resources* 21 (Spring 1986): 238–51; Evelyn M. Kitagawa and Philip M. Hauser, *Differential in Mortality in the United States: A Study in Socioeconomic Epidemiology* (Cambridge, Mass.: Harvard University Press, 1973); Eugene Rogot, Paul Sorlie, and Norman Johnson, "Life Expectancy by Employment Status, Income, and Education in the National Longitudinal Mortality Study," *Public Health Reports* 107 (July–August 1992): 457–61; and Howard Iams and John McCoy, "Predictors of Mortality among Newly Retired Workers," *Social Security Bulletin* 54 (March 1991): 2–10.

As a result, Garrett concludes that "differences in mortality eliminated the progressive spread in returns across income categories."[17]

In addition, the long-term progressivity of Social Security benefits is further reduced by the tendency of low-income workers to enter the labor force at a younger age.[18] The poor tend to start work right after high school, if not sooner, while the middle class and wealthy are more likely to delay full-time entry into the workforce until after they have completed college. Therefore, the poor will begin paying taxes several years earlier than the wealthy, but paying taxes for those additional years does not earn any additional benefits.[19]

The poor also have much higher death rates before age 65 than do the nonpoor.[20] Individuals who die before age 65 never receive any retirement benefits at all from Social Security. Their survivors will, of course, receive survivors' benefits, which at least partially offset the loss of retirement benefits. However, for a tiny fraction of what the workers paid in Social Security taxes, they could have purchased life insurance policies that would have paid at least as much as Social Security. Moreover, the largest part of Social Security taxes is earmarked, not to pay for survivors' benefits, but for the retirement benefits that individuals who die before age 65 will never receive. Indeed, a person who is single or has no survivors and dies before age 65 receives nothing at all in exchange for years of payroll taxes—the worst possible deal from Social Security—and that person

---

[17]Daniel Garrett, "The Effects of Differential Mortality Rates on the Progressivity of Social Security," *Economic Inquiry* 33 (July 1995): 457. Not all economists agree on this point. For example, Eugene Steuerle and Jon M. Bakija conclude that while differentials in mortality rates do weaken the progressivity of Social Security, those differences are not sufficient to completely offset the progressive benefit structure. Therefore, the system still results in a net redistribution of wealth from rich to poor. The transfer is smallest for single men and largest for one-wage-earner couples. C. Eugene Steuerle and Jon M. Bakija, *Retooling Social Security for the 21st Century: Right and Wrong Approaches to Reform* (Washington: Urban Institute, 1994), pp. 115–19.

However, everyone agrees that proposed reforms such as raising the retirement age or reducing cost-of-living increases would tilt the equation strongly in the favor of higher income retirees.

[18]Ibid., p. 119.

[19]One of the earliest discussions of this problem was Milton Friedman and Wilbur Cohen, *Social Security: Universal or Selective?* (Washington: American Enterprise Institute, 1972).

[20]Rogot, Sorlie, and Johnson.

Figure 7.3
LIFE EXPECTANCY BY RACE AND SEX, 1995

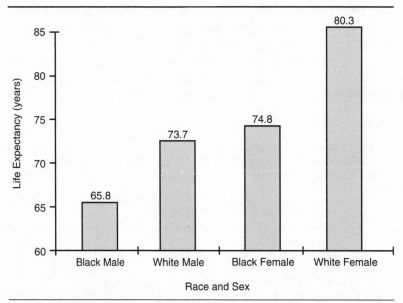

SOURCES: Based on data from the U.S. National Center for Health Statistics, *Vital Statistics of the United States,* annual, and *Monthly Vital Statistics Reports,* cited in Bureau of the Census, *The American Almanac: Statistical Abstract of the United States* (Austin: Reference Press, 1995), Table 114, p. 86.

is likely to be poor.[21] As Figure 7.3 shows, that is particularly damaging to African-Americans. The life expectancy of a black man today is just 65.8 years.[22] Clearly, many poor black men are not benefiting from our current Social Security system.

Changing to a Chilean-style system of mandatory private savings would solve both problems and have the beneficial side effect of increasing the amount of retirement income the poor could expect

[21]Peter J. Ferrara, *Social Security: The Inherent Contradiction* (Washington: Cato Institute, 1980), pp. 229–30.

[22]Based on middle mortality assumptions. Bureau of the Census, *The American Almanac: Statistical Abstract of the United States* (Austin: Reference Press, 1995), Table 114, p. 86.

to receive.[23] Low-income workers are far more likely to be dependent on Social Security when they retire than are their high-income counterparts. The poorest 20 percent of the elderly depend on Social Security for 81 percent of their income, while Social Security provides only 20 percent of income for the wealthiest 20 percent of retirees.[24]

William Shipman of State Street Global Advisors, one of the nation's largest financial management companies, estimates that a poor person could expect to receive as much as three times more

[23]The Chilean system, which went into effect May 1, 1981, mandates contributions of 10 percent of earnings for program participants. The pension available from the system is simply that which is actuarially computed from the accumulated contributions.

When the new system began, those in the old system were given the option of switching to the new. After 1982 all new employees were required to join the new system. As of 1992 approximately 90 to 95 percent of all persons who had been under the old system had shifted.

Contributions to the system are paid entirely by the employee; there is no employer payroll tax to support it. At the initiation of the system, however, all employers were required to give all employees a wage increase of 18 percent, approximately the increased cost of the new system to workers but less than the reduced cost to employers.

Pension funds are invested in security portfolios administered by private organizations known as AFPs. Twenty-one AFPs, which compete with each other on the basis of investment returns and service, are closely regulated to ensure compliance with government-mandated financial and investment requirements. Each worker chooses the AFP in which he wants to participate and may transfer fund balances at his own discretion up to four times a year. Like any other mutual fund, an AFP invests fund balances in a portfolio of securities and charges the portfolio an administrative fee for its services. Fees are a combination of a flat monthly percentage plus a percentage of earnings, and AFP fees are well publicized so that workers may consider those charges in their choice of funds. Fees average 1 percent of total wages, down from more than 2 percent since the system was started. Several of the funds, in fact, are owned and operated by U.S. investment firms. Provida, with 25 percent of the system's assets and the largest AFP, is 42 percent owned by New York–based Bankers Trust, and Santa Maria, the second-largest AFP, is 51 percent owned by Aetna Life & Casualty of Hartford, Connecticut.

Minimum retirement ages are 65 for men and 60 for women. Participants may, however, retire earlier if the pension payable is at least 50 percent of their average earnings over the previous 10 years and 100 percent of the legal minimum monthly wage. See Karl Borden, "Dismantling the Pyramid: The Why and How of Privatizing Social Security," Cato Institute Social Security Paper no. 1, August 14, 1995.

[24]Neil Gilbert and Neung-Hoo Park, "Privatization, Provision, and Targeting: Trends and Policy Implications for Social Security in the United States," *International Social Security Review* 49 (January 1996): 22.

Figure 7.4
MONTHLY BENEFITS OF SOCIAL SECURITY AND PRIVATE CAPITAL
MARKETS
(for a person earning $12,800 per year)

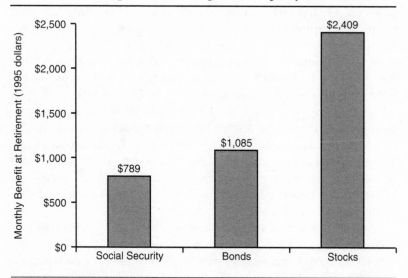

SOURCES: Derived from Social Security Administration, *Social Security Bulletin, Annual Statistical Supplement, 1994* (Washington: Government Printing Office, 1994); *Stocks, Bonds, Bills and Inflation* (Chicago: Ibbotson Associates, 1995); and "IFC Investible Index," International Finance Corporation, Washington, 1995, cited in William G. Shipman, "Retiring with Dignity: Social Security vs. Private Markets," Cato Institute Social Security Paper no. 2, August 14, 1995, p. 4.

from investing in private capital markets than from Social Security (Figure 7.4).[25]

Beard points out that, in a private savings system, a person who never earns more than minimum wage would, if allowed to invest his Social Security payroll taxes privately, retire with more than $1 million in the bank.[26] Moreover, individuals would have direct

[25]William G. Shipman, "Retiring with Dignity: Social Security vs. Private Markets," Cato Institute Social Security Paper no. 2, August 14, 1995.

[26]Beard, pp. 74–75. Beard uses nominal dollars. In 1995 dollars, the amount would be $300,000.

property rights to their savings. If they died before using up their savings, the money would become part of their estates, providing a new supply of capital for their heirs.[27]

The second tax that is especially hard on the poor is the capital gains tax. On the surface, that may seem surprising, since few poor people pay capital gains taxes. In fact, the capital gains tax is generally portrayed as a tax on the rich. However, it is also a tax on investment—investment that is needed to create jobs for poor people. As economist Jude Wanniski explains, "When the government puts a high tax on capital gains, the people who lose the most from a high rate are the poorest, the youngest, those at the beginning of their careers, those who are furthest from the sources of capital."[28]

When capital gains taxes are high, investment capital grows scarce. The areas that are the first to feel the lack of capital are areas where investments are most risky—inner-city neighborhoods with high crime rates, a poorly educated workforce, and high business bankruptcy rates.[29]

Historical evidence suggests that when capital gains taxes fall, investment seeps back into those neighborhoods. According to the U.S. Civil Rights Commission, after the capital gains tax was reduced from 49 percent to 28 percent in 1978, "the number of black-owned businesses increased in a five-year period by one-third." After the tax rate was cut again to 20 percent, the number of black-owned businesses increased by an additional 38 percent. But after the rate was raised back to 28 percent in 1986, the commission noted that the "expansion has slowed significantly."[30] That led the commission to conclude,

> The best hope for getting critically needed seed money into Los Angeles and other tense urban areas is by cutting the capital gains tax.
>
> Just as the fruit of a tree contains the seeds for more trees, so the fruits of success—capital gains—contain the seeds

[27]Ibid., p. 38.

[28]Jude Wanniski, Testimony before the U.S. Senate Committee on Finance, *Hearing on Tax Treatment of Capital Gains,* 104th Cong., 1st sess., February 15, 1995, p. 102.

[29]Stephen Moore and John Silvia, "The ABCs of the Capital Gains Tax," Cato Institute Policy Analysis no. 242, October 4, 1995, p. 34.

[30]Cited in Arthur Fletcher et al., "Help the Poor, Cut the Cap Gains Tax," *Wall Street Journal,* August 25, 1993.

Table 7.2
CAPITAL GAINS TAX RATES AROUND THE WORLD
(assets held more than one year)

Country	Tax Rate (%)
United States	28.0
Belgium	0.0
Canada	23.8
France	18.1
Germany	0.0
Hong Kong	0.0
Italy	25.0
Japan	20.0
Netherlands	0.0
Singapore	0.0
South Korea	0.0
Sweden	16.8
Taiwan	0.0

SOURCE: Stephen Moore and John Silvia, "The ABCs of the Capital Gains Tax," Cato Institute Policy Analysis no. 242, October 4, 1995, Table 4, p. 18. Figures are from the American Council for Capital Formation.

> that generate new investment and success for more people. Policies that punish success ultimately kill the seeds that promise enterprise and jobs to the poor. . . .
> Give us the seed capital for inner-city jobs and investment, and we will use our rich potential to rebuild our city and transform America.[31]

As Jesse Jackson says, "Capitalism without capital is just an 'ism.'"[32] Yet, as Table 7.2 shows, America has one of the world's highest capital gains tax rates. In fact, many countries have no tax on capital gains at all.[33]

Regulation

Someone starting a business today needs a battery of lawyers just to comply with the myriad government regulations promulgated

---

[31]Quoted in ibid.

[32]Quoted in Dick Armey, "The GOP's Fiscal Challenge," *Washington Post*, October 25, 1995.

[33]Moore and Silvia, p. 18.

Figure 7.5
FEDERAL REGULATORS VS. PRIVATE-SECTOR JOB GROWTH

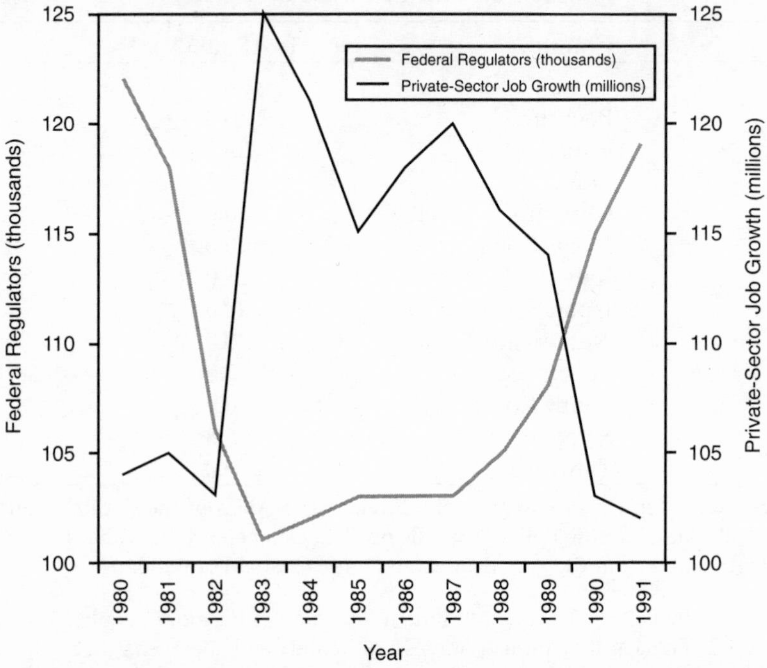

SOURCE: William Laffer, "How Regulation Is Destroying American Jobs," Heritage Foundation Backgrounder no. 926, February 16, 1993, p. 4.

by a virtual alphabet soup of government agencies: OSHA, EPA, FTC, CPSC, and so on. It is estimated that the current annual cost of government regulations is more than $570 billion.[34] At the current rate of growth, that cost will exceed $634 billion by the year 2000. That is $634 billion that cannot be used to create jobs and lift people out of poverty.

In fact, as Figure 7.5 shows, there is an inverse relationship between the number of federal regulators and job creation. During the Reagan administration, when there was a brief rollback in federal

[34]Estimate derived from Thomas D. Hopkins, "The Cost of Federal Regulations," Policy Analysis, National Chamber Foundation, Washington, January 1992, p. 21. Hopkins's figure has been converted to 1995 dollars.

regulation, job creation was strong, but as regulation surged under President Bush, job creation fell.

Although federal regulations are most damaging to the economy at large, state and local regulations are a particular hindrance to the poor. Zoning and occupational licensing laws, for example, are particularly damaging to the types of small businesses that may help people work their way out of poverty.

Given that impact, it is worth noting that many of the licensing requirements and other restrictions were originally developed to prevent African-Americans from fully participating in the free market.[35] In the aftermath of slavery, plantation owners found themselves without their former supply of cheap labor, as blacks were able to enter the competitive labor market. Many former slaves had developed valuable skills as craftsmen and were setting up small businesses. Others began to contract their services to plantation owners. The available labor supply became increasingly scarce, and stiff competition drove up wages.

The plantation owners tried to resist that trend. First, they attempted to form a cartel, mutually agreeing to hold down wages. But, as is the case with all cartels, individual members soon began cheating, the cartel collapsed, and competition again began to force up wages. Unable to succeed on their own, the plantation owners turned to the power of government to enforce their will, seeking laws to restrict the economic freedom of African-Americans. The first of those laws were explicitly based on race and were soon struck down by the courts. In addition, Congress passed federal legislation prohibiting the states from interfering with the right to contract.

Frustrated in their attempts to enact explicitly race-based restrictions, the plantation owners and their political allies turned to subtler legislation that appeared neutral but, nonetheless, acted to restrict opportunities for African-Americans. Enticement laws, for example, made it illegal for an employer to try to hire a worker already under contract to another employer. Vagrancy laws made it a crime to be unemployed, thus making it extremely difficult to quit a job in order

[35]For an excellent discussion of the history of occupational licensing and minorities, see Clint Bolick, *Unfinished Business: A Civil Rights Strategy for America's Third Century* (San Francisco: Pacific Research Institute, 1990).

to look for another one. Emigrant-agent laws made it illegal to entice people to move to other areas of the country.

Near the beginning of the century, as large numbers of blacks began to move into trades such as plumbing and carpentry, trade unions began to advocate occupational licensure laws to keep blacks out. Often those licensing laws contained testing and other requirements only tangentially related to the job in question. An examination of union journals and newspaper accounts at the time many of those laws were passed leaves little doubt as to their racist intent.[36]

Several studies have shown that although occupational licensing is no longer race based, it continues to have a disproportionate impact on minorities.[37] Take, for example, cosmetology licensing in Missouri. As is the case in many states, in addition to fulfilling costly training requirements, potential hairstylists must pass both a practical examination—demonstrating their skill at hairdressing—and a written examination, which includes detailed esoteric questions about biology and chemistry. A study by economist Stuart Dorsey found that black candidates passed the practical examination at the same rate as white candidates but failed the written portion

---

[36]Typical was this letter in the January 1905 edition of the *Plumbers, Gas, and Steam Fitters Official Journal*:

> There are about 10 Negro skate plumbers working around here [Danville, Va.], doing quite a lot of jobbing and repairing, but owing to the fact of not having an examination board it is impossible to stop them, hence the anxiety of men here to organize.

Quoted in Walter E. Williams, *The State against Blacks* (New York: McGraw-Hill, 1982), pp. 91–92.

African-Americans were not the only targets of the discriminatory laws. Regulations were also used to limit the access of other minorities to the economy. For example, one of the nation's earliest zoning laws was an 1885 Modesto, California, ordinance aimed at Chinese immigrants:

> [It is] unlawful for any person to establish, maintain, or carry on the business of a public laundry . . . within the City of Modesto, except that part of the city which lies west of the railroad track and south of G Street.

Cited in Michael Goldberg and Peter Horwood, *Zoning: Its Costs and Relevance for the 1980s* (Vancouver: Fraser Institute, 1980), p. 11.

[37]See, for example, Susan Michalik and Louise G. Trubek, "Regulating Occupations: Legal Challenges to Licensing Examinations in Wisconsin," Center for Public Representation, Madison, Wis., 1988; Simon Rottenberg, ed., *Occupational Licensure and Regulation* (Washington: American Enterprise Institute, 1980); and S. David Young, *The Rule of Experts: Occupational Licensing in America* (Washington: Cato Institute, 1987).

at vastly disproportionate rates.[38] The study concluded that "occupational licensing can restrict the labor market opportunities for groups of workers whose alternatives are already limited."[39]

We know that entrepreneurship is one major road out of poverty. Moreover, small businesses are the leading source of new jobs in this country. Nearly two-thirds of all new jobs are created by small businesses.[40] Yet African-Americans, for example, own fewer than 4 percent of all small businesses in America.[41] One reason is that poor blacks lack the legal and financial resources to deal with the regulatory roadblocks to starting new businesses. Creating prosperity and helping the poor to become self-sufficient will therefore require the elimination of unnecessary rules and regulations that limit entrepreneurship.

Minimum Wage and Mandated Benefits

Government regulations such as minimum wage laws and mandated benefits drive up the cost of employing additional workers. Minimum wage laws increase wages beyond the natural market rate, thereby increasing costs and prices, skewing the job market, and increasing unemployment.[42] The General Accounting Office,

[38]Stuart Dorsey, "The Occupational Licensing Queue," *Journal of Human Resources* 15, no. 3 (1980): 424–34.

[39]Ibid., p. 424.

[40]Personal communication from the Small Business Administration, Office of Advocacy, February 15, 1996.

[41]U.S. Department of Commerce, "Black-Owned Business Firms Up 46 Percent over Five Years, Census Bureau Survey Finds," Press release, December 12, 1995. Moreover, black-owned small businesses tend to be smaller than average. Approximately 80 percent are family-owned enterprises, employing no outside workers. About half of black-owned businesses have gross receipts of less than $5,000 per year. In addition, black-owned small businesses are disproportionately dependent on government contracts. Approximately 60 percent of their receipts come from government. National Urban League, *The State of Black America, 1993* (New York: AG Publishing, 1993), pp. 94, 101.

[42]Recent legislation, which would increase the minimum wage to $5.15 an hour by 1997, will almost certainly lead to increased unemployment. See, for example, Edward Gramlich, "Impact of Minimum Wages on Other Wages, Employment, and Family Incomes," Brookings Papers on Economic Activity, Brookings Institution, Washington, 1976, pp. 409–51; Finis Welch and James Cunningham, "Effects of Minimum Wages on the Level and Age Composition of Youth Employment," *Review of Economics and Statistics* 60 (1978): 140–45; David Parsons, *Poverty and the Minimum Wage* (Washington: American Enterprise Institute, 1980); Charles Brown, Curtis Gilroy, and Andrew Kohen, "The Effect of Minimum Wage on Employment and Unemployment," *Journal of Economic Literature* 20 (June 1982): 487–528; Charles Brown, "Minimum

summarizing 50 years of economic studies on the issue, concluded, "Employment is lower than if no minimum wage existed."[43]

Most often, employers do not lay off workers; they simply create fewer new jobs or do not replace workers who leave voluntarily.[44] The biggest job loss occurs among teenagers, the unskilled, and potential entrants to the job market.[45]

Employers may also reduce other benefits, such as health insurance or free meals, to compensate for increased wages, leaving the worker worse off. Richard McKenzie estimates that minimum wage workers receive a reduction in overall compensation of 2 percent for every 10 percent increase in the minimum wage.[46]

There is even evidence that at least some minimum wage laws, like occupational licensing laws, were originally intended to discriminate

Wage Laws: Are They Overrated?" *Journal of Economic Perspectives* 2, no. 3 (1988): 133–46; and David Neumark, "Employment Effects of Minimum and Subminimum Wages: Panel Data on State Minimum Wage Laws," *Industrial and Labor Relations Review* 46, no. 1 (1992): 55–81.

Recently, advocates of increasing the minimum wage have cited a study by Princeton economists David Card and Alan Krueger that showed no loss of jobs in the New Jersey fast-food industry after that state's increase in its minimum wage. David Card and Alan Krueger, "Minimum Wages and Employment: A Case Study of the Fast-Food Industry in New Jersey and Pennsylvania," *American Economic Review* 84, no. 4 (September 1994): 772–93. However, at least two recent studies have demonstrated that the Card-Krueger study was seriously flawed in its methodology. For example, Card and Krueger relied on telephone interviews with the managers of fast-food restaurants to determine their employment histories. However, subsequent examination of actual payroll records showed strikingly different results. University of Michigan economists David Neumark and William Wascher found a substantial loss of jobs as a result of the minimum wage hike. David Neumark and William Wascher, "The Effect of New Jersey's Minimum Wage Increase on Fast-Food Employment: A Re-Evaluation Using Payroll Records," January 1996, awaiting publication. See also Donald Deere, Kevin Murphy, and Finis Welch, "Sense and Nonsense on the Minimum Wage," *Regulation* 18, no. 1 (1995): 47–56.

[43]General Accounting Office, *Minimum Wage Policy Questions Persist*, Report to the U.S. Senate Committee on Labor and Human Resources (Washington: Government Printing Office, 1983), p. i.

[44]Alan Reynolds, "Cruel Costs of the 1991 Minimum Wage," *Wall Street Journal*, July 7, 1992.

[45]Neumark.

[46]Richard McKenzie, *The American Job Machine* (New York: Universe Books, 1988), p. 211.

against minorities.[47] For example, the Davis-Bacon Act, which requires prevailing wages (in practice, usually standard union wages) to be paid on all government contracts, was originally promoted to keep black workers, who were generally not allowed to join unions, from competing with unionized whites. One of the law's early supporters, the notorious racist Rep. Clayton Allgood (D-Miss.), candidly explained that the law would put an end to "cheap colored labor . . . that is in competition with white labor throughout the country."[48]

Other mandated benefits, from health insurance to family leave, have the same impact. By raising the cost of employment, they decrease the likelihood that a person will be hired. For a typical small business, the total tax and regulatory burden for hiring an additional worker is more than $5,400.[49] At best, that is $5,400 that is not going to the worker. At worst, the cost prevents the hiring of the worker. As a general rule, if we want poor people to work, we should avoid policies that punish employment.

Health Care

Government policies are also one of the most important barriers the poor face in attempting to gain access to health care. For example, federal tax policy provides a very generous tax break for the purchase of health care—but only on two conditions: health care must be purchased through insurance, and the insurance must be provided by an employer.

Current federal (and state) tax laws exclude from taxable wages the cost of health insurance provided by an employer. Therefore, the vast majority of Americans, those who receive health insurance through their employers, do not pay federal, state, or Social Security taxes on the value of their policies. Moreover, the employer can deduct the full premium cost as a business expense. Employers do not even pay Social Security payroll taxes on those benefits. In short, the entire cost of employer-provided insurance is paid with *before-tax* dollars.[50]

---

[47]Michael Bernstein, "Economic Regulation and Discrimination," *Lincoln Review* 8, no. 1 (Spring 1990): 19–28.

[48]Quoted in Williams, p. 122.

[49]Gwartney and Stroup, p. 92.

[50]The tax treatment of employer-provided health insurance is largely a historical accident. During World War II the United States simultaneously experienced a labor

However, those Americans not fortunate enough to receive employer-provided health insurance face entirely different tax laws. Part-time workers, students, the unemployed, and everyone else not receiving employer-provided health insurance—including most employees of small businesses—are unable to deduct *any* of the cost of health insurance. (Individuals may deduct out-of-pocket medical expenses only if they itemize deductions and the expenses exceed 7.5 percent of adjusted gross income. Fewer than 5 percent of American taxpayers are eligible for that deduction.)[51]

The difference in tax treatment creates a disparity that effectively doubles the cost of health insurance for people who must purchase their own. For example, the family of a self-employed person who earns $35,000 per year, has to pay federal and state taxes with only a 25 percent deduction, and has to pay Social Security taxes must earn $7,075 to pay for a $4,000 health insurance policy. A person working for a small business that offers no health insurance has to earn $8,214 to pay for that $4,000 policy.[52]

The distortions caused by that tax policy leave poor Americans worse off in several ways. First, the poor are far less likely to receive employer-provided insurance than are the wealthy. Only 28.4 percent of families with incomes under $20,000 per year receive insurance through work, while 78 percent of those with incomes above $20,000 do so.[53] Since the poor are likely to find it extremely costly to purchase health insurance, they are much more likely to be uninsured. Workers who must purchase their insurance with after-tax dollars are 24 times more likely to be uninsured than are those who

---

shortage and wage and price controls. Unable to attract scarce workers by raising wages, American businesses began offering health insurance as a recruitment aid. During the 1950s the Internal Revenue Service decided that employer-provided health insurance was not a part of a worker's wages for tax purposes. For a complete discussion of the tax treatment of health insurance and its consequences, see John C. Goodman and Gerald L. Musgrave, *Patient Power: Solving America's Health Care Crisis* (Washington: Cato Institute, 1992), pp. 270–78.

[51]Internal Revenue Service, *Statistics of Income Bulletin* and *Statistics of Income, Individual Tax Returns*, annual, cited in Bureau of the Census, *The American Almanac: Statistical Abstract of the United States* (Austin: Reference Press, 1995), Table 533, p. 345.

[52]Health Care Solutions for America, "Federal Tax Policy and the Uninsured: How U.S. Tax Laws Deny 10 Million Americans Access to Health Insurance," Washington, January 1992, p. 4.

[53]Ibid., p. 3.

are eligible for tax-free employer-provided coverage.[54] Significantly, the poor and minorities, who are less likely to have employer-provided insurance, are most likely to be left without access to health insurance.[55] Thus, the perverse impact of our tax policies is to penalize those who are least able to afford health insurance. It is estimated that if individually purchased health insurance received the same tax treatment as employer-provided insurance, as many as 10 million of America's 41 million uninsured could purchase health insurance.[56]

Second, because insurance is so closely linked with employment, if a worker loses his job, he is in danger of losing his insurance. Of the 41 million Americans without health insurance at any given time, half are uninsured for four months or less, and only 15 percent are uninsured for more than two years.[57] Essentially, those are people who lost their jobs and, therefore, lost their insurance. Since the poor have less stability in their jobs, they are at far greater risk for interruptions in their health insurance. However, if the tax code did not give preference to insurance purchased through an employer, people would be more inclined to purchase insurance individually (with employers acting as little more than brokers) or through non-employer groups. In that case, the individual, not the employer, would own the insurance policy, and it would be fully portable.

Finally, the tax treatment of health insurance has encouraged a third-party payment system that increases the cost of health care. Economists from across the political spectrum understand that one of the major factors driving health care costs is our third-party payment system that insulates consumers from the cost of their health care decisions.[58] There are numerous studies that show that health care consumers do make cost-conscious decisions when given a financial incentive to do so. For example, the RAND Corporation

[54]Jill Foley, *The Uninsured in the United States: The Nonelderly Population without Health Insurance* (Washington: Employee Benefits Research Institute, April 1991), p. 10.

[55]Ibid.

[56]Health Care Solutions for America, p. 3.

[57]Katherine Swartz and Timothy McBride, "Spells without Health Insurance: Distributions of Durations and Their Link to Point-in-Time Estimates of the Uninsured," *Inquiry* 27, no. 3 (Fall 1990): 17.

[58]For a detailed discussion of how third-party payment increases health care costs, see Stan Liebowitz, "Why Health Care Costs Too Much," Cato Institute Policy Analysis no. 211, June 23, 1994.

conducted a study of how people's health care decisionmaking changed in relation to the size of the consumer's copayment. The study found that an individual who had to pay 50 percent of the cost of health care spent 25 percent less than an individual with no copayment. The study also showed that, contrary to the assertions of some critics, those reduced expenditures are not caused by individuals' forgoing truly necessary health care. (Health outcomes were virtually identical.) Rather, the savings result from reduced use of optional services and cost-based selection among competing providers.[59]

Obviously, the poor are hurt most by increased health care costs. Several mechanisms have been proposed to equalize the tax treatment of individually purchased health insurance and out-of-pocket health care expenses, including medical savings accounts.[60] In the meantime, the government's tax policy leaves the poor at a distinct disadvantage.

Access of the poor to affordable health care is also limited by medical licensing laws and other restrictions on the scope of practice of nonphysician professionals. First, there is strong evidence that such restrictions drive up the cost of health care, while doing little to protect public health and safety.[61] Second, because high-poverty areas such as rural communities and inner cities may suffer from a shortage of physicians, restrictions on nonphysician health care professionals may lead to difficulties in finding proper care.[62]

Needed: A Holistic Approach

One government policy after another penalizes the poor. Agricultural price supports drive up the cost of milk, bread, and meat.[63]

---

[59]Joseph Newhouse et al., "Some Interim Results from a Controlled Trial of Cost Sharing in Health Insurance," *New England Journal of Medicine* 305, no. 25 (December 17, 1981): 95–112; and Willard Manning et al., "Health Insurance and the Demand for Medical Care: Evidence from a Randomized Experiment," *American Economic Review* 77 (June 1987): 251–73.

[60]For a complete discussion of medical savings accounts, see Goodman and Musgrave, pp. 439–63.

[61]See Sue A. Blevins, "The Medical Monopoly: Protecting Consumers or Limiting Competition?" Cato Institute Policy Analysis no. 246, December 15, 1995.

[62]Goodman and Musgrave, pp. 633–51.

[63]See, for example, James Bovard, *The Farm Fiasco* (San Francisco: Institute for Contemporary Studies, 1989).

The poor suffer. Tariffs and trade barriers prevent the importation and sale of low-cost foreign goods. The poor are hurt.[64]

Government policies hurt the poor in noneconomic ways as well. For example, poor neighborhoods will never be revitalized while they are being torn apart by crime. But, like alcohol prohibition before it, the war on drugs has turned inner-city streets into war zones.[65]

No single program, however well intentioned, can bring about the kind of economic prosperity necessary to successfully fight poverty. Rather, we need a holistic approach that works simultaneously on the whole body politic, removing the impediments of government and allowing the natural genius and creativity of the American people to flourish.

The holistic interaction of programs can be seen on the negative side as well. Programs never exist in a vacuum; they interact with one another. Thus, the same members of Congress vote for farm price supports, which drive up the cost of food, then vote for food stamps to enable the poor to purchase the food at inflated prices. The result is no net benefit to the poor but an increase in the power of government.[66]

Supporters of the civil society must adopt a holistic approach, too, pursuing liberty and free markets across the full range of government programs. For example, both food stamps and agricultural subsidies should be eliminated. Welfare should be eliminated, but so should taxes and regulations that prevent economic growth and limit the availability of jobs.

Education

A detailed discussion of education reform is well beyond the scope of this book. Still, there can be no serious attempt to solve the problem of poverty in America without addressing our failed government-run school system. Analysts as diverse as President Clinton's secretary of labor Robert Reich and social scientist Charles Murray have warned that our society is becoming more and more

---

[64]James Bovard, *The Fair Trade Fraud* (New York: St. Martin's, 1991).

[65]For a discussion of how the war on drugs increases crime and violence, see David Boaz, ed., *The Crisis in Drug Prohibition* (Washington: Cato Institute, 1992).

[66]It is, however, a good *political* strategy. Thus, Bob Dole is a champion of both farm price supports and food stamps, thereby earning the gratitude (and support) of Kansas farmers.

Table 7.3
CHANGE IN AVERAGE REAL EARNINGS BY EDUCATION LEVEL,
1979–92 (percentage)

Education	Men	Women
Less than high school	− 23	− 7
High school graduate	− 17	+ 1
College graduate	+ 5	+19

SOURCE: Don Boroughs, "Winter of Discontent," *US News & World Report,*
January 22, 1996.

divided between those with the skills and education needed to function in the increasingly competitive global economy and those without such skills and education. For example, as we saw in Chapter
1, the poverty rate for families at least one member of which finished
college is just over 2 percent; it is 10.5 percent for high school graduates and 24.2 percent for those who did not finish high school.[67]

Moreover, the "education gap" is growing steadily worse. As
Table 7.3 shows, average annual earnings for high school dropouts
have been declining in real terms, while the income of college graduates has been increasing.

At the same time that education is becoming increasingly crucial,
government schools are doing more and more poorly at educating
children. The failures of government schools are well documented
and need not be dwelled on at length here. Test scores plummeted
throughout the 1960s and 1970s. There was a slight upturn in the
1980s, but they have stagnated since.[68] One in five students drops out
of school, and dropout rates in some inner cities exceed 80 percent.[69]

Supporters of government education have long argued that the
solution to our growing crisis in education lies in increased spending.
However, there is no evidence that increasing the money spent on
government schools will lead to increased educational performance.
Education economist Eric Hanushek of the University of Rochester

[67]Christopher Jencks and Kathryn Edin, "The Real Welfare Problem," *American
Prospect* 1, no. 1 (Spring 1990): 31–50.

[68]Samuel Brunelli, ed., *Report Card on American Education 1994: A State-by-State
Analysis* (Washington: American Legislative Exchange Council, 1994).

[69]Chester Finn Jr., "The High School Dropout Puzzle," *Public Interest*, no. 87 (Spring
1987): 3–22.

Figure 7.6
EDUCATIONAL SPENDING VS. TEST SCORES

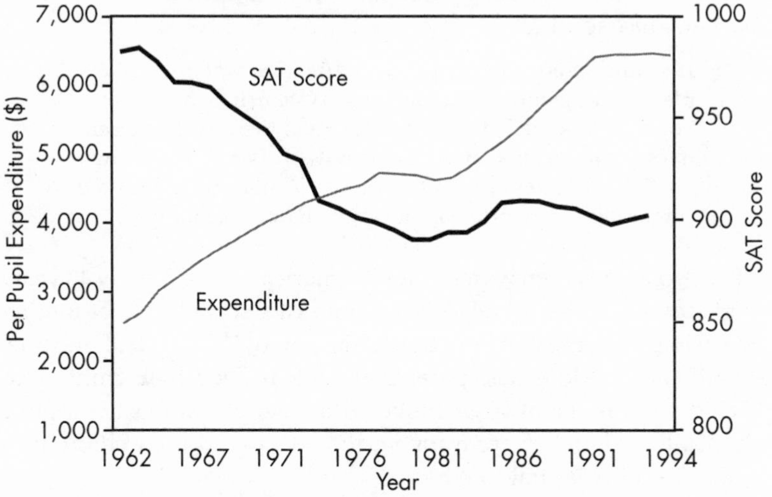

SOURCE: Educational Testing Service; and U.S. Department of Education, *Digest of Education Statistics 1994* (Washington: National Center for Education Statistics, 1994), Tables 127, 165, cited in *The Cato Handbook for Congress: 104th Congress* (Washington: Cato Institute, 1995), p. 121.

NOTE: SAT scores for 1961–67 are means for all students; subsequent scores are for college-bound seniors.

reviewed 147 studies of the relationship between spending on education and student performance and concluded that "there appears to be no systematic relationship between school expenditures and student performance."[70] Likewise, John Chubb and Terry Moe of the Brookings Institution concluded, "As for money, the relationship between it and effective schools has been studied to death. The consistent conclusion is that there is no connection between school funding and school performance."[71] Figure 7.6 shows how educational spending has been increasing, even as test scores have fallen.

[70]Eric Hanushek, "The Economics of Schooling: Production and Efficiency in Public Schools," *Journal of Economic Literature* 24 (September 1986): 1161–62.

[71]John E. Chubb and Terry M. Moe, *Politics, Markets, and America's Schools* (Washington: Brookings Institution, 1990), p. 193.

175

The real problem lies, not with the level of education funding, but with the very nature of the government-run education monopoly. As even Albert Shanker, president of the American Federation of Teachers, has admitted,

> It's time to admit that public education operates like a planned economy, a bureaucratic system in which everybody's role is spelled out in advance and there are few incentives for innovation and productivity. It is no surprise that our school system doesn't improve: it more resembles the communist economy than our own market economy.[72]

The problem is even worse among America's poor. Nearly 40 years after *Brown v. Board of Education*, America's schools are becoming increasingly segregated, on the basis not of race but of income. Wealthy and middle-class parents are able to send their children to private schools, or at least move to a district with better public schools. Poor families are trapped, forced to send their children to public schools that fail to educate.

It is time to break up the public education monopoly and give all parents the right to decide what schools their children will attend. That can be done through a variety of mechanisms, from tuition tax credits to educational vouchers. Whatever the mechanics, educational control must be returned to parents.

Injecting competition, market forces, and parental choice into education will improve education for all Americans. But the greatest impact will be in the inner cities and among poor parents. Instead of being forced to send their children to the drug-infested, crime-ridden inner-city schools of today, poor parents will have the choice of a wide variety of competing schools—religious, Afrocentric, Montessori, traditional. Some children will still be born into poverty, but they will have a far better opportunity to get a good education, which has always been one of the best tickets out of poverty.[73]

Conclusion

The largest part of getting out of poverty has to do with personal behavior—finishing school, avoiding pregnancy, getting a job. But

---

[72]Quoted in "Reding, Writing & Erithmatic," *Wall Street Journal*, October 2, 1989.

[73]For a discussion of how educational choice will benefit the poor, see David Boaz, ed., *Liberating Schools: Education in the Inner City* (Washington: Cato Institute, 1991).

few would deny that economic growth and prosperity are important factors in the civil society's fight against poverty.

That means that we must end those government policies—high taxes and regulatory excess—that inhibit growth and job creation. We must protect capital investment and give people the opportunity to start new businesses. We must reform our failed government school system.

Ending welfare is only the start. Creating opportunity is the rest of the story.

8. Conclusion: A New Debate

"Crisis" is a much overused word in Washington. It is used to describe everything from the health care situation to the budget situation. We sometimes seem incapable of dealing with an issue unless it is presented as apocalyptic. That leaves us jaded when a true crisis comes along.

Welfare may be the real thing. It is certainly a crisis for the people trapped in the system. Take a walk through a government housing project. Look at the people. Look at the faces of the children growing up in a system that offers them no hope for a better tomorrow.

Consider the case of eight-year-old Eric Morse. In 1994 two 10-year-old boys hurled Eric to his death from a 14th floor window of the public housing project where they lived. The *New York Times* described the housing project as "an island of poverty and pathology," noting that

> Chicago's Ida B. Wells housing project has few adult men. The women are disproportionately teenagers. At the time [of the crime], a third of the complex's 2,800 apartments were abandoned, used primarily by drug dealers who hawked heroin from the windows. In a survey at a nearby high school, half the students said they had been shot at; 45 percent said they had seen someone killed.[1]

That is the environment in which poor children are growing up today. That is the world that welfare has created. That *is* a crisis!

We know that welfare is a failure. It has failed to either reduce poverty or make the poor self-sufficient. It has torn at the social fabric of the country. It has been a significant factor in the increase in out-of-wedlock births, with all their attendant social problems. It has weakened the work ethic and added to rising crime rates. Most tragic of all, the pathologies it engenders are being passed from mother to child, from generation to generation.

[1]Brent Staples, "The Littlest Killers," *New York Times*, February 6, 1996.

We also know that traditional liberal welfare reform will not work. Yet another job-training program will be no more successful than the 163 we already have. More child care will not address the underlying problems of the welfare system. Economists speak of the Samaritan's dilemma: an attempt to do good may actually cause increased harm.[2] That is the nature of the welfare system.

Traditional conservative welfare reforms do not hold the answer either. Workfare, LEARNfare, and all the other programs designed to micromanage the lives of the poor are doomed to fail. The ability to fine-tune moral and spiritual values is well beyond the capability of government. It is better simply to get government out of the way.

A New Debate

The American public understands that welfare has failed. Public opinion polls consistently show majorities of around 90 percent in favor of welfare reform.[3] Nearly half the public believes that the current system is "fundamentally flawed."[4]

As a result, welfare reform has become perennial fodder for political campaigns and congressional grandstanding. But recent debates over welfare reform have provided more heat than light. What is needed is a new and different debate on welfare.

The new debate is not about motives. Most liberals, conservatives, and libertarians want the same thing—a country where all Americans have the opportunity to realize their full potential, where as few people as possible live in poverty and no one must go without the basic necessities of life. We want an America where every mother can look at her children and see hope for their future. It is a question of means. How do we get there from here?

The new debate is not about funding levels. Welfare programs are not basically good programs that just need to be better funded

---

[2]In the Biblical story (Luke 10), a Samaritan finds on the road to Jerusalem a man who has been robbed and beaten. The Samaritan cares for his injuries, thereby performing a good deed. However, the economist asks, what if knowledge of the Good Samaritan's efforts cause more people to travel the road to Jerusalem alone? What if some of them are then beaten and robbed when there is no one to assist them? By saving one man, the Samaritan may set in motion a chain of events that leads to the death of even more men. Hence, the Samaritan's dilemma.

[3]See, for example, Douglas Muzzio and Richard Behn, "What to Do about Welfare," *Public Perspective*, February–March 1995, pp. 35–46.

[4]Ibid., p. 41, citing Gallup poll for CNN/*USA Today*, December 2–5, 1994.

or made more efficient. They are fundamentally flawed programs that would not succeed at *any* level of funding. Liberals need to understand that we could pour every available penny into welfare and still do little or nothing to relieve the plight of the poor. Conservatives must realize that even if welfare cost next to nothing, it would still be wrong, if it produced the same misery it does today.

Rather, the new debate is about the role of government—about the balance between government and the civil society. Should government be involved in fighting poverty? Can government programs lift people out of poverty? What alternatives does the civil society offer?

The evidence clearly demonstrates that the answer to the first two questions is no. Government should not be involved in fighting poverty. There is no way to design a government welfare program that will work—that will do more good than harm. The answer to the third question is less clear. However, the poor would probably be far better off in the civil society.

The Civil Society and the Poor

The civil society will remove the incentives of the welfare state that entice people into poverty-inducing behavior. Without welfare, there will be fewer children born to poor single mothers who cannot afford to raise them. Those young women will be more likely to complete their education and marry before giving birth.

Since welfare will no longer be a better economic choice than a job, the poor will work more. True, in many cases their first jobs will be low paying. Many will have to struggle. But once on the ladder of economic opportunity, they will have the chance to move up, rung by rung, toward independence and self-sufficiency.

The first rung of that ladder will be easier to reach. With taxes and regulation dramatically reduced, more jobs will be created. Many poor people will be able to start their own businesses and eventually give employment to others. By breaking the government's monopoly on education and reducing the crime spawned by the war on drugs, we can revitalize our inner cities. The middle class, which fled the cities to escape bad schools and high crime rates, will return, bringing new jobs to our urban centers.

Some people will undoubtedly remain poor, will still need a helping hand; a reinvigorated private charitable sector will provide the type of help they really need. A new ethic of giving will emerge. Small, local charities will encourage neighbor to help neighbor, forging stronger community ties.

Most important of all, there will be hope for the next generation. The intergenerational transmission of the pathologies of poverty will be broken.

The civil society will stop treating the poor like children. It will accord them the dignity of holding them responsible for their actions. Poor people are poor—they are not stupid or lazy. If we give them responsibility for their own lives, they will respond. No one claims it will be easy. Their lives may be a struggle, particularly at first.

The civil society will also demand more of the rest of us. We will no longer be able to ignore the poor, content that government will solve the problem for us. We will have to become involved. We will have to give of ourselves—with genuine compassion.

But the benefits will be clear, both for society and for the poor themselves: a dramatic reduction in out-of-wedlock births and single-parent families, the restoration of the inner-city family, less crime and violence, a stronger work ethic, the movement of the underclass into the lower middle class and beyond, and a renewed sense of charity and community. That is a vision worth pursuing.

One hundred years ago, Herbert Spencer summed up the argument for letting the civil society fight poverty. "It must be admitted," he said,

> that individual ministration to the poor is the normal form of ministration; and that, made more thoughtful and careful, as it would be if the entire responsibility of caring for the poor devolved upon it, would go a long way toward meeting the needs; especially as the needs would be greatly diminished when there had been excluded the artificially generated poverty with which we are surrounded.[5]

Is there a 100 percent guarantee that the proposals offered here will work? No, there is not. Will some people fall through the cracks of the civil society and suffer? Probably. Perfection is not attainable.

What we do know is that there is a 100 percent chance that current policies will fail. They are failing today. People are suffering today.

[5]Herbert Spencer, *The Principles of Ethics* (1897; Indianapolis: Liberty Classics, 1978), vol. 2, pp. 403–4.

To remain with a system that we know has failed, because we fear change, is to prolong their suffering.

Of course, we should not be satisfied as long as one person is left behind. We must constantly strive to ensure that every man, woman, and child has a chance at the American dream. It is the civil society, built on personal responsibility, opportunity, and true compassion, that offers the best hope for the future.

Take one last look at the legacy of welfare. We can do better. For the sake of our future, our society, and our children, we *must* do better.

Appendix: Major Welfare Programs

When most people think of welfare, they think of Aid to Families with Dependent Children (AFDC). Certainly, that program has been at the center of the American social welfare system. However, the welfare state is far, far bigger than any one program. In fact, there are more than 77 major federal welfare programs. A vast majority of those are means tested: the programs provide aid directly to low-income persons in the form of cash, food, housing, medical care, and so forth, with eligibility individually determined on the basis of the recipients' incomes. The remaining programs are either community-targeted programs, which provide aid to communities that have large numbers of poor people or are economically distressed, or categorical programs, eligibility for the benefits of which is based on belonging to a needy or disadvantaged group, such as migrant workers or the homeless. Some welfare programs are well known. Others are largely unheard of.

Two of those programs, AFDC and the Job Opportunities and Basic Skills program, are eliminated by the Personal Responsibility and Work Opportunity Reconciliation Act of 1996. However, the rest of the welfare state is intact. An examination of the remaining programs shows how far we still have to go.

Cash Assistance Programs

Aid to Families with Dependent Children

AFDC, eliminated by the 1996 act, has been the primary cash benefit program targeted to the poor and the program most often considered "welfare." AFDC began in 1935 (it was then called Aid to Dependent Children) as part of the Social Security Act. The program provides cash payments to children of families whose fathers or mothers are absent, incapacitated, deceased, or unemployed and to certain others in the households of those children. All 50 states, the District of Columbia, Puerto Rico, and Guam operate AFDC

Table A.1
AFDC Benefits, 1995
(mother and two children)

Rank	Jurisdiction	Monthly Benefit ($)	Yearly Benefit ($)
1	Alaska	923	11,076
2	Hawaii	712	8,544
3	New York	703	8,436
4	Connecticut	680	8,160
5	Vermont	638	7,656
6	California	607	7,284
7	Massachusetts	579	6,948
8	Rhode Island	554	6,648
9	New Hampshire	550	6,600
10	Washington	546	6,552
11	Minnesota	532	6,384
12	Wisconsin	517	6,204
13	Michigan	489	5,868
14	Oregon	460	5,520
15	Kansas	429	5,148
16	Iowa	426	5,112
17	New Jersey	424	5,088
18	Pennsylvania	421	5,052
19	District of Columbia	420	5,040
20	Maine	418	5,016
21	South Dakota	417	5,004
22	Utah	414	4,968
23	North Dakota	409	4,908
24	Montana	401	4,812
25	Illinois	367	4,404
26	Maryland	366	4,392
27	Nebraska	364	4,368
28	Wyoming	360	4,320
29	New Mexico	357	4,284
30	Colorado	356	4,272
31	Virginia	354	4,248
32	Nevada	348	4,176
33	Arizona	347	4,160

Rank	Jurisdiction	Monthly Benefit ($)	Yearly Benefit ($)
34	Ohio	341	4,092
35	Delaware	338	4,056
36	Oklahoma	324	3,888
37	Idaho	317	3,804
38	Florida	303	3,636
39	Missouri	292	3,504
40	Indiana	288	3,456
41	Georgia	280	3,360
42	North Carolina	272	3,264
43	West Virginia	249	2,988
44	Kentucky	228	2,736
45	Arkansas	204	2,448
46	South Carolina	200	2,400
47	Louisiana	190	2,280
48	Tennessee	185	2,220
49	Texas	184	2,208
50	Alabama	164	1,968
51	Mississippi	120	1,440

SOURCE: Carmen Solomon, "Aid to Families with Dependent Children (AFDC): Need Standards, Payment Standards, and Minimum Benefits," Congressional Research Service Report for Congress no. 95-229 EPW, January 18, 1995, pp. 30–32; and Cato Institute telephone survey of state welfare managers, conducted May–June 1995.

programs. American Samoa has been eligible for the program but has chosen not to participate.[1]

Each state determines its own benefit levels and (within certain federal restrictions) eligibility requirements. Funding comes from both the federal and state governments, with the federal portion varying from a high of 80 percent to a low of 50 percent. On average, the federal government provides 55 percent of funding.[2]

The amount of AFDC benefits a mother and two children receive ranges from a high of $923 per month in Alaska to a low of $120

[1]For an overview of AFDC, see U.S. House of Representatives, Committee on Ways and Means, *1994 Green Book: Background Material and Data on Programs within the Jurisdiction of the Committee on Ways and Means* (Washington: Government Printing Office, 1994), pp. 324–454.

[2]Ibid., p. 324.

per month in Mississippi. The national average AFDC benefit was $399 per month in 1995.[3] Table A.1 ranks jurisdictions by the generosity of their benefits in 1995.

The 1996 act eliminates AFDC. States will administer their own cash assistance programs, which the federal government will fund through block grants.

Supplemental Security Income

Supplemental Security Income (SSI), which was added to the Social Security Act as Title XVI in 1972, began operating in 1974. SSI is a means-tested cash assistance welfare program for low-income aged, blind, and disabled persons. Although administered by the Social Security Administration, SSI is funded from general revenues, not the Social Security payroll tax. A person's entitlement to cash assistance under SSI does not depend on the previous payment of payroll taxes.[4]

Earned Income Tax Credit

Described in detail in Chapter 4, the Earned Income Tax Credit (32 U.S.C.) is a refundable tax credit available to lower income working families and individuals. The EITC is intended to provide a financial incentive for work to lower income working families and families in transition from welfare to work. The maximum available credit in 1995 was $3,110. The credit is phased in when annual income is below $8,400 and phased out starting at $11,290 until it is stopped completely at $26,673 for a family of four.[5]

Title IV Foster Care Program

Under Title IV-E of the Social Security Act, the Foster Care program provides matching funds to the states to help place low-income children in foster homes, public institutions for children, and private

[3]Carmen Solomon, "Aid to Families with Dependent Children (AFDC): Need Standards, Payment Standards, and Minimum Benefits," Congressional Research Service Report for Congress no. 95-229 EPW, January 18, 1995, pp. 30–32; and Cato Institute telephone survey of state welfare managers, conducted May–June 1995.

[4]U.S. House of Representatives, pp. 207–62. For a discussion of abuses in the SSI program, see Christopher Wright, "SSI: Black Hole of the Welfare State," Cato Institute Policy Analysis no. 224, April 27, 1995.

[5]For a complete discussion of the Earned Income Tax Credit, see U.S. Department of the Treasury, Internal Revenue Service, "Earned Income Credit," Catalog no. 15173A, publication 596, 1994. See also U.S. House of Representatives, pp. 699–704.

nonprofit child-care institutions. The amount of funding is based on a state's Medicare matching rate. To be eligible for funding, a child must qualify for AFDC and the parents or guardian of the child must have requested foster care or the child must have been removed from the home pursuant to a judicial determination that remaining in the home would be against the child's welfare.[6]

Refugee and Entrant Assistance

The refugee and entrant assistance programs provide subsidies to state governments for cash, medical assistance, and social services provided to eligible refugees and Cuban and Haitian entrants.[7]

Emergency Assistance to Needy Families with Children

Emergency assistance consists of cash payments, in-kind payments, medical care, and other remedial care. The Social Security Act gives states permission to provide emergency assistance to needy families with children for no more than 30 days per year. Most emergency assistance is given as a result of natural disasters, although other qualifying causes include eviction, homelessness, utility shutoff, loss of employment or strike, and emergency medical needs.[8]

Adoption Assistance

Adoption assistance under Title IV-E of the Social Security Act provides federal matching funds to states to subsidize the costs of adopting low-income children with special needs. In order for adoptive parents to be eligible, the child must be legally free for adoption and must have special needs, as determined by the state, that prevent adoption without assistance payments. Assistance is available from the time of placement for adoption until the age of 18 (or 21 if deemed necessary by the state).[9]

---

[6]U.S. House of Representatives, p. 606; and Office of Management and Budget, *1995 Catalog of Federal Domestic Assistance* (Washington: General Services Administration, 1995), p. 1229.

[7]Robert Rector and William F. Lauber, *America's Failed $5.4 Trillion War on Poverty* (Washington: Heritage Foundation, 1995), pp. 49–50; and Office of Management and Budget, pp. 1191–92, 1210–13.

[8]U.S. House of Representatives, p. 360.

[9]U.S. House of Representatives, p. 618; Rector and Lauber, pp. 50–51; and Office of Management and Budget, pp. 1229–30.

General Assistance to Indians

General assistance to Indians under the Snyder Act of 1921 is designed to provide financial assistance for basic needs (e.g., food, clothing, shelter) of Indians and Alaskan natives who live on or near reservations when such assistance is not available from state or local agencies.[10]

Food Assistance Programs

Food Stamps

As the name implies, the food stamp program provides vouchers to low-income households for the purchase of food. Participating households are expected to spend 30 percent of their monthly cash income on food. The food stamp program contributes the difference between that amount and the amount judged to be sufficient to purchase an adequate diet. The food stamp program operates in all 50 states, the District of Columbia, Guam, Puerto Rico, and the Virgin Islands. Eligibility standards and benefit levels are defined by the federal government and, with the exception of Alaska, Hawaii, and the territories, are uniform nationally. The maximum benefit level is derived from the U.S. Department of Agriculture's "Thrifty Food Plan," varied by household size, and adjusted annually for inflation.[11]

Recipients of AFDC are automatically eligible for food stamps. However, the amount of food stamps received varies depending on the amount of the AFDC payment and the cost of food. As shown in Table A.2, in 1995 a mother with two children would have received the largest amount in food stamps, $422, in Hawaii and the lowest, $192, in Connecticut. The high benefit level in Hawaii is due largely to the high price of food in that state. The low benefit in Connecticut is due largely to the extremely high AFDC benefits that Connecticut provides. The nationwide average was $278.[12]

---

[10]Rector and Lauber, p. 51; and Office of Management and Budget, pp. 327–28.

[11]For an overview of the food stamp program, see U.S. House of Representatives, pp. 757–82.

[12]Solomon, pp. 30–32.

Table A.2
MAXIMUM FOOD STAMP BENEFITS WHILE RECEIVING MAXIMUM
AFDC BENEFITS, 1995
(mother and two children)

Rank	Jurisdiction	Monthly Benefit ($)	Yearly Benefit ($)
1	Hawaii	422	5,064
2	Alabama	295	3,540
	Arkansas	295	3,540
	Delaware	295	3,540
	Florida	295	3,540
	Georgia	295	3,540
	Idaho	295	3,540
	Indiana	295	3,540
	Kentucky	295	3,540
	Louisiana	295	3,540
	Maryland	295	3,540
	Mississippi	295	3,540
	Missouri	295	3,540
	North Carolina	295	3,540
	Ohio	295	3,540
	Oklahoma	295	3,540
	South Carolina	295	3,540
	Tennessee	295	3,540
	Texas	295	3,540
	West Virginia	295	3,540
3	Oregon	293	3,516
4	Arizona	292	3,504
	Nevada	292	3,504
5	Illinois	291	3,492
6	Virginia	290	3,480
7	New Mexico	289	3,468
	Colorado	289	3,468
8	Wyoming	288	3,456
9	Nebraska	287	3,444
10	Alaska	285	3,420
11	Kansas	284	3,408
12	Montana	276	3,312
	New Jersey	276	3,312

continued

Table A.2
MAXIMUM FOOD STAMP BENEFITS WHILE RECEIVING MAXIMUM
AFDC BENEFITS, 1995
(mother and two children), *continued*

Rank	Jurisdiction	Monthly Benefit ($)	Yearly Benefit ($)
13	North Dakota	273	3,276
14	Utah	272	3,264
15	Maine	271	3,252
	South Dakota	271	3,252
16	Pennsylvania	270	3,240
	District of Columbia	270	3,240
17	Rhode Island	268	3,216
	Iowa	268	3,216
18	Washington	258	3,096
19	Michigan	249	2,988
20	Wisconsin	241	2,892
21	Minnesota	236	2,832
22	New Hampshire	231	2,772
23	Massachusetts	222	2,664
24	California	214	2,568
25	Vermont	205	2,460
26	New York	201	2,412
27	Connecticut	192	2,304

SOURCE: Carmen Solomon, "Aid to Families with Dependent Children (AFDC): Need Standards, Payment Standards, and Minimum Benefits," Congressional Research Service Report for Congress no. 95-229 EPW, January 18, 1995, pp. 30–32.

Special Supplemental Food Program for Women, Infants, and Children

The Special Supplemental Food Program for Women, Infants, and Children (WIC), under the Child Nutrition Act of 1966, as amended, provides food assistance and nutritional screening for pregnant and postpartum women and their infants, as well as for low-income children up to the age of five. Beneficiaries receive vouchers for the purchase of specific food items (or occasionally actual foodstuffs). The actual food package differs according to the ages of the children, whether the mother is pregnant, and whether a postpartum mother

Table A.3
WIC BENEFITS, 1994

Rank	Jurisdiction	Monthly Benefit ($)	Yearly Benefit ($)
1	Hawaii	144.18	1,730.16
2	Alaska	114.18	1,370.16
3	Connecticut	105.78	1,269.36
4	New York	103.11	1,237.32
5	Arizona	101.01	1,212.12
6	Washington	99.18	1,189.92
7	Rhode Island	97.59	1,171.08
8	Louisiana	97.23	1,166.76
9	Vermont	96.96	1,163.52
10	North Dakota	95.52	1,146.24
11	Illinois	95.04	1,140.48
12	New Mexico	93.54	1,122.48
13	Wisconsin	93.48	1,121.76
14	Idaho	93.33	1,119.96
15	Virginia	93.12	1,117.44
16	Kansas	92.16	1,105.92
17	Montana	91.98	1,103.76
18	Oklahoma	91.02	1,092.24
19	Alabama	90.93	1,091.16
20	California	90.81	1,089.72
21	District of Columbia	90.33	1,083.96
	Nebraska	90.33	1,083.96
22	Michigan	89.58	1,074.96
	Tennessee	89.58	1,074.96
23	Kentucky	89.31	1,071.72
24	Pennsylvania	89.04	1,068.48
25	Missouri	88.86	1,066.32
26	Colorado	87.84	1,054.08
27	Florida	86.82	1,041.84
28	West Virginia	86.73	1,040.76
29	Delaware	86.22	1,034.64
30	Wyoming	86.19	1,034.28
31	Maryland	85.68	1,028.16
32	Iowa	85.14	1,021.68

continued

Table A.3
WIC BENEFITS, 1994, *continued*

Rank	Jurisdiction	Monthly Benefit ($)	Yearly Benefit ($)
33	New Jersey	85.05	1,020.60
34	Georgia	84.69	1,016.28
35	South Dakota	82.83	993.96
36	Minnesota	82.74	992.88
37	Maine	82.41	988.92
38	Massachusetts	82.35	988.20
39	North Carolina	82.17	986.04
40	Nevada	81.72	980.64
41	Arkansas	81.21	974.52
42	Utah	80.04	960.48
43	New Hampshire	79.95	959.40
44	Oregon	79.17	950.04
45	Indiana	78.60	943.20
46	Ohio	75.81	909.72
47	Texas	75.27	903.24
48	Mississippi	74.01	888.12
49	South Carolina	71.94	863.28

SOURCE: U.S. Department of Agriculture, Food and Consumer Service, "Nutrition Program Facts: Special Supplemental Nutrition Program for Women, Infants, and Children," October 1994, pp. 1–2; U.S. Department of Agriculture, Food and Consumer Service, "National Databank Statistics," June 2, 1995.

is nursing; but food packages generally include milk, cheese, eggs, infant formula, cereals, fruit, and vegetable juices.[13]

The actual benefit a household receives depends on availability of funds and prioritization of need. Table A.3 shows the average benefit in each jurisdiction for a mother with two children in 1994.

School Lunch Program

The School Lunch program, established by the National School Lunch Act of 1946, as amended, is a federally financed program that

[13]U.S. Department of Agriculture, Food and Consumer Service, "Nutrition Program Facts: Special Supplemental Nutrition Program for Women, Infants, and Children," October 1994, pp. 1–2; and Office of Management and Budget, pp. 73–74.

provides cash grants for each free or reduced-price lunch served to needy children in participating schools and residential child-care institutions. For a child to qualify for a free lunch, the family income must be at or below 130 percent of the federal poverty line; for a reduced-price lunch, the family income must be more than 130 percent but not more than 185 percent of the federal poverty line.[14]

School Breakfast Program

The School Breakfast program, created by the Child Nutrition Act of 1966, as amended, provides breakfast for school students through a guaranteed federal subsidy. The amount of the subsidy granted to schools varies depending on need, as determined by the state education agency, and income. Free breakfast is provided to children whose family incomes are at or below 130 percent of the federal poverty line; reduced-price breakfast is provided to children whose family incomes are above 130 percent but not more than 185 percent of the federal poverty line.[15]

Emergency Food Assistance Program

Under the Emergency Food Assistance program of the Temporary Emergency Food Assistance Act of 1983, the federal government is responsible for the cost of providing food commodities and the initial packaging and processing needed to make them appropriate for distribution by local emergency feeding organizations. Benefits provided to the "needy" are commonly provided in the form of packages of commodities for at-home consumption or through soup kitchens and shelters.

States set the criteria for individual eligibility. By law, those eligible must be "needy," and by federal regulation, need is defined as having a low income or receiving federal benefits under a low-income program (such as food stamps or cash welfare). States, however, decide the actual income eligibility criteria.[16]

---

[14]Department of Agriculture, Food and Nutrition Service, "Food Program Update: A Review of FNS Food Assistance Program Activity," 1993; and Office of Management and Budget, pp. 71–72.

[15]Department of Agriculture, Food and Nutrition Service, "Food Program Update"; and Office of Management and Budget, pp. 70–71.

[16]Rector and Lauber, p. 57; and Office of Management and Budget, p. 83.

Nutrition Program for the Elderly

The Older Americans Act of 1965, as amended, established the Nutrition Program for the Elderly, which provides congregate and home-delivered meal service for elderly persons. All people aged at least 60 and their spouses are eligible. In addition, handicapped or disabled persons under 60 who reside in housing facilities occupied by the elderly where congregate meals are provided are also eligible for congregate meals. The program provides at least one meal daily, five or more days per week.[17]

Child and Adult Care Food Program

Under the Child and Adult Care Food Program (established by the National School Lunch Act of 1946, as amended), the federal government, through grants-in-aid and other means, provides food service programs for low-income children and elderly or impaired adults in nonresidential care institutions, family day care homes for children, and some private for-profit centers. The program serves meals and snacks approved by the U.S. Department of Agriculture.[18]

Summer Food Service Program for Children

The Summer Food Service Program for Children (National School Lunch Act of 1946, as amended) provides grants-in-aid for food service programs for needy children during the summer months and at other approved times when area schools are closed for vacation. The number of meals served is limited to two per day, except in summer camps and programs serving primarily migrant children. This aid is targeted to low-income communities, and eligible programs must operate in areas where at least 50 percent of the children are from families that meet the eligibility for free and reduced-price school lunches.[19]

Food Distribution Program on Indian Reservations

The Needy Families Food Distribution Program on Indian reservations, enacted under the Agricultural Act of 1949, as amended, is offered as an alternative to food stamp assistance, if requested by

---

[17]Rector and Lauber, pp. 57–58; and Office of Management and Budget, pp. 83–84.

[18]Rector and Lauber, pp. 58–59; and Office of Management and Budget, p. 74.

[19]U.S. Department of Agriculture, Food and Nutrition Service, "Food Program Update"; and Office of Management and Budget, pp. 76–77.

the appropriate tribal organization. Benefits consist of food packages that comply with U.S. Department of Agriculture guidelines for nutritional adequacy.[20]

Commodity Supplemental Food Program for Mothers, Children, and Elderly Persons

The Commodity Supplemental Food Program, under the Agriculture and Consumer Protection Act of 1973, as amended, aims to improve the nutritional status of low-income mothers, children, and elderly persons through food packages. Persons served include pregnant, postpartum, and breast-feeding women; infants and children up to the age of six; and elderly persons.[21]

Special Milk Program for Children

The Child Nutrition Act of 1966, as amended, provides for the Special Milk program, which makes available funds for free milk for children in participating schools and residential child-care institutions to encourage the consumption of fluid milk by children. This program operates in schools and institutions that do not participate in other federally subsidized meal programs.[22]

Health and Medical Programs

Medicaid

The Medicaid program, Title XIX of the Social Security Act, was begun in 1965 and is the nation's primary program for providing health care to low-income people. Adults and children in low-income families make up nearly 75 percent of Medicaid beneficiaries, but the program also covers many services not included in the Medicare program for the elderly and disabled. The elderly and disabled actually are responsible for the majority (approximately 59 percent) of Medicaid spending because of their intensive use of acute and long-term care services.[23] As is AFDC, Medicaid is administered

---

[20]U.S. Department of Agriculture, Food and Nutrition Service, "Food Program Update," p. 98; and Office of Management and Budget, pp. 81–82.

[21]U.S. Department of Agriculture, Food and Nutrition Service, "Food Program Update," pp. 98–99; and Office of Management and Budget, pp. 79–80.

[22]Ibid., pp. 72–73.

[23]Kaiser Commission on the Future of Medicaid, "Medicaid Facts," San Francisco, February 1995, p. 1.

by the states within broad federal guidelines. Funding is divided between the federal and state governments, with the federal government's share ranging from 50 to 80 percent of the total. On average, the federal government covers about 57 percent of Medicaid costs.[24]

The federal government requires all state Medicaid programs to include coverage for certain services: inpatient hospital services; outpatient hospital services; physicians' services; laboratory and x-ray services; nursing facility services for adults; family planning services; rural health clinic services; nurse-midwife services; prenatal care; federally qualified health center services; early and periodic screening, diagnostic, and treatment services for children under age 21, including treatment for conditions identified in screening; and services of certified pediatric or family nurse-practitioners. However, states have the option of paying for additional services, ranging from mental health services to dental care, from eyeglasses to prescription drugs. Some states, such as Wisconsin, have chosen to cover most optional services. Others, such as Delaware and Louisiana, cover relatively few optional services.[25]

Maternal and Child Health Services Block Grant

Title V of the Social Security Act, the Maternal and Child Care Health Services Block Grant, supports inpatient, preventive, and primary health care services for low-income mothers, infants, and children and children with special health care needs.[26]

Community Health Centers

The Community Health Centers program, under the Public Health Service Act of 1987, as amended, supports the development and operation of community and migrant primary care service delivery centers that provide medically underserved populations with a range of primary health services including diagnostic, treatment, preventive, emergency, transportation, and preventive dental services.[27]

---

[24]For a complete overview of the Medicaid program, see U.S. House of Representatives, pp. 783–819.

[25]Health Care Financing Administration, "Medicaid Services by State," October 1, 1994.

[26]Rector and Lauber, p. 53; and Office of Management and Budget, pp. 1383–84.

[27]Rector and Lauber, p. 54; and Office of Management and Budget, pp. 1036–37.

Migrant Health Centers

The Migrant Health Centers program of the Public Health Service Act, as amended, is a federally financed program that supports the development and operation of health centers and projects that provide primary health care services, supplemental health services, and environmental health services to migrant and seasonal farm workers and their families. In addition to federal aid, some migrant health centers also seek aid from state and local governments, patient fees, and programs such as Medicare and Medicaid.[28]

Medicare

Many people with incomes below the federal poverty level have dual eligibility for Medicare and Medicaid. Under a provision termed the "Medicaid Buy-In," a state government may shift a Medicaid-eligible recipient into the Medicare program. Under the buy-in provision, the state uses Medicaid funds to pay for the individual's insurance premium for Part B Medicare coverage (and in some cases the premium for Part A coverage as well). The individual then receives health care coverage as part of the Medicare system while the state government continues to use Medicaid funds to pay for health costs not covered by Medicare, such as copayments and deductibles.[29]

Housing and Energy Programs

Section 8 Housing

Housing Assistance Payments, created by section 8 of the Housing Act of 1937, as amended, can be subdivided into three separate programs: the section 8 Rental Voucher Program, the section 8 Rental Certificate Program, and the section 8 Moderate Rehabilitation Program.[30]

A family is considered eligible for housing assistance if its household income falls below 50 percent of the median family income for a family of that size in the county in which they reside. AFDC payments are counted as income, but food stamps and other forms

---

[28]Rector and Lauber, pp. 54–55; and Office of Management and Budget, pp. 1128–29.

[29]Rector and Lauber, p. 55. See also U.S. House of Representatives, pp. 123, 130–31.

[30]For a description of Section 8 housing and rental assistance programs, see Office of Management and Budget, pp. 313–16.

Table A.4
Housing Assistance Benefits, 1994

Rank	Jurisdiction	High Monthly Benefit ($)	Low Monthly Benefit ($)	Median Monthly Benefit ($)	Median Annual Benefit ($)
1	District of Columbia	718.00	718.00	718.00	8,616.00
2	Massachusetts	1,065.30	342.30	703.80	8,445.60
3	Hawaii	896.40	473.40	684.90	8,218.80
4	Connecticut	915.00	421.00	668.00	8,016.00
5	New Jersey	808.80	517.80	663.30	7,959.60
6	Rhode Island	630.80	482.80	556.80	6,681.60
7	California	821.90	246.90	534.40	6,412.80
8	Maryland	734.20	243.20	488.70	5,864.40
9	Alaska	707.10	239.10	473.10	5,677.20
10	New York	794.10	152.10	473.10	5,677.20
11	Virginia	737.80	196.80	467.30	5,607.60
12	New Hampshire	543.00	377.00	460.00	5,520.00
13	Delaware	524.60	381.60	453.10	5,437.20
14	Florida	674.10	199.10	436.60	5,239.20
15	Nevada	580.60	281.60	431.10	5,173.20
16	Maine	550.60	297.60	424.10	5,089.20
17	Colorado	628.20	196.20	412.20	4,946.40
18	South Carolina	501.00	251.00	376.00	4,512.00
19	Pennsylvania	561.70	165.70	363.70	4,364.40
20	Arizona	513.90	207.90	360.90	4,330.80
21	Wyoming	500.00	219.00	359.50	4,314.00
22	Illinois	547.90	150.90	349.40	4,192.80
23	New Mexico	519.90	176.90	348.40	4,180.80
24	Texas	511.80	184.80	348.30	4,179.60
25	Idaho	490.90	192.90	341.90	4,102.80
26	Utah	498.80	184.80	341.80	4,101.60
27	Indiana	430.60	234.60	332.60	3,991.20
28	Mississippi	455.00	210.00	332.50	3,990.00
29	Michigan	497.30	163.30	330.30	3,963.60
30	Washington	493.20	159.20	326.20	3,914.40
31	North Carolina	463.40	187.40	325.40	3,904.80

Rank	Jurisdiction	High Monthly Benefit ($)	Low Monthly Benefit ($)	Median Monthly Benefit ($)	Median Annual Benefit ($)
32	Vermont	452.60	185.60	319.10	3,829.20
33	Georgia	505.00	132.00	318.50	3,822.00
34	Arkansas	400.80	226.80	313.80	3,765.60
35	Ohio	408.70	212.70	310.70	3,728.40
36	Louisiana	403.00	214.00	308.50	3,702.00
37	Kentucky	416.60	189.60	303.10	3,637.20
38	West Virginia	403.30	201.30	302.30	3,627.60
39	Alabama	424.80	168.80	296.80	3,561.60
40	Wisconsin	441.90	147.90	294.90	3,538.80
41	Tennessee	456.50	127.50	292.00	3,504.00
42	Minnesota	437.40	144.40	290.90	3,490.80
43	Oregon	391.00	169.00	280.00	3,360.00
44	Missouri	390.40	169.40	279.90	3,358.80
45	Iowa	385.20	163.20	274.20	3,290.40
46	Oklahoma	332.80	154.80	243.80	2,925.60
47	South Dakota	342.90	139.90	241.40	2,896.80
48	Kansas	364.30	117.30	240.80	2,889.60
49	Nebraska	381.80	84.80	233.30	2,799.60
50	Montana	297.70	161.70	229.70	2,756.40
51	North Dakota	311.30	102.30	206.80	2,481.60

SOURCE: "HUD Fair Market Rent Values by County," *Federal Register* 58, no. 189 (October 1993): S1410–86.

of public assistance are not.[31] Although a family may be eligible for housing assistance, whether they receive benefits depends on, among other things, the availability of housing units and the amount of funding appropriated for rental assistance.

Section 8 rent payments are based on fair market rental values, determined county by county.[32] Table A.4 shows the high, low, and median section 8 benefit for each jurisdiction in 1994.

[31]U.S. Department of Housing and Urban Development, Office of Policy Development and Research, Research Utilization Division, *Fiscal Year 1995 Income Limits for Low-Income and Very-Low Income Families under the Housing Act of 1937* (Washington: U.S. Department of Housing and Urban Development, 1995), pp. 2–4.

[32]24 CFR parts 813, 888.

Public and Indian Housing

This program provides aid through authorized local Public Housing Authorities to lower income families in conventional public housing. Families include individuals aged 62 or older, the disabled, and the handicapped.[33]

Section 502 Rural Housing Loans

Section 502 of the Housing Act of 1949, as amended, provides direct loans to lower income rural families to facilitate the purchase, construction, sanitation, or repair of a home if a family is unable to obtain credit on reasonable terms. Examples of acceptable loan uses are to provide adequate sewage facilities or a safe water supply, or both; for weatherization; to purchase essential equipment normally sold with dwelling units; or in some cases to purchase an adequate site on which to construct a dwelling.[34]

Sections 515 and 521 Rural Rental Housing Loans

Rural rental housing loans (sections 515 and 521 of the Housing Act of 1949, as amended) are intended to make available rental and cooperative housing for low- or moderate-income families, handicapped persons, or persons over the age of 62 who reside in rural areas. Loans can be used to construct, purchase, improve, or repair rental or cooperative housing or to develop manufactured housing projects.[35]

Section 521 Rural Rental Assistance Payments

Rural Rental Assistance Payments lower the rent paid by low-income families occupying Rural Rental Housing (section 515 of the Housing Act of 1949, as amended), Rural Cooperative Housing (section 514), and Farm Labor Housing (section 516). The program is financed through the Farmers Home Administration, which makes rental assistance payments to the owners of such housing. Rents are intended to be reduced for low-income senior citizens and families whose rents exceed 30 percent of their monthly adjusted family income or 10 percent of monthly income and for welfare recipients

[33]Office of Management and Budget, pp. 309–10.
[34]Ibid., pp. 48–49.
[35]Ibid., pp. 50–51.

whose monthly rent exceeds the portion of welfare payments designated for housing.[36]

Adjustable Rate Mortgage

Under the National Housing Act of 1949, as amended, the U.S. Department of Housing and Urban Development provides mortgage insurance for adjustable rate mortgages. Individuals or families intending to occupy the property may use the loan to purchase, construct, or refinance a home.[37]

Indian Housing Improvement Grants

This program, enacted under the Snyder Act of 1921, is mainly devoted to housing improvement, but funds are also used for housing construction in cases in which no other program will meet the need. Applicants must be Indians or Alaskan natives living in substandard housing. Priority is given to families according to a point system based on six factors: annual income, family size, overcrowded living conditions, age of family members, handicap or disability, and potential ownership of a house financed by the HUD Indian Housing Authority, which results in negative points.[38]

Section 504 Rural Housing Loans and Grants

Section 504 of the Housing Act of 1949, as amended, provides direct loans and project grants to very low-income rural homeowners to allow them to remove health hazards and to make necessary safety repairs to their homes. Loans have a 20-year term at a 1 percent interest rate. In 1992 the average loan amount was $4,400, and grants averaged $4,300. Loans and grants may be combined; however, the total may not exceed $15,000.[39]

Sections 514 and 516 Farm Labor Housing Loans and Grants

Under sections 514 and 516 of the Housing Act of 1949, as amended, individual farm owners, farm owners' associations, local broad-based nonprofit organizations, Indian tribes, and agencies or subdivisions of state or local governments can obtain low-interest

---

[36]Ibid., pp. 55–56.
[37]Ibid., pp. 266–67.
[38]Rector and Lauber, p. 65; and Office of Management and Budget, pp. 330–31.
[39]Rector and Lauber, pp. 65–66; and Office of Management and Budget, pp. 52–53.

loans to provide low-rent housing for farm laborers. Applicants must demonstrate a need for housing for farm labor and must show that other credit, which would make housing available to farm workers at reasonable rates, cannot be obtained.[40]

Section 523 Rural Housing Self-Help Technical Assistance Grants

Technical Assistance Grants, under the Housing Act of 1949, as amended, are distributed by the Farmers Home Administration to state and local governments and public and private not-for-profit organizations to pay a portion or all of the cost of developing programs of technical and supervisory assistance for families that are building their own homes by the mutual self-help method. Construction costs are reduced as groups of 6 to 10 families join forces, each contributing at least 700 hours of labor to building homes for group members.[41]

Section 533 Rural Housing Preservation Grants for Low-Income Rural Homeowners

Section 533 of the Housing Act of 1949, as amended, provides grants to elderly, very low-income rural homeowners to use to repair or rehabilitate their housing in order to bring it up to code standards. Grants are made to very low-income homeowners, aged 62 or older, whose income is so low that they would be unable to pay back any part of a loan. Grants of up to $5,000 may be awarded.[42]

Energy Aid Programs

Low-Income Home Energy Assistance Program

The Low-Income Home Energy Assistance Program (LIHEAP), under the Low-Income Home Energy Assistance Act of 1981, as amended, actually consists of a variety programs designed to help poor individuals meet their heating and energy costs. LIHEAP funds include federal block grant allotments, federal emergency contingent allotments, a federal leveraging incentive award, and state funds. Funds are available to the states, the District of Columbia, Indian tribal governments, and some territories.

---

[40]Rector and Lauber, p. 66; and Office of Management and Budget, pp. 45–46.

[41]Rector and Lauber, pp. 66–67; and Office of Management and Budget, pp. 53–54.

[42]Rector and Lauber, pp. 67–68; and Office of Management and Budget, pp. 56–57.

Table A.5
Utilities Assistance, Fiscal Year 1994

Rank	Jurisdiction	Average Monthly Benefit ($)	Average Annual Benefit ($)
1	Texas	83.33	999.96
2	Vermont	60.92	731.04
3	Minnesota	59.83	717.96
4	Connecticut	52.67	632.04
5	Mississippi	51.83	621.96
6	Wisconsin	51.25	615.00
7	South Dakota	51.08	612.96
8	Virginia	48.67	584.04
9	New Jersey	48.58	582.96
10	North Dakota	48.25	579.00
11	Alaska	45.92	551.04
12	Illinois	45.00	540.00
13	Iowa	44.42	533.04
14	Louisiana	44.17	530.04
15	Colorado	43.00	516.00
16	Rhode Island	42.83	513.96
17	Kansas	40.00	480.00
	Tennessee	40.00	480.00
18	New Hampshire	38.33	459.96
19	Wyoming	37.92	455.04
20	Indiana	36.67	440.04
21	Nebraska	36.42	437.04
22	Kentucky	36.08	432.96
23	Montana	35.17	422.04
24	Nevada	35.08	420.96
25	Massachusetts	34.75	417.00
26	Michigan	34.08	408.96
27	Pennsylvania	32.83	393.96
28	District of Columbia	32.75	393.00
29	Idaho	32.67	392.04
30	Washington	32.50	390.00
31	Georgia	32.33	379.96

continued

Table A.5
UTILITIES ASSISTANCE, FISCAL YEAR 1994, *continued*

Rank	Jurisdiction	Average Monthly Benefit ($)	Average Annual Benefit ($)
32	California	30.67	368.04
	Delaware	30.67	368.04
33	Missouri	30.42	365.04
34	New York	29.75	357.00
35	Alabama	29.00	348.00
36	Utah	28.58	342.96
37	Ohio	28.42	341.04
38	Oregon	27.08	324.96
39	Hawaii	25.83	309.96
40	Maryland	24.42	293.04
41	South Carolina	22.17	266.04
42	Maine	21.67	260.04
43	West Virginia	21.50	258.00
44	Arizona	20.00	240.00
45	Oklahoma	18.92	227.04
46	Florida	17.83	213.96
47	North Carolina	17.58	210.96
48	Arkansas	16.33	195.96
49	New Mexico	12.08	144.96

SOURCE: U.S. Department of Health and Human Services, Administration for Children and Families, Office of Community Services, Energy Assistance Division, "Results of Summer Telephone Survey of Fiscal Year 1994 Low-Income Home Energy Assistance Program (LIHEAP) Estimates," LIHEAP Information Memorandum, March 14, 1995.

LIHEAP funds operate several programs including heating assistance, cooling assistance, winter crisis assistance, and summer crisis assistance. Because states may consolidate those programs and some states are not eligible for crisis assistance in a given year, states may operate from one to four energy assistance programs. Although originally conceived as a program to provide heating fuel, the program has expanded into a full range of energy assistance. A large portion of the program's funds actually goes to provide air conditioning.

Eligible beneficiaries include households whose income does not exceed the greater of 150 percent of the poverty level or 60 percent of the median income in the state and households receiving AFDC, SSI, food stamps, or certain income-tested veterans' benefits. States may establish lower eligibility standards, but income eligibility standards may not be set below 110 percent of the poverty level.[43]

The actual benefit a household receives varies according to availability of funds and prioritization of need. Table A.5 shows the average benefit per recipient household in each jurisdiction in 1994.

Weatherization Assistance

The Energy Conservation and Production Act of 1976 provides low-income persons full federal funding for weatherization and insulation. States' average expenditure per dwelling may not exceed $1,697, adjusted annually for inflation.[44]

Education and Training Programs

Pell Grants

Pell grants, under the Higher Education Act of 1965, as amended, provide monetary assistance to undergraduate students enrolled in a higher education program on at least a half-time basis. Eligibility is limited to U.S. citizens or eligible noncitizens enrolled in participating schools and making satisfactory academic progress.[45]

Head Start

Head Start, begun in 1965 pursuant to the Economic Opportunity Act of 1964, provides a wide range of services to low-income children aged five and under, including instruction in cognitive language development; medical, dental, and mental health services (including screening and immunization); and nutritional and social services. At least 90 percent of children enrolled in the program must be from

---

[43]U.S. Department of Health and Human Services, Administration for Children and Families, Office of Community Services, Energy Assistance Division, "Results of Summer Telephone Survey of Fiscal Year 1994 Low-Income Home Energy Assistance Program (LIHEAP) Estimates," LIHEAP Information Memorandum, March 14, 1995; and Office of Management and Budget, pp. 1193–95.

[44]Rector and Lauber, p. 69; and Office of Management and Budget, pp. 760–61.

[45]Rector and Lauber, p. 69; and Office of Management and Budget, pp. 851–52.

families with incomes below the poverty line. In practice, approximately 55 percent of Head Start children are from families receiving AFDC.[46]

Title 1 Grants to Local Education Authorities for Educationally Deprived Children under the Elementary and Secondary Education Act

Title 1 grants are used by state and local educational agencies to supply educational services not normally provided by states and localities in order to meet the needs of educationally disadvantaged children. Grant eligibility is restricted to state and local education agencies in areas with the highest concentrations of children from low-income families.[47]

Supplemental Educational Opportunity Grants

Supplemental educational opportunity grants, under the Higher Education Act of 1965, as amended, provide assistance to postsecondary institutions to help students demonstrating financial need pay for their educations.[48]

Chapter One Migrant Education Program

The Migrant Education Program, authorized by the Elementary and Secondary Education Act of 1965, distributes funds to state educational agencies to use to provide programs for children in families headed by a migrant agricultural worker or a migratory fisherman. The amount of the grant is based on the number of eligible children and the average per pupil expenditure in the various states.[49]

Special Programs for Students from Disadvantaged Backgrounds

The Higher Education Act of 1965, as amended, provides five special low-income educational programs: Upward Bound, Student Support Service, Talent Search, Educational Opportunity Centers, and the Ronald E. McNair Postbaccalaureate Achievement Awards.

---

[46]U.S. House of Representatives, p. 834; and Office of Management and Budget, pp. 1215–16. Although Head Start is widely praised, there is evidence that it actually has little impact on child development. See John Hood, "Caveat Emptor: The Head Start Scam," Cato Institute Policy Analysis no. 187, December 18, 1992.

[47]Rector and Lauber, pp. 70–71; and Office of Management and Budget, pp. 811–12.

[48]Rector and Lauber, p. 71.

[49]Ibid., pp. 71–72; and Office of Management and Budget, p. 812.

In general, at least two-thirds of beneficiaries must be "low income."[50]

State Student Incentive Grants for Needy Students

State Student Incentive Grants under the Higher Education Act of 1965, as amended, provide funds to postsecondary students who demonstrate substantial financial need. Funds may be disbursed as grants or provided as work-study financial assistance to students. Federal formula grants must be matched by state funds.[51]

Fellowships for Graduate and Professional Study for Disadvantaged Minorities

Fellowships for graduate and professional study, created by the Higher Education Act of 1965, are available through institutions for higher education to graduate students in financial need. Two kinds of fellowships are supported under the program. Students from groups underrepresented in graduate or professional programs are eligible for Graduate and Professional Opportunity Fellowships. Those who hope to pursue careers in fields of high national priority or in public interest fields are eligible for Public Sector Education Fellowships. To qualify for either fellowship, applicants must show financial need.[52]

Follow Through

The Follow Through Act of 1983 provides education and nutrition services to children in the primary grades from low-income families. Family members are encouraged to participate.[53]

Even Start

Even Start of the Elementary and Secondary Education Act of 1965, as amended, establishes family-centered education projects that encourage parents to take part in the education of their children.[54]

---

[50]Rector and Lauber, pp. 72–73; and Office of Management and Budget, pp. 840–43, 852, 925.

[51]Rector and Lauber, pp. 73–74; and Office of Management and Budget, pp. 852–53.

[52]Rector and Lauber, pp. 73–74; and Office of Management and Budget, pp. 860–61.

[53]Rector and Lauber, p. 74; and Office of Management and Budget, pp. 814–15.

[54]Rector and Lauber, pp. 74–75; and Office of Management and Budget, pp. 921–23.

Training for Disadvantaged Adults and Youth (JTPA II-A) Block Grant

Title II-A of the Job Training Partnership Act of 1982, as amended, provides education and training services to participants who are deemed "economically disadvantaged." Services include on-the-job training, work experience, and support services. Participants includes people with limited English-speaking ability, displaced homemakers, school dropouts, teenage parents, the handicapped, older workers, veterans, offenders, alcoholics, and addicts.[55]

Summer Youth Employment Program (JTPA II-B)

Title II-B of the Job Training Partnership Act of 1982, as amended, which is fully funded by the federal government, provides education, training, and summer jobs that pay the applicable minimum wage to "economically disadvantaged" youths. Those youths are either unemployed, underemployed, or in school and aged 16–21. At local discretion, youths aged 14–15 may also be included.[56]

Job Corps (JTPA-IV)

Title IV of the Job Training Partnership Act is a program, funded fully by the federal government, that provides basic education, vocational skills training, counseling, work experience, and health services to "economically disadvantaged" youths. The recipients must be aged 14 through 21 and live in a "disorienting" environment. Job Corps enrollees live in residential centers where they are helped to accomplish regular school work, qualify for other suitable training programs, satisfy armed forces requirements, or secure and hold "meaningful employment."[57]

Senior Community Service Employment Program

Title V of the Older Americans Act of 1965 makes eligible for the Senior Community Service Employment Program (SCSEP) persons aged at least 55 whose income does not exceed 125 percent of the poverty line. Participants are placed in part-time community service jobs subsidized by the federal government and, when possible, placed in unsubsidized jobs. SCSEP workers transport the elderly; assist them with household chores; and also assist in libraries,

---

[55]Rector and Lauber, p. 75; and Office of Management and Budget, pp. 447–48.
[56]Rector and Lauber, pp. 75–76; and Office of Management and Budget, pp. 447–48.
[57]Ibid.

schools, and nutrition programs. Upon placement, SCSEP workers receive either the prevailing wage or the applicable federal minimum, whichever is higher.[58]

Job Opportunities and Basic Skills Training

The Family Support Act of 1988 established the Job Opportunities and Basic Skills (JOBS) training program, which replaced the work incentive (WIN) program and other provisions of prior law. The JOBS program is administered at the federal level by the assistant secretary for children and families in the Department of Health and Human Services and at the state level by the state welfare agency. The state welfare agency may offer services and activities directly or through arrangements or contracts with Job Training Partnership Act administrative entities, state and local educational agencies, and other public agencies or private organizations (including community-based organizations).

Services have included (1) education activities, including high school or equivalent education, basic and remedial education to achieve a basic literacy level, and education for individuals with limited English proficiency; (2) job skills training; (3) job readiness activities; (4) job development and job placement; and (5) supportive services.[59] The JOBS program is eliminated by the Personal Responsibility and Work Opportunity Reconciliation Act of 1996.

Foster Grandparents

The Foster Grandparents Program (FGP) of the Domestic Volunteer Service Act of 1973, as amended, provides both part-time volunteer service opportunities for low-income persons and person-to-person support services to children with special or exceptional needs, with special emphasis on terminally ill children, juvenile delinquents, pregnant teenagers, and runaway youth. FGP grants are used to provide foster grandparents with stipends, insurance, transportation, and meals during service to offset the costs of volunteering.[60]

---

[58]Rector and Lauber, pp. 76–77; and Office of Management and Budget, pp. 441–42.
[59]U.S. House of Representatives, pp. 337–43.
[60]Office of Management and Budget, pp. 1393–94; and Rector and Lauber, pp. 77–78.

Senior Companions

The Senior Companions Program of the Domestic Volunteer Service Act of 1973, as amended, provides both volunteer service opportunities for low-income older persons and community care for adults with mental or physical impairments. Volunteers must be aged 60 or older with incomes below 125 percent of the federal poverty line. They provide community-based support to adults, primarily older persons with mental, emotional, and physical impairments. The law requires a stipend for low-income volunteers plus transportation and meal costs.[61]

Migrant and Seasonal Farm Workers Training Program

Title IV of the Job Training Partnership Act of 1982 authorizes the Migrant and Seasonal Farmworker Program, which provides federal funds for job training, job search assistance, and other supportive services such as health care, temporary shelter, meals, and emergency assistance for those individuals who suffer chronic seasonal unemployment and underemployment in the agricultural industry.[62]

Indian and Native American Employment and Training Program

The Native American Employment and Training Program provides federal funds to support a set of comprehensive job training services for low-income, underemployed, and unemployed persons of Native American descent. In addition to employment and training programs, funding may be used for day care, drug and alcohol counseling, transportation and relocation assistance, and similar services.[63]

Social Services and Community Development Programs

Social Services Block Grant (Title XX of the Social Security Act of 1935, as amended)

The Social Services Block Grant provides federal funds to states and insular areas for a wide variety of programs to assist low-income persons. Each state, within specific statutory limitations, determines

[61]Rector and Lauber, p. 78; and Office of Management and Budget, pp. 1395–96.
[62]Rector and Lauber, pp. 78–79; and Office of Management and Budget, pp. 444–45.
[63]Rector and Lauber, p. 79; and Office of Management and Budget, pp. 448–50.

which social services are best suited to the needs of the individuals residing in the state.[64]

Community Services Block Grant

The Community Services Block Grant (CSBG), under the Omnibus Budget Reconciliation Act of 1981, makes federal funds available to states, insular areas, and Indian tribes and tribal organizations to help address the causes of poverty in communities. States and other primary grantees may provide the services they feel best meet the needs of the low-income population in individual states. In general, CSBG services seek improvements in employment, education, budgeting, housing, nutrition, energy, emergency services, and health.[65]

Legal Services Corporation

The Legal Services Corporation (LSC) provides federal funding for support programs that offer legal services in civil proceedings to low-income persons. LSC provides legal aid in the following areas of law: family, employment, consumer, housing, civil rights, and public welfare.[66]

Emergency Shelter Program

The Emergency Shelter Program, enacted under the Stewart B. McKinney Homeless Assistance Act of 1987, as amended, provides funds to public and private organizations that provide shelter and other essentials such as food assistance to the homeless.[67]

Title X Family Planning

Title X of the Public Health Service Act of 1987, as amended, provides grants to public and nonprofit private organizations to provide family-planning services. The program provides services and information to help people, particularly those from low-income families, plan how many children to have and when to have them. Services provided include counseling, pregnancy testing, physical examinations, laboratory services, screening for sexually transmitted

[64]Rector and Lauber, p. 79; and Office of Management and Budget, pp. 1232–33.
[65]Rector and Lauber, p. 80; and Office of Management and Budget, pp. 1195–96.
[66]Rector and Lauber, p. 80.
[67]Rector and Lauber, p. 81; and Office of Management and Budget, pp. 282–83.

diseases, infertility services, sterilization, and provision of contraceptives.[68]

Volunteers in Service to America (VISTA)

VISTA, enacted under the Domestic Volunteer Service Act of 1973, as amended, employs volunteers on projects intended to directly benefit low-income persons, including youth programs that combat illiteracy and drug abuse, food distribution, aiding the homeless, and addressing the needs of elderly and handicapped persons.[69]

Title III-B Supportive Services for the Aging

Title III of the Older Americans Act of 1965 is a federally funded program that covers some of the costs of supportive services for the elderly. Some of the services provided include information, referrals to public and private programs, transportation, employment services, legal aid counseling, health education and screening, home repairs and maintenance, and in-home services such as homemaker or home health aids to avoid institutionalization. All persons 60 years old or older are eligible. However, particular attention is directed toward those persons with the greatest economic and social need.[70]

Day Care Assistance for Families "At Risk" of Welfare Dependence

The federal government provides matching grants to states for the at-risk child-care program, pursuant to the Omnibus Budget Reconciliation Act of 1990. The program provides day care aid to families at risk of becoming dependent on AFDC. Under the program, children receive subsidized care, for which their families must pay a fee based on a sliding schedule set by the state (unless their income is below the poverty level). States are free to provide child care by any method they choose, including direct provision, vouchers, contracts, reimbursement, and cash advance.[71]

---

[68]Rector and Lauber, pp. 81–82; and Office of Management and Budget, pp. 1111–12.

[69]Rector and Lauber, p. 82; and Office of Management and Budget, pp. 1394–95.

[70]Rector and Lauber, pp. 82–83; and Office of Management and Budget, pp. 996–97.

[71]U.S. House of Representatives, pp. 550–56; and Office of Management and Budget, pp. 1203–4.

Child Care and Development Block Grant

The Child Care and Development Block Grant, under the Omnibus Budget Reconciliation Act of 1990, is a federally funded program that provides child-care services, early childhood development, and before- and after-school social services for children. Special priority for the program is given to children in very low-income families and to those with special needs. Under federal law, parents are given the choice of obtaining care from a state provider or using certificates that are payable for child care from a provider of their choice.[72]

Child Care for Recipients (and Ex-Recipients) of AFDC

Under this program, established by Title IV-A of the Social Security Act of 1935, as amended, AFDC recipients receive free day care and ex-recipients enrolled in the "transitional" program receive subsidized day care. The law allows states to guarantee day care by direct provision or through the use of vouchers, reimbursement, or other "appropriate" arrangements. All AFDC recipients who need child care in order to engage in schooling, work, or training are eligible for the "regular" child-care program. Families who need day care in order for a family member to accept a job offer or retain a present job, and who lost AFDC eligibility because of increased hours of work or higher earnings, are eligible for the "transitional" program. Transitional child-care benefits begin with the first month of eligibility and continue for 12 consecutive months.[73]

Economic Development Administration

The Economic Development Administration was set up by the Public Works and Economic Development Act of 1965 to promote long-term economic development and assist in the construction of public works and development facilities needed to initiate and encourage the creation of permanent jobs in the private sector in areas experiencing severe economic distress.[74]

Appalachian Regional Development Program

The Appalachian Regional Development Program, created under the Appalachian Regional Development Act of 1965, as amended,

[72]Rector and Lauber, pp. 574–78; and Office of Management and Budget, pp. 1204–5.
[73]Ibid., pp. 548–49.
[74]Rector and Lauber, p. 86.

aims to stimulate substantial public investments in public services and facilities that will attract private-sector investments and start Appalachia on the road to social and economic development. A multitude of programs is offered to this "distressed" region, including community development, highway development, health care delivery, housing, and child-care services, among other things.[75]

Legalization Impact Aid

Under the Immigration Reform and Control Act (IRCA) of 1986, a temporary program of State Legalization Impact Assistance Grants was established. Those grants relieve the states and localities of health, welfare, and education costs associated with the legalization of aliens under IRCA.[76]

State Programs

In addition to the federal welfare programs listed above, all 50 states fund and operate their own welfare programs. The two most common are described below. However, this is by no means a comprehensive list. States offer a wide variety of programs. For example, Massachusetts provides a clothing allowance for poor children.

General Assistance

Also called General Relief in some states, General Assistance provides cash payments to low-income persons who do not qualify for AFDC, SSI, or Emergency Assistance to Needy Families with Children. In practice, that usually means individuals without children, often unemployed single men. Benefits and eligibility standards vary widely from state to state.[77] Michigan has abolished its General Assistance program and Massachusetts has restricted its program to disabled persons.

General Assistance Medical Care

Similar to the cash General Assistance program, General Assistance Medical Care provides medical assistance to poor individuals who do not qualify for Medicaid. Eligibility and the services provided vary widely from state to state.[78]

[75]Ibid.
[76]Ibid., p. 87.
[77]Rector and Lauber, p. 48.
[78]Ibid., p. 52.

Local Programs

Many counties and municipalities also finance and operate welfare programs, usually providing short-term cash, medical, and shelter assistance to individuals who do not qualify for federal programs. However, some assistance may be in addition to that provided by federal and state programs.[79]

---

[79]See, for example, Thomas Carroll, "The Real Price Tag of New York's Welfare Benefits," Empire Foundation/Change-NY, Albany, New York, August 1994.

Index

Acs, Gregory, 80
African-Americans
  charitable institutions of, 41–44
  incomes of immigrant and native-
    born, 26
  labor market barriers, 165–67
  out-of-wedlock births, 70, 81–82
  poverty rates, 11–16, 20, 24–28
  racism and, 24–25
Agricultural price supports, 172
Agriculture and Consumer Protection
  Act (1973), 197
Aid to Dependent Children (ADC)
  federal funding, 59
  under Social Security Act (1935),
    49–51, 185
  See also Aid to Families with
    Dependent Children (AFDC)
Aid to Families with Dependent
  Children (AFDC)
  cash payments and benefits (1995),
    185–88
  child-care provisions, 215
  expansion of services, 52–53
  family cap, New Jersey, 82–83
  federal funding, 55, 59
  food stamp eligibility, 190–92
  Head Start eligibility, 208
  as part of total value of welfare, 81
  under recent welfare reform
    legislation (1996), 185, 188
  Republican proposals for, 60
  under Social Security Act, 49
  and teenage childbearing, 73–74
  total spending for, 63
Allgood, Clayton, 169
Almy, Frederic, 36, 41, 147
America Works, 119
Anderson, Martin, 120
Anderson v. Burson (1968), 54n
Anti-poverty programs
  current federal, 62–63
  effect and intent of, 151–52
  Johnson administration, 52–54, 57
  Nixon administration, 54

Appalachian Regional Development
  Program, 215–16
Aramony, William, 141
Auletta, Ken, 89

Bane, Mary Jo, 59
Bartlett, Bruce, 7, 151
Bastiat, Frederic, 153–54
Beard, Sam, 156, 161
Berstam, Mikhail, 79
Better Child Care Act (1990), 102
Births, out-of-wedlock
  to African-Americans, 81–82
  noneconomic outcomes of, 74–76
  relation to receipt of welfare, 76–80
  relation to welfare availability, 132
  rise in number (1960–90), 70–73
Blankenhorn, David, 91
Block grants
  Child Care and Development Block
    Grant, 215
  Community Services Block Grant,
    213
  disadvantages and inefficiency of,
    124–25
  entitlement status with, 60–61
  maternal and child health services,
    198
  purpose of state-level, 123–24
  in recent welfare reform legislation
    (1996), 61–62
  Social Services Block Grant, 212–13
Brock, William, 50
Browning, Edgar, 108
Brown v. Board of Education (1954), 176
Burkhauser, Richard, 30
Burroughs, Charles, 35n
Burtless, Gary, 133–34
Bush administration, 56

Capital gains tax, 162
Card-Krueger minimum wage study,
  167–68n42
Carter administration, 54

219

225

About the Author

Michael Tanner is director of health and welfare studies at the Cato Institute in Washington, D.C. Before joining Cato, he served as director of research for the Georgia Public Policy Foundation in Atlanta. Tanner also spent five years as legislative director with the American Legislative Exchange Council. He is the author of six previous books on health and welfare reform.

His work has appeared in such publications as the *Wall Street Journal*, the *Baltimore Sun*, the *Washington Times*, the *Indianapolis Star*, the *Cleveland Plain Dealer*, the *Detroit News*, the *Portland Oregonian*, *USA Today*, and the *National Review*. A frequent media guest, he has appeared on *ABC World News Tonight*, *CBS Evening News*, *NBC Dateline*, and *Good Morning America*, among other programs.

Cato Institute

Founded in 1977, the Cato Institute is a public policy research foundation dedicated to broadening the parameters of policy debate to allow consideration of more options that are consistent with the traditional American principles of limited government, individual liberty, and peace. To that end, the Institute strives to achieve greater involvement of the intelligent, concerned lay public in questions of policy and the proper role of government.

The Institute is named for *Cato's Letters*, libertarian pamphlets that were widely read in the American Colonies in the early 18th century and played a major role in laying the philosophical foundation for the American Revolution.

Despite the achievement of the nation's Founders, today virtually no aspect of life is free from government encroachment. A pervasive intolerance for individual rights is shown by government's arbitrary intrusions into private economic transactions and its disregard for civil liberties.

To counter that trend, the Cato Institute undertakes an extensive publications program that addresses the complete spectrum of policy issues. Books, monographs, and shorter studies are commissioned to examine the federal budget, Social Security, regulation, military spending, international trade, and myriad other issues. Major policy conferences are held throughout the year, from which papers are published thrice yearly in the *Cato Journal*. The Institute also publishes the quarterly magazine *Regulation*.

In order to maintain its independence, the Cato Institute accepts no government funding. Contributions are received from foundations, corporations, and individuals, and other revenue is generated from the sale of publications. The Institute is a nonprofit, tax-exempt, educational foundation under Section 501(c)3 of the Internal Revenue Code.

CATO INSTITUTE
1000 Massachusetts Ave., N.W.
Washington, D.C. 20001